RODIN

Sculpture and Drawings

RODIN

Sculpture and Drawings

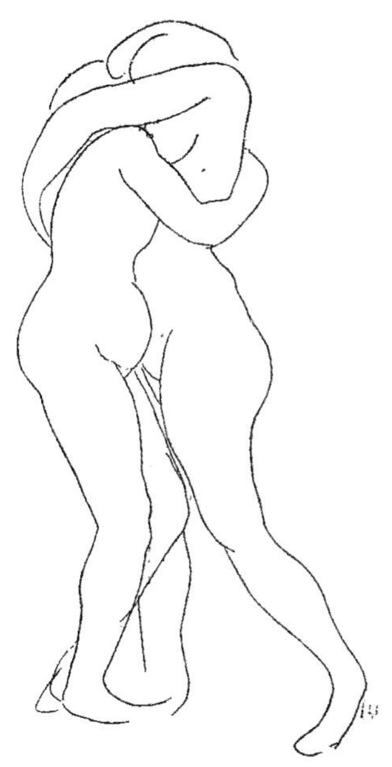

■ national gallery of **australia**

This publication accompanies the exhibition

RODIN:
A MAGNIFICENT OBSESSION
Sculpture from the Iris and B. Gerald Cantor Foundation, Los Angeles

National Gallery of Australia, Canberra
14 December 2001 – 24 February 2002
McClelland Gallery, Langwarrin, Victoria
9 March – 19 May 2002
Singapore Art Museum, Singapore
5 June – 25 August 2002

Lenders to the Exhibition
Iris and B. Gerald Cantor Foundation, Los Angeles
Musée Rodin, Paris
Fondation Pierre Gianadda, Martigny
National Gallery of Victoria, Melbourne

National Gallery of Australia exhibition curated by the
Department of International Art: Jörg Zutter, Lucina Ward and Anthony White

First published in Australia in 2001 by the Publications Department of the National Gallery of Australia, Parkes Place, Canberra, ACT 2601 **www.nga.gov.au**

Designer Kirsty Morrison
Editor Susan Hall
Printer Inprint

Cataloguing-in-Publication data

Rodin: sculpture and drawings: catalogue accompanying the exhibition Rodin: a magnificent obsession.

Bibliography.
ISBN 0 642 54189 2.

1. Rodin, Auguste, 1840-1917 - Exhibitions.
2. Rodin, Auguste, 1840-1917 - Criticism and interpretation. I. National Gallery of Australia.

730.92

front cover: Auguste RODIN *Pierette c.*1900 (cat. 100)
back cover: Auguste RODIN *The Thinker (reduction)* 1880 (cat. 33)
title page: Auguste RODIN *'Never again will we know the bitter taste of her kisses! …'* from *The Torture Garden* by Octave Mirbeau (detail) (cat. 127)

Contributors
Jaynie Anderson
University of Melbourne
Peter Brown
Australian National University
Claudie Judrin
Musée Rodin
Antoinette Le Normand-Romain
Musée Rodin
Paul Paffen
University of Melbourne
Lucina Ward
National Gallery of Australia
Jörg Zutter
National Gallery of Australia

Distributed in Australia by
Thames and Hudson
11 Central Boulevard Business Park
Port Melbourne, Victoria 3207

Distributed in the United Kingdom by
Thames and Hudson
30–34 Bloomsbury Street
London WC1B 3QP

Distributed in the United States of America by
University of Washington Press
1326 Fifth Avenue, Ste 555
Seattle, WA 98101-2604

CONTENTS

FOREWORD

Rodin was considered the most famous sculptor of his time, not only in France, but also throughout Europe, America and Australia. Despite the time and distance involved, young Australian artists, collectors and museum directors of the early 1900s regarded a trip to Europe and its cultural capital, Paris, as essential. Many of these travellers visited Rodin's studio – the expressive liberty and emotional intensity of Rodin's figures had an enormous impact on the culture of his time and the art of the entire twentieth century. In the light of this, it is not surprising to find that his work is represented in State galleries in Melbourne, Sydney, Adelaide and Perth.

Since the National Gallery of Australia opened in 1982, Rodin has been a powerful presence. His *Burghers of Calais* – two nude studies and casts of four of the six figures – stand sentinel in the Sculpture Garden. The Gallery also holds a maquette of the final monument. These works have allowed our visiting public to become familiar with Rodin's work and its impact on generations of sculptors.

The National Gallery is now delighted to present this splendid Rodin exhibition, a significant group of works, which is representative of Rodin's entire artistic career: sculptures, drawings and watercolours, as well as contemporary photographs.

The late B. Gerald Cantor and his wife, Iris, built up the most comprehensive private collection of Rodin's works, and we are very grateful that the Iris and B. Gerald Foundation has allowed an important selection of sculptures to come to Canberra. The exhibition is supplemented by outstanding drawings made by Rodin around 1900, at the height of his career. The presentation of these exciting works on paper along with the sculptures gives insight into Rodin's working process. They also reveal a more intense and less dramatic side of his genius. Most of these works on paper are on loan from the Musée Rodin, Paris, and we are grateful to the director, Jacques Vilain, and the chief curators, Antoinette Le Normand-Romain and Claudie Judrin for their generous support.

The Fondation Pierre Gianadda at Martigny, Switzerland, has also loaned drawings and watercolours, and we acknowledge the support of Léonard Gianadda. The Director of the National Gallery of Victoria, Melbourne, Dr Gerard Vaughan has been accommodating and generous in agreeing to important loans. We acknowledge with gratitude the loan of a fine bronze Rodin nude study of *Eustache de Saint-Pierre*, a promised bequest by Tony Gilbert.

We thank in particular the authors of this catalogue: Antoinette Le Normand-Romain, Claudie Judrin, Jörg Zutter, Jaynie Andersen and Paul Paffen.

The exhibition has been made possible by the Iris and B. Gerald Cantor Foundation and we thank especially Iris Cantor, Judith Sobol, Executive Director, and her predecessor Rachel Blackburn. We appreciate the support of Alan Dodge, Director, Art Gallery of Western Australia, in introducing the Cantor Foundation to us and in whose gallery the Cantor collection was first displayed in Australia. At the National Gallery, Lucina Ward has managed the curatorship of the show with the support of her colleagues, Jörg Zutter and Anthony White. Kirsty Morrison designed the catalogue and Susan Hall edited it. Patrice Riboust designed the exhibition and Ron Ramsey managed all aspects of it with his colleagues led by Adam Worrall. Staff from all the Gallery's departments have worked long and well to make the exhibition a major event.

We hope you enjoy this opportunity to experience not only Rodin's magnificent sculpture but also his original and influential drawings, here shown together in Australia for the first time.

Brian Kennedy
Director, National Gallery of Australia

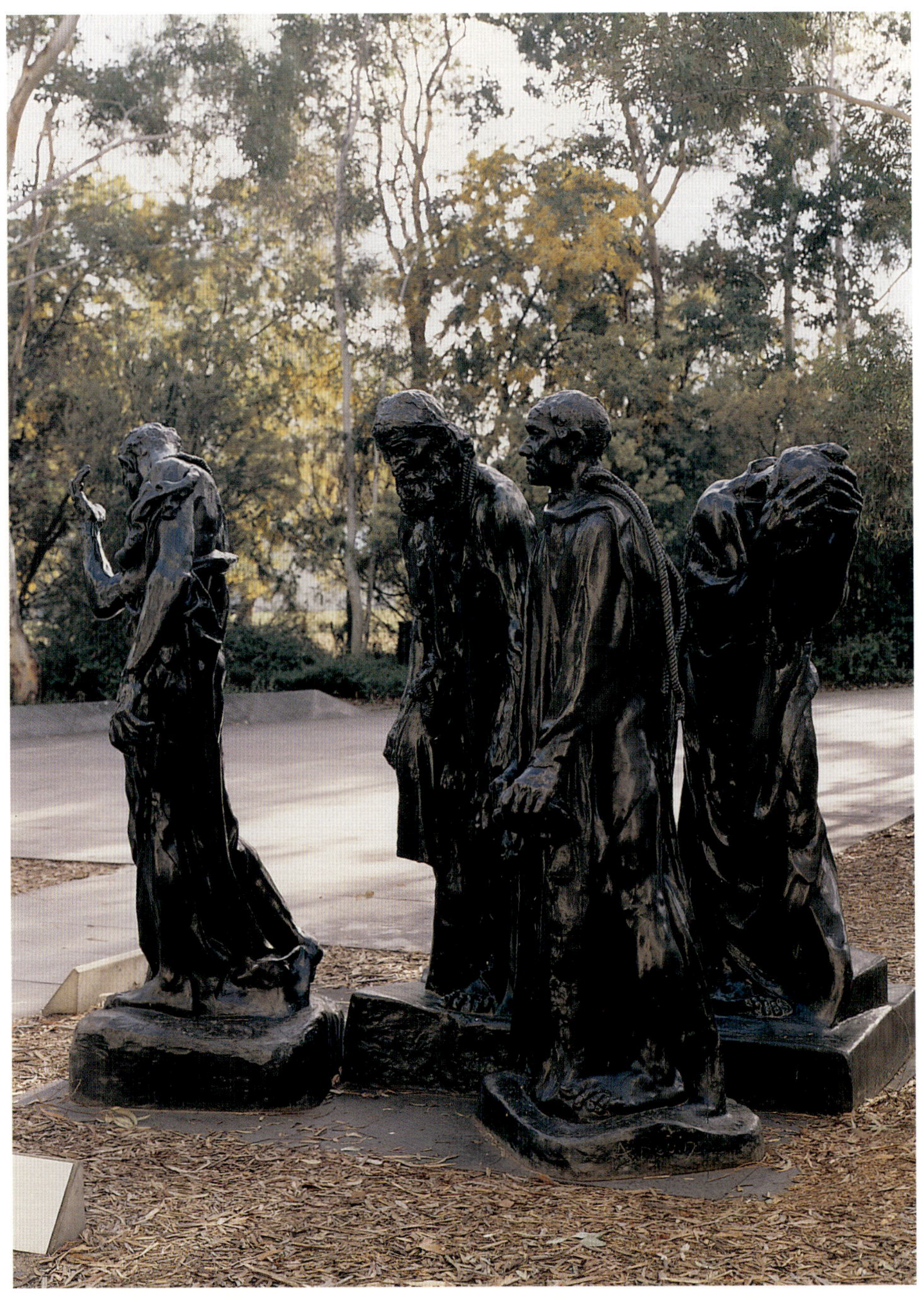

The Burghers of Calais (detail): *Pierre de Weissant* c.1885–86; *Eustache de Saint-Pierre* 1885–86; *Jean d'Aire* c.1885–86 and *Andrieu d'Andres* c.1886 (cat. 123, 124, 121 and 125)

RODIN: AN INTRODUCTION

Jörg Zutter

Auguste Rodin (1840–1917) was born in Paris in the same year as Claude Monet, one year after Paul Cézanne and Alfred Sisley and one year before Auguste Renoir. Clearly Rodin was a contemporary of the French Impressionist painters, whose work had received growing attention in Paris since the Second Empire (1852–70), but was he really an Impressionist? Should we not rather associate his work with international currents at the end of the nineteenth century such as Symbolism, the art of the *fin de siècle* and, in a more general sense, with an art historical period which saw the dissolution of traditional form and the first experiments with abstraction?[1] To put the question another way, should Rodin's work be placed at the end of a classical tradition that began with Michelangelo and ended in the late nineteenth century, or at the beginning of the modern era of sculpture, alongside artists such as Aristide Maillol, Medardo Rosso and Constantin Brancusi?

To understand Rodin today, we have to step back one hundred years in history and look more closely at the cultural situation in Paris at that time. By 1900, official authority in art had been challenged by independent exhibitions organised by artists' associations, art critics and dealers. In those days, Paris was disseminating its cultural taste internationally and attracting foreign artists from all over the world. The Republic embraced the pluralism of this situation in an opportunistic way in the Exposition Universelle (Universal Exhibition) of 1900, which asserted the technical achievements and cultural dominance of Paris as an international capital. This forms the background to Rodin's career when he was in his sixties.[2]

By 1900, Auguste Rodin had produced the major works of his career – *L'Age d'airain* (*The Age of Bronze*), *Saint Jean-Baptiste* (*Saint John the Baptist Preaching*), the different monuments for *Les Bourgeois de Calais* (*The Burghers of Calais*), for *Balzac*, for *Victor Hugo* – and had become a leading figure in the cultural life of France. He had also become very much a focus of attention because he had been working, since 1880, on a large-scale public project intended for the future Musée des Arts Décoratifs (Museum of Decorative Arts) called *La Porte de l'Enfer* (*The Gates of Hell*). Rodin, who presented the unfinished version of this work in different temporary exhibitions, wrestled with *The Gates* until the end of his life without ever completing them. Many famous sculptures evolved

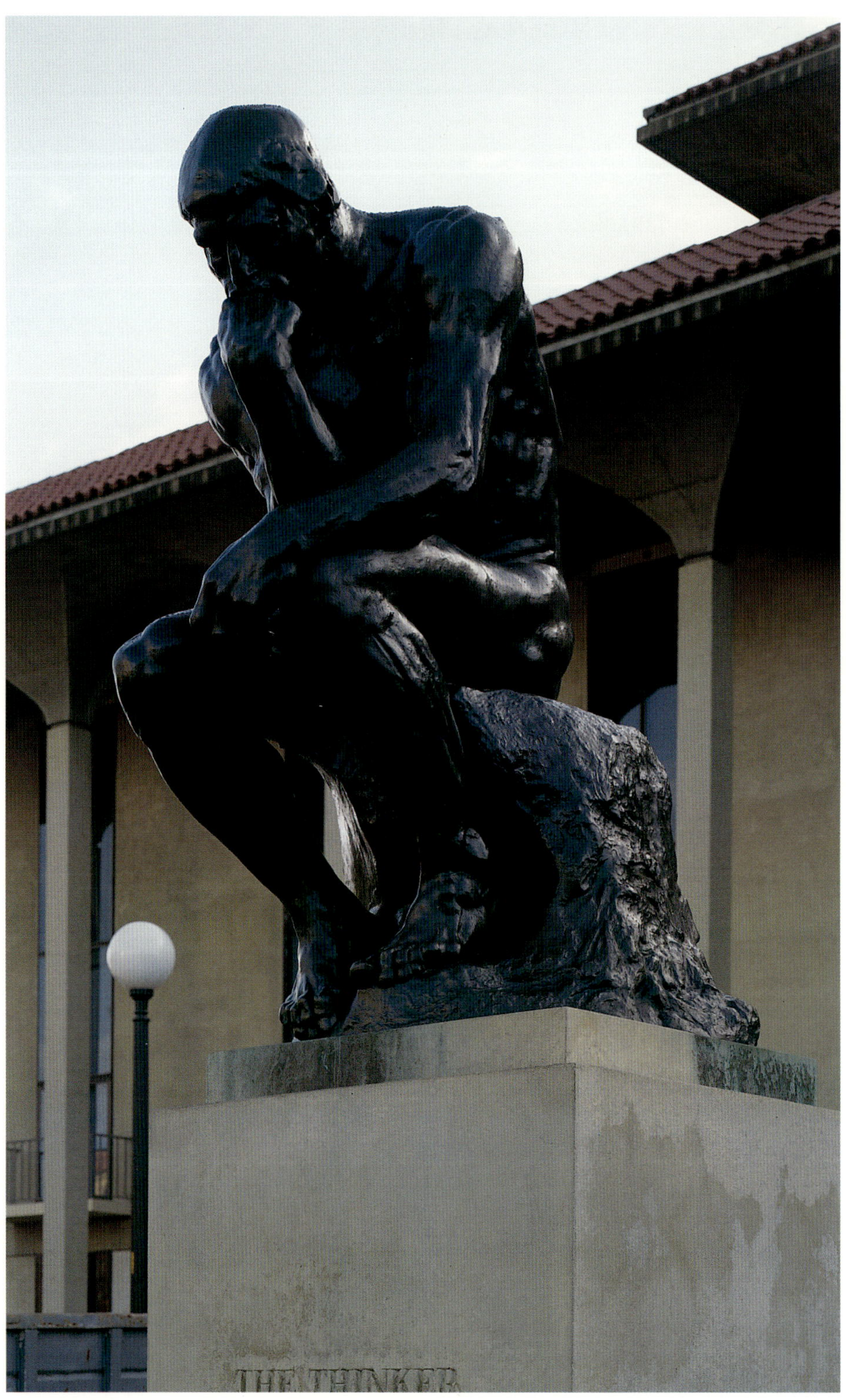

The Thinker 1880 (cat. 32)

from this project, including *Le Penseur* (*The Thinker*), *Le Baiser* (*The Kiss*) and *Eve*. In 1900, Rodin was among the few living French artists who had gained world-wide recognition; he had accepted major commissions for monuments and had sold various sculptures to museums and private collections not only in France but also abroad.

Indeed, at the time of the Exposition Universelle of 1900, Rodin was at the pinnacle of his career. Paris promoted its artists through this exhibition and Paris was, in turn, promoted by them. Rodin was not only represented in the artistic section of this world exhibition but also organised – following the example of Gustave Courbet and Edouard Manet – his own retrospective exhibition in a special rented and privately financed venue, the so-called Pavillon de l'Alma in the neighbourhood near the Exposition Universelle. There he exhibited for the first time the entire unfinished plaster version of *The Gates* together with a selection of 168 sculptures, drawings and photographs.[3] At the Exposition Universelle itself, Rodin's work was on display in the so-called Exposition Décennale located in the recently-opened Grand Palais, a modern steel and glass construction destined for temporary exhibitions, where twenty-nine countries were represented with paintings, works on paper, sculptures and works of architecture. In the Grand Palais, Rodin's *The Kiss* was exhibited alongside works by artists from all over the world, including his compatriot Alfred Guillou, the Russian Valentin Serov, the Czech

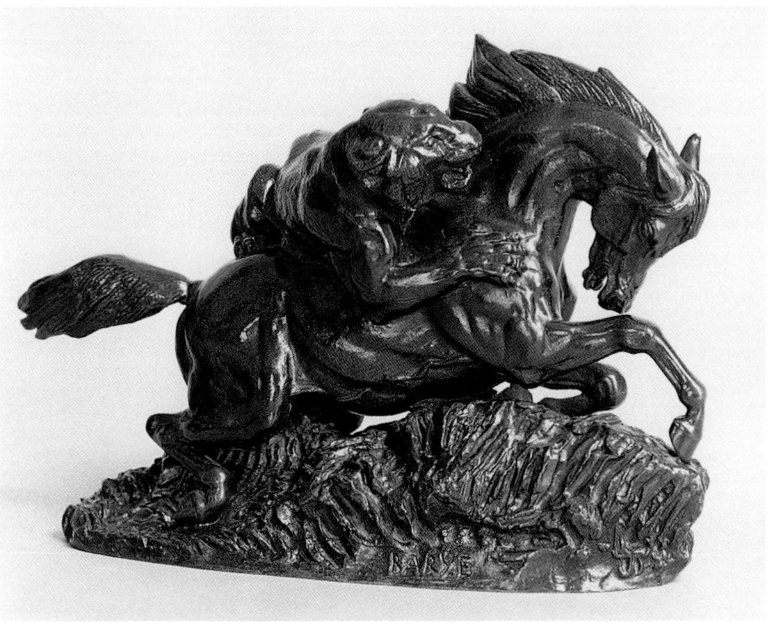

Antoine-Louis BARYE *A Horse Attacked by a Tiger* c.1837 Bronze
24.3 x 37.2 x 14.8 cm National Gallery of Australia

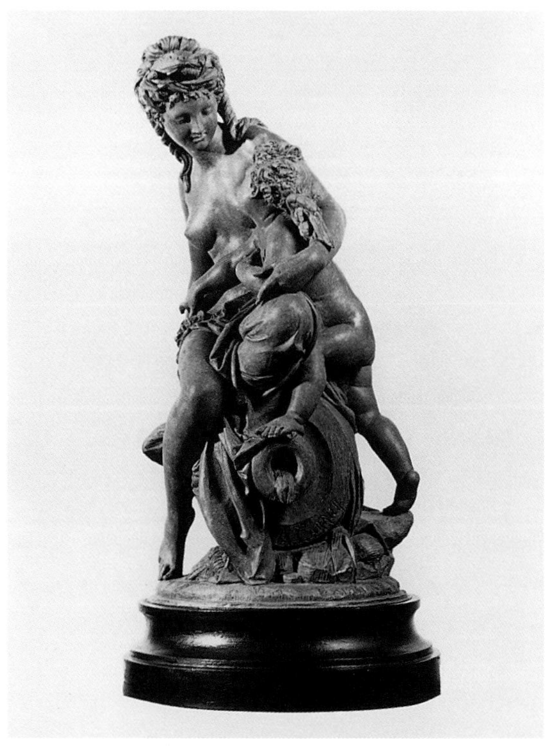

Albert-Ernest CARRIER-BELLEUSE *Venus Disarming Cupid* before 1869 Terracotta 74.8 x 39.2 x 36.2 cm National Gallery of Australia

František Kupka and the Japanese, western-style artist, Ichiro Yuasa. Such a diverse group was representative of the artistic pluralism of the time, and of the widespread *fin de siècle* mood which characterised the international taste of the period, a taste that has to be taken into consideration in regard to Rodin's work. In particular, the sculpture and painting displays of nudes, bathers and other unclothed and flying female figures in the Décennale exhibition, which today provide ample material for interpretations by psychologists and feminists, should be seen in the light of this turn of the century context. To give only one example of the type of events that characterised that period, Freud's *The Interpretation of Dreams* had been published in 1899.[4]

1900 also marked the end of Rodin's long quest for artistic recognition and financial success. At the very beginning of his career, from 1854 on, Rodin was in touch with the artists Alphonse Legros and Charles Cazin and – after his failure in the entrance exam for the Ecole des Beaux-Arts (Fine Arts Academy) – with the animal sculptor Antoine-Louis Barye, whose classes he attended at the Musée d'Histoire Naturelle (Natural History Museum) and whose work is represented in the collection of the National Gallery of Australia. The details of Rodin's artistic development are discussed in

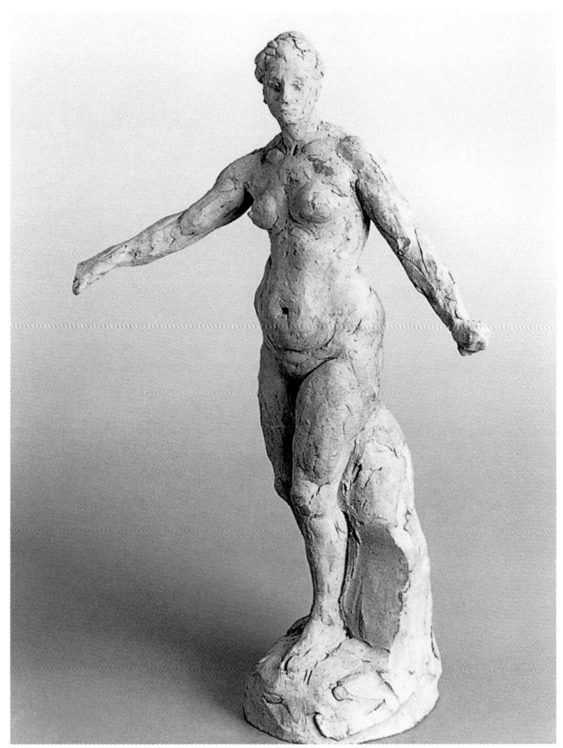

Jules DALOU Study for the figure of the Republic for *The Triumph of the Republic* 1879 Terracotta 27.6 x 18.0 x 10.8 cm National Gallery of Australia

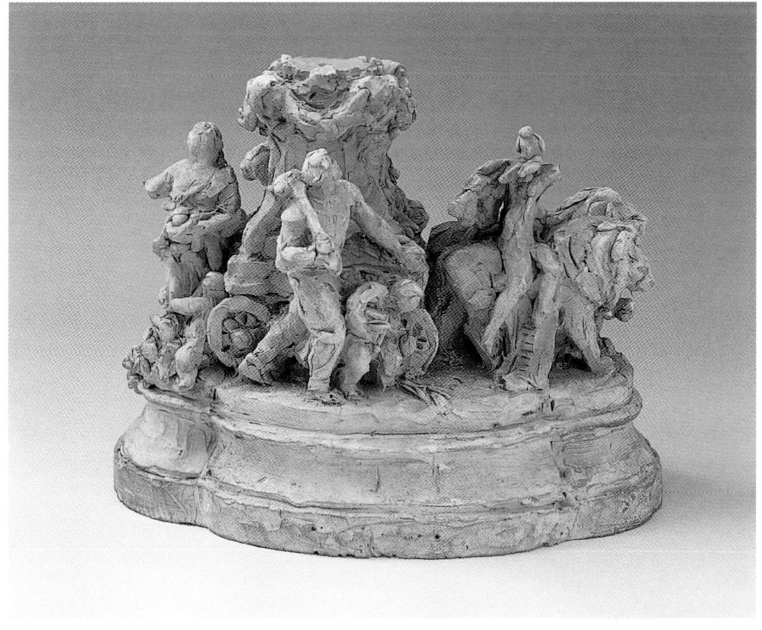

Jules DALOU Study for the chariot for *The Triumph of the Republic* 1879 Terracotta 22.2 x 20.8 x 29.2 cm National Gallery of Australia

Antoinette Le Normand-Romain's catalogue essay. In 1864, the artist became an assistant to Albert-Ernest Carrier-Belleuse, for whom he worked in Brussels. As Le Normand-Romain argues, Rodin's official career has to be seen in the larger context of the Salons of the 1870s,[5] where the sculptor was admitted at different times: in 1875 with the marble bust of *L'Homme au nez cassé* (*The Man with the Broken Nose*), in 1877 with a plaster of *The Age of Bronze*, and in 1878 with the bust of *Saint John the Baptist Preaching*. The anatomical accuracy of *The Age of Bronze* led to the famous accusations that he had used life casts of his model. The whole controversy about the appropriate style, execution and movement of contemporary sculpture – whether academic or realistic – is typical of Rodin's time and of the difficult choices each successful sculptor had to make.[6]

In the 1870s, the success at the Salon of the heroic and patriotic works of Antoine Mercié, Louis-Ernest Barrias and Frédéric Auguste Bartholdi encouraged Rodin to express in his sculpture the disillusionment experienced among artists and intellectuals after the defeat of France in the Franco-Prussian War. Instead of using images of heroism and bravery, he expressed the horror of war and the desire for revenge. One of Rodin's contemporaries was Jules Dalou who, due to his involvement in the Paris Commune of 1871,[7] had to live in exile in London until the general amnesty was announced in 1879. Dalou returned to Paris and was invited to participate in a competition honouring the Republic.[8] His terracotta studies for *The Triumph of the Republic* of 1879, in the collection of the National Gallery of Australia, underline the sculptor's goal as a public educator and spokesman for the people and, for that reason, situate him close to Rodin.

In the late 1870s, Rodin had still to fight for recognition and to be admitted to official and prestigious exhibitions which were so crucial to get the necessary attention from art lovers, collectors and art critics and which were therefore so important for his forthcoming career. To give only one example: although contemporary sculpture occupied a prominent place in various prestigious group exhibitions in Paris, Rodin's work was not on display at the Exposition Universelle of 1878, where there was an art exhibition with a significant sculpture section. The art critic Anatole de Montaiglon wrote about this show in the *Gazette des Beaux-Arts*: 'French sculpture is stronger than painting; it is better than every other school of sculpture; its primacy cannot be put in jeopardy.'[9] Rodin was not yet recognised by the various experts and critics associated with the leading group of contemporary French sculptors.

In 1880, Rodin was admitted to the Salon with a plaster of the *Saint John the Baptist Preaching* and a bronze of *The Age of Bronze,* which was acquired by the French Government together with *The Thinker*. It was at this time that Rodin

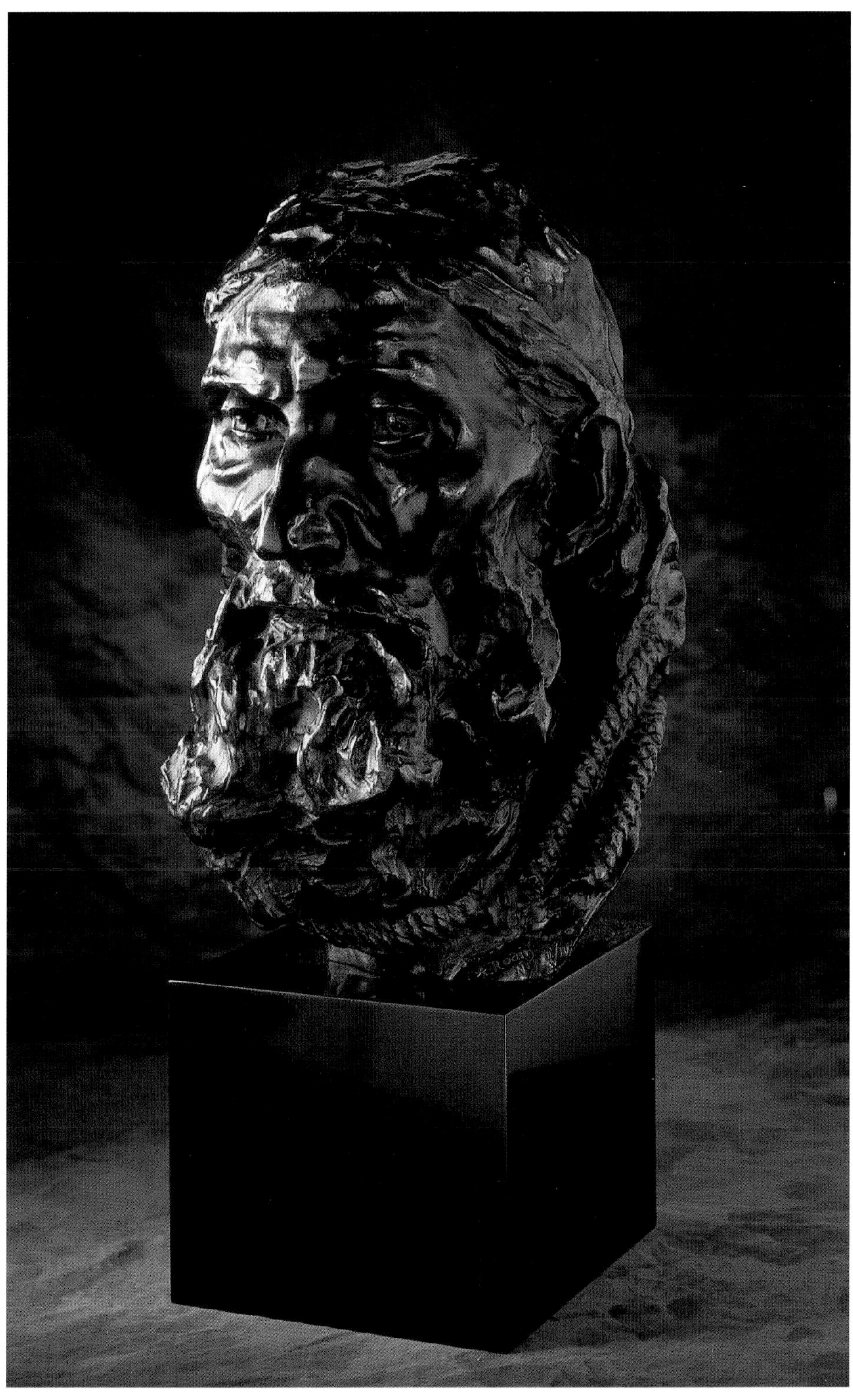

Final Head of Eustache de Saint-Pierre c.1886 (cat. 55)

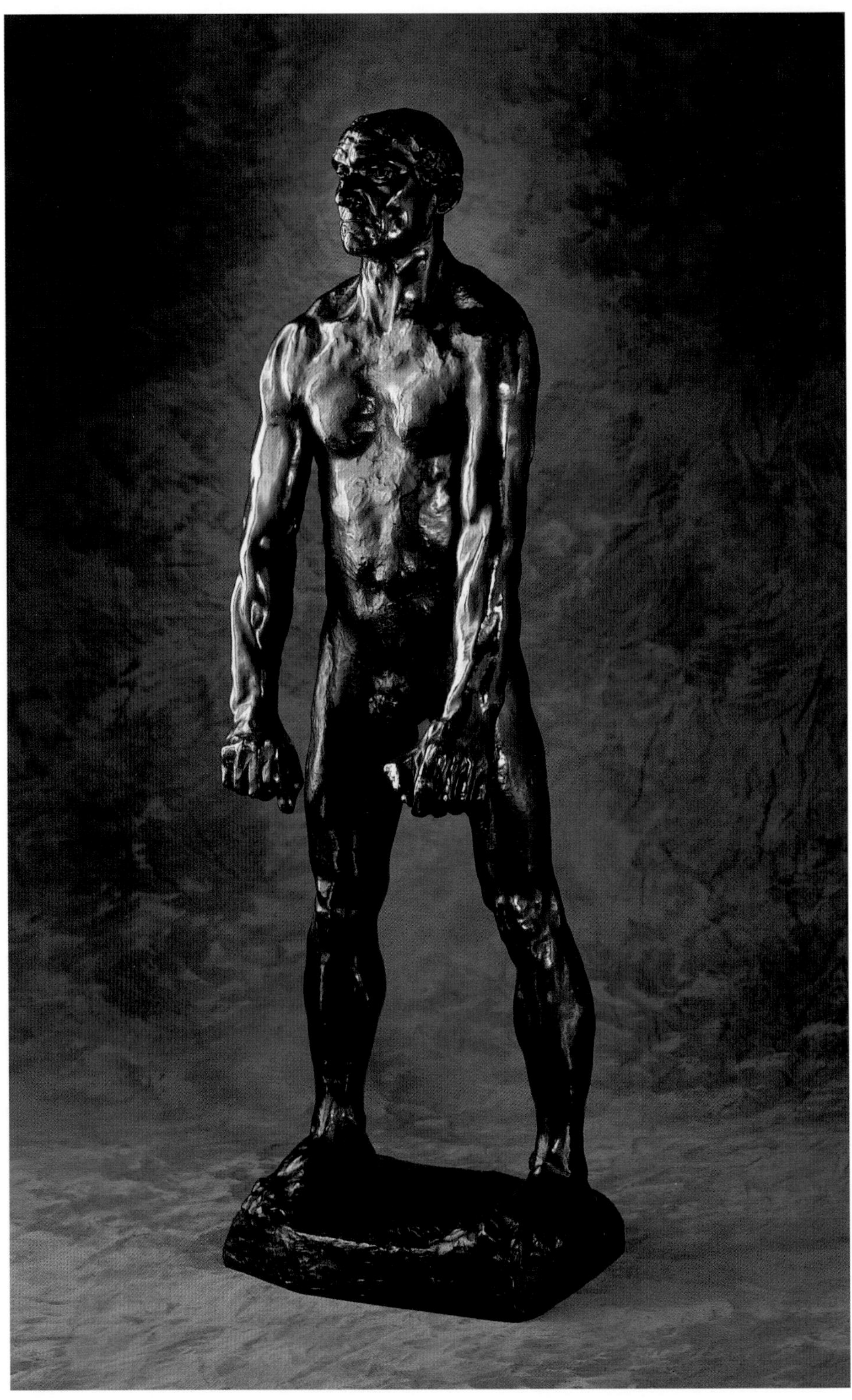

Nude Study for Jean d'Aire (reduction) 1885–86 (cat. 53)

received the commission for *The Gates of Hell* and it was his decision to choose Dante's *Inferno* (the part of the *Divine Comedy* entitled *Hell*) as the source for his theme and iconography. The enthusiasm for sculpture in Salon reviews of 1878 did not last forever and, in 1889, it was replaced by an enthusiasm for painting, although the situation later changed back in favour of sculpture. Some critics highlighted Rodin's affinity with Impressionism, especially when he exhibited together with his friend Claude Monet in 1889 in the fine art section of the Exposition Universelle and when, in that same year, the two artists showed together at the Galérie Georges Petit in Paris. At the latter exhibition Rodin presented thirty-five sculptures, among them – for the first time – *The Burghers of Calais* and also the *Bust of Mrs Russell, The Thinker* and *The Dream*. Monet presented a large retrospective of his work including 145 paintings, mainly landscapes of the years 1864–1889, including his famous *Impression, Sunrise* of 1872 which he had shown in the first Impressionist group exhibition of 1874.[10]

Gustave Geffroy, who wrote the main essay on Rodin in the catalogue of his exhibition at the Galérie Georges Petit, outlines in another text how he had liberated sculpture from the academic tradition and he compares the immeasurable number of natural poses in Rodin's work to Impressionist painting: 'I have shown Rodin in the presence of the natural, easy transformations of his model, intoxicated with the truth, which reveals itself to him through all aspects of this form, at once fixed and changing, resembling all that exists, all the *fugitif durable* of nature, the sky, the sea, the universe animated by light.'[11] In this passage, Geffroy does not assert that Rodin's modelling dematerialises his forms but claims that it creates a unity and harmony of the figure with its environment. The unique opportunity to present a large selection of Rodin's sculptures and drawings, only a few months after the closure of the successful exhibition *Monet &Japan* at the National Gallery of Australia, offers an excellent occasion to re-examine and analyse at close range the artistic similarities and correspondences between the sculptor and the painter, both of whom are represented in the National Gallery of Australia's collection – Rodin with a maquette, two nude studies and four of the six final figures for *The Burghers* and Monet with *Haystacks, Midday* and *Waterlilies*.[12]

By the 1890s, Rodin had gained a considerable reputation because of his successful exhibitions and the invitations for commissions: *Claude Lorraine, Victor Hugo* and *Balzac*. In contrast to the Impressionist painters who, by the 1880s, had already turned their backs on the Salon, Rodin showed regularly at the official group exhibitions newly founded in 1882 in Paris: the Salon of the Société des Artistes Français (Association of French Artists), a reincarnation of the old Salon. He also showed at the more progressive Salon, organised in the

1890s by the Société Nationale des Beaux-Arts (National Society of Fine Arts), which had been created by a number of artists, including the painters Pierre Puvis de Chavannes, Eugène Carrière and Albert Besnard, as well as Rodin himself. Rodin exhibited regularly at the Nationale until 1913; in 1898 his marble *The Kiss* was given pride of place in the centre of the colonnaded circle in the middle of the exhibition. Facing it was the plaster *Monument to Balzac*, Rodin's audacious sculpture and a strong example of his mature work, which was roundly criticised and finally refused by the Société des Gens de Lettres (Society of Authors) who had commissioned it. Whereas *The Kiss* is described as a kind of old-fashioned work in Rodin's 'ancienne manière' by the art critic Camille Mauclair, who saw the artist as adhering to a conservative kind of perfection, the *Balzac* was considered instead as a product of artistic boldness and arrogance.[13] From this moment on, Rodin's sculpture parallels Symbolist taste and is both admired and criticised in particular because of its expressive effects, disproportion, transformation, contortion and fragmentation, as many exhibition reviews demonstrated.

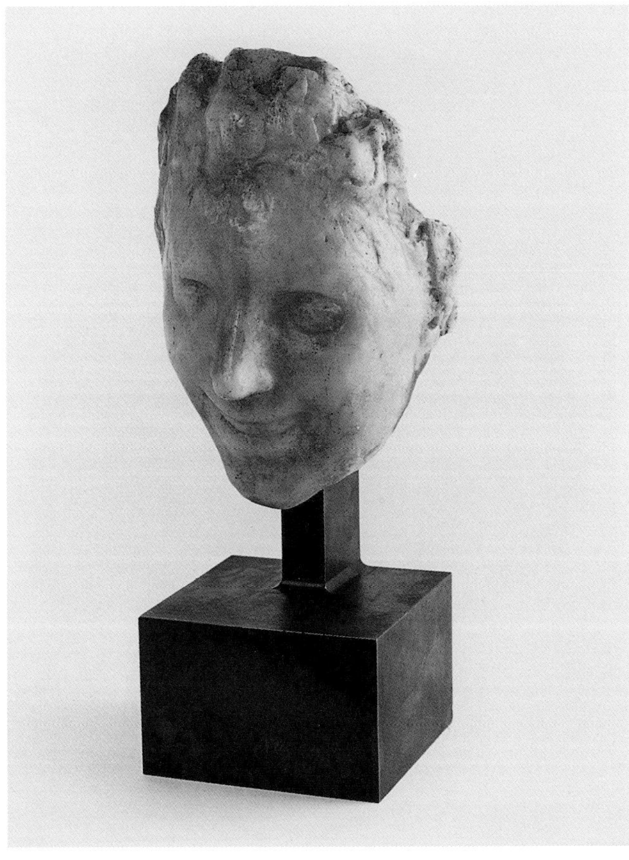

Medardo ROSSO *Laughing Woman* 1890
Modelled wax on plaster 23.0 x 16.5 x 11.0 cm National Gallery of Australia

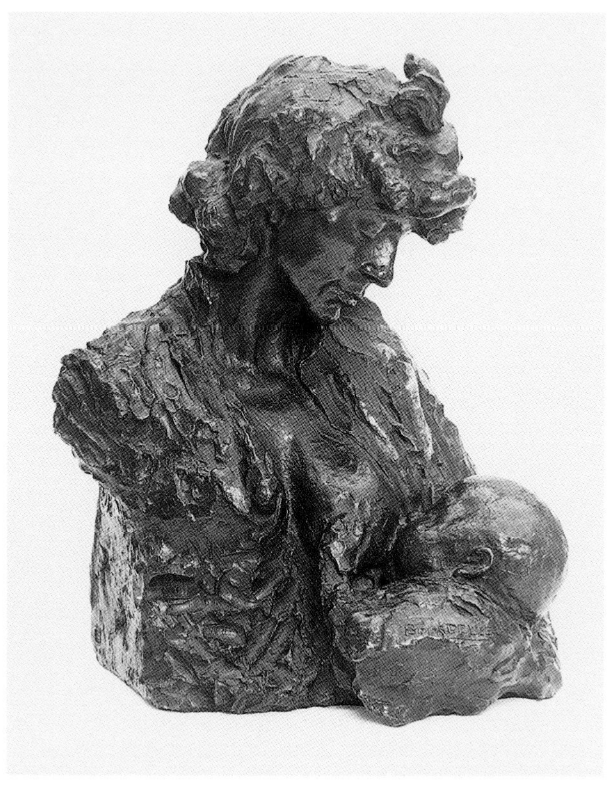

Emile Antoine BOURDELLE *Maternity* 1893
Bronze 53.0 x 35.6 x 34.8 cm National Gallery of Australia

Within the context of the growing number of independent and sometimes juryless exhibitions, Rodin remained an active participant in the artistic life of Paris after 1900. From 1897 to 1905 he was president of the sculpture section of the Société Nationale des Beaux-Arts. He had considerable influence in this position where he judged and encouraged younger sculptors like Maillol and Brancusi.[14] The collection of the National Gallery of Australia includes sculptures by both these artists, who were in contact with Rodin and were influenced by his work, and also by Emile Antoine Bourdelle, his studio assistant, and his friend Medardo Rosso.[15] It is, of course, the nature of sculptural projects, which are first produced in terracotta or plaster, to be reproduced and disseminated in bronze and/or marble to a wide circle of collectors. With the help of his studio assistants, founders and art dealers, Rodin made his art widely available and authorised large bronze and marble editions which have been acquired by private collectors and museum directors worldwide.[16] As Jaynie Anderson and Paul Paffen document in their catalogue essay about Rodin and the National Gallery of Victoria, important sculptures by Rodin were purchased for Melbourne as early as 1905, during the visit of the Gallery's director Bernard Hall to Europe. The correspondence between Hall and Rodin, which is partly held in the National Gallery of Australia Research Library,[17] makes it clear that Hall first acquired the bronze bust of *Jean-Paul Laurens* and thereafter the so-called *Minerve sans casque* (*Minerva Without a Helmet*) for which John Russell's wife was a model. On the other hand, lesser-known figures drawn from previously created but not fully accomplished works – that is to say experimental and intimate studies on paper, in plaster and assembled in new compositions, or cut in marble – have become known thanks to scholarly research on these issues and also thanks to the exhibition *Le Corps en Morceaux (The Body in Fragments)*, organised by the Musée d'Orsay in Paris in 1990.[18] These events have revealed a hitherto unknown aspect of Rodin's work and have helped to dispel the perception of him as the operator of an exclusively mechanical workshop production.

The growing interest in the artist's individual working process which followed from that revelation has also been stimulated by the research activity of the Musée Rodin in Paris. In 1916, the French Government designated the Hôtel Biron on the rue de Varenne, where Rodin had been in subtenancy since 1908, as a future Musée Rodin and received three donations of works, including marble and bronze sculptures and a large number of plasters and works on paper. This was the result of four years of difficult negotiations between Rodin and his friends and the French Government, which finally accepted the donation of the artist's estate, including the rights for reproducing and copying it, in exchange for the creation of a museum bearing his name. The debate in Parliament had been lively and ardent, since some members were opposed to the idea of immortalising the works in this way and other members rejected the idea of a museum dedicated to a single living artist. The present exhibition includes more than seventy sculptures from the Iris and B. Gerald Cantor Foundation, Los Angeles (many of them issued posthumously by the Musée Rodin), and also works in bronze and marble from the Musée Rodin in Paris, the National Gallery of Victoria in Melbourne and the National Gallery of Australia in Canberra. The Musée Rodin has also lent thirty works on paper. These are complemented by six drawings from the Fondation Pierre Gianadda in Martigny, Switzerland, which give insight in Rodin's life-long studies of the female figure.[19] As Claudie Judrin maintains in her catalogue essay, Rodin was a prolific and innovative draughtsman; the Musée Rodin, with its eight thousand sheet collection, holds only a part of his massive legacy. Rodin's highly erotic life drawings, works which stand alone from his sculptural practice, are not the result of using professional models but of depicting the casual, non-academic poses of standing, reclining, sleeping or dancing figures. These exciting and spontaneous drawings are of great interest for us today since they not only give detailed insight in the artist's working process and its evolution but they also reveal another, more personal and less heroic side of Rodin's genius.

1 See Petr Wittlich, 'Les yeux clos, le symbolisme et les nouvelles formules du pathos', in *Paradis Perdus: L'Europe Symboliste* ex. cat., Montreal: Musée de Beaux-Arts de Montréal, 1995, pp. 235–241.

2 MaryAnne Stevens, 'The Exposition Universelle: This vast competition of effort, realisation and victories', in *1900 Art at the Crossroads* ex. cat., London: Royal Academy; New York: Solomon R. Guggenheim Museum, 2000, pp. 55–71.

3 *Rodin en 1900. L'Exposition de l'Alma* ex. cat., Paris: Musée du Luxembourg, 2001.

4 In fact, the article with the title *The Interpretation of Dreams* had been published in 1899 but the date of the physical book is recorded as 1900 (Leipzig: F. Deuticke). See also Wittlich, op.cit., p. 235.

5 During the first half of the nineteenth century, the Salon was the premier venue for the displaying of works of art. The jury had enormous power to 'make or break' an artist by excluding any painter of whom it did not approve. That this system was open to abuse was generally accepted by the 1860s and, in 1863, a Salon des Refusés allowed the public to judge the rejected works for themselves. By 1870, the jury was entirely elected by artists. Eventually there were four competing exhibitions – the Salon des Artistes Français (1881), the Salon des Indépendants (1884), the Société Nationale des Beaux-Arts (1890) and the Salon d'Automne (1903).

6 Ruth Butler, 'Rodin and the Paris Salon', in Albert E. Elsen (ed.), *Rodin Rediscovered* ex. cat., Washington: National Gallery of Art, 1982, pp. 19–50.

7 The Paris Commune was the socialist government elected in Paris in 1871 after the defeat of France in the Franco-Prussian War and the collapse of the Second Empire. It was suppressed by the National Assembly in a battle where 33,000 were killed.

8 Michael Lloyd and Michael Desmond, *European and American Paintings and Sculptures 1870–1970 in the Australian National Gallery*, Canberra: National Gallery of Australia, 1992, p. 48.

9 Butler, op.cit., p. 37, note 69.

10 *Claude Monet – Auguste Rodin. Centenaire de l'exposition de 1889* ex. cat., Paris: Musée Rodin, 1989.

11 JoAnne Culler Paradise, 'The Sculptor and the Critic: Rodin and Geffroy', Elsen, op.cit., p. 265, note 39.

12 Lloyd and Desmond, op.cit., pp. 56–63; 72–79.

13 Daniel Rosenfeld, 'Rodin's Carved Sculptures', Elsen, op.cit., p. 86, note 18.

14 Butler, op.cit., p. 46.

15 Lloyd and Desmond, op.cit., pp. 68–71, 82–87, 192–201, 202–205.

16 Rosenfeld, op.cit., p.81; Antoinette Le Normand-Romain, *Rodin*, Paris: Flammarion, 1997, p. 117.

17 Bernard Hall Archive. National Gallery of Australia Research Library, items 1:71-2, 74, 77, 79; 2:7; 232-3, 341.

18 *Le Corps en Morceaux* ex. cat., Paris: Réunion des Musées Nationaux, 1990.

19 See in particular *Rodin: Dessins et aquarelles des collections suisses et du Musée Rodin* ex. cat., Martigny: Fondation Pierre Gianadda, 1994.

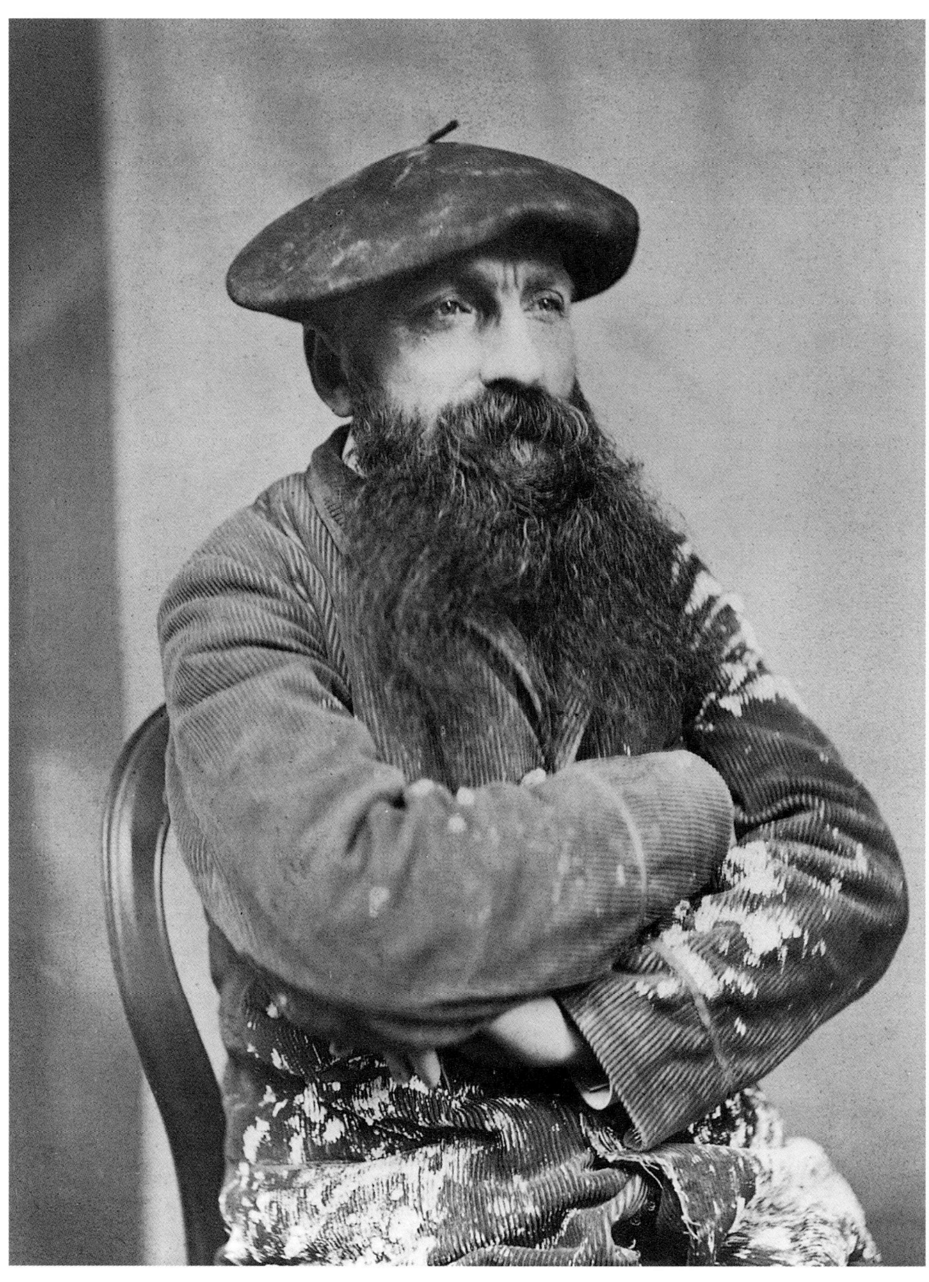

Anonymous photographer *Portrait of Rodin in a Beret and a Plaster-splattered Coat* c.1880
Albumen photograph 21.8 x 16.8 cm Musée Rodin

RODIN AND HIS ART

Antoinette Le Normand-Romain

> Rodin was a god. Whenever I went to see him, I had the impression of being received by a benevolent god. He was a profound thinker who never said anything foolish. Nor would he ever say anything bad about an artist. He would happily show those works of his fellow artists that he found beautiful, without any trace of jealousy. He either expressed strong ideas or kept silent. I listened to him without chancing a reply, as I had too much respect for his genius. We rarely spoke about sculpture, there being a mutual understanding without any need for words.[1]
>
> Aristide Maillol (1861–1944)

A benevolent god is how Auguste Rodin (1840–1917) represented himself in his symbolic self-portraits such as *Pygmalion*, *Le Sculpteur et sa Muse (The Sculptor and his Muse)*, or in the bottom right bas-relief of *La Porte de l'Enfer (The Gates of Hell)*. There he appears as God the Father, the Creator. But we know that behind this apparent self-assurance lay hidden a tormented soul in search of a perfection that forever eluded him. As he once confided to Austrian poet Rainer Maria Rilke (1875–1926), the sculptor has, in his awkward way, to make a superhuman effort to understand the Muse.

At first sight, Rodin appeared shy, almost gauche, but as the symbolist writer and critic Camille Mauclair put it 'gradually the dominant impression … became one of calm and exceptional authority. There was nothing bombastic about this man, but nothing gauche either'.[2] For Rilke, 'he was someone of few words, like all men of action',[3] something confirmed by Paul Gsell:

> In general, he spoke little. He seemed to be someone self-absorbed, who would listen to others as he slowly stroked his long beard. From time to time, he let out a short sentence or two in a hushed voice and as if in a dream-like state. If a subject interested him, however, he would suddenly hold forth passionately on it, as he would smile at ideas that met his approval, and get worked up against men and things that he found objectionable while falling back the next moment into resolute silence.[4]

Mauclair wrote that: 'He was really like an elemental force of nature. And his own simplicity was the root of his way of simplifying things. He brought everything back to a question of values. He only saw the overall design, in morality as in art. His life was based on two or three principles, which could be summarised as an aversion for all that was not essential.'[5] Rilke, who was Rodin's secretary for a few months in 1905, shared Mauclair's view of him as a single-minded person, escaping time, who went ' back upstream like a river God and (looked) forwards like a prophet ... Exactly (defined) in his uniqueness, he nonetheless lost himself in a kind of medieval anonymity, he had this humility of greatness that made one think of the builders of great cathedrals. His isolation was not a sign of any desire to keep aloof, being rather based on his relationship with nature'.[6]

These texts were all written after 1900, the year of the great Rodin exhibition organised by the artist himself in Paris, in the Pavillon de l'Alma, on the fringe of the Exposition Universelle (Universal Exhibition). By then he already had behind him a certain number of prestigious commissions, even if few of them had actually amounted to anything, and he was now perceived as the champion of sculpture, both in France and beyond. He divided his time between his home at Meudon (purchased in 1895) where he returned every evening, and the Dépôt des Marbres (Storehouse for Marble Sculptures), at the Champ-de-Mars end of the rue de l'Université, where he had studios put at his disposal by the head of the Ecole des Beaux-Arts (Fine Arts Academy). It was there that *The Gates of Hell* stood, there also that he worked on the monuments to the French authors Victor Hugo and Honoré de Balzac. *The Gates* reflected the passionate admiration he felt for Dante, Michelangelo (1475–1564) and the Italian Renaissance, while in later works it was the influence of Antiquity that was to be paramount. 'On Sundays, when I go up to the Samothrace I feel an eternal youth, an inspiration of happiness', he wrote in 1904.[7] He had long studied both traditions, however, to the point of being able to give, within a few moments, and from just a handful of clay, a demonstration of the principles of composition in both Greek and Renaissance art. Moreover, as soon as he could, he collected works from Antiquity (marble statues, pottery), a period he loved as much as he did the eighteenth century. His passion for the latter led him to the Hôtel Biron that he discovered, thanks to Rilke, in 1908, and also led him to acquire and relocate at Meudon the portico of the château of Issy, destroyed during the 1871 Commune.[8]

Above all, however, he had a reverence for Nature, both inanimate and animate beings: 'Nature is always beautiful. All one has to do is look and understand', as André Fontainas recalled him saying.[9] It is well known that women were the object of his passionate interest, as thousands of his drawings attest.

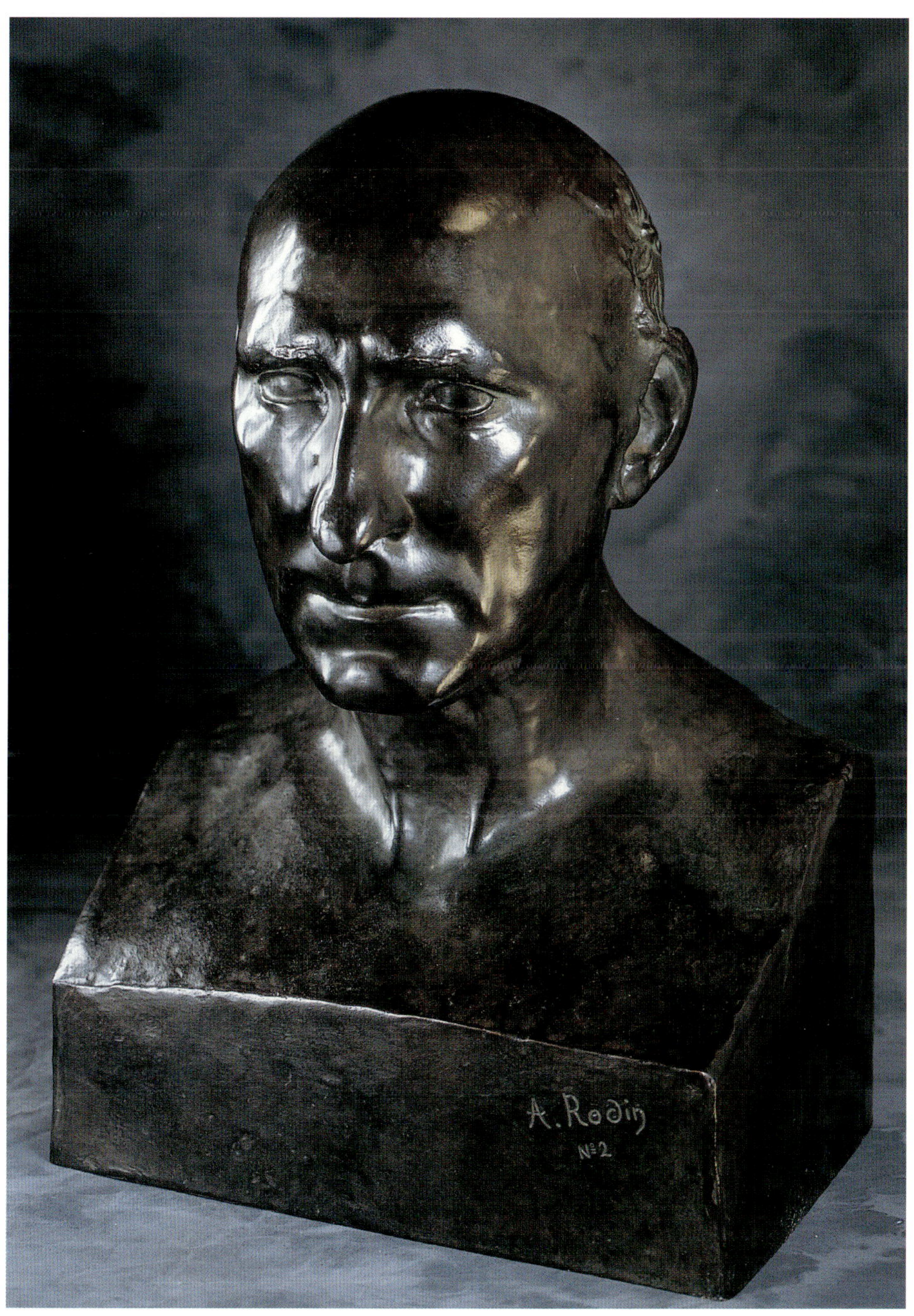

Bust of Jean-Baptiste Rodin 1860 (cat. 1)

'He was forever drawing. He would move around the model … admiring her shapes, caressing them with his eyes, and sometimes with his hand, pointing out their beauty to me', as William Rothenstein recalls.[10] Some of his female models mattered a great deal to him – Rose Beuret (1842–1917), his life-long companion, who gave him a son (whom he never recognised) and whom he married a few months before his death, plus a string of mistresses, of whom Camille Claudel (1864–1943) was the most significant. Indeed, with her immense talent and strong personality, Claudel was probably the great love of Rodin's life – although his art came before everything.

THE EARLY YEARS

The young Auguste Rodin, an indifferent albeit conscientious student, clearly had only one passion – for drawing. In 1854, he was finally able to devote himself wholeheartedly to it, when his elder sister, Maria, helped him persuade his parents to enrol him at the Ecole Impériale Spéciale de Dessin et de Mathématiques (Special Imperial School of Drawing and Mathematics) known as the 'Petite Ecole'. Rodin worked relentlessly, spending his spare time at the Louvre where he did drawings after Michelangelo, Raphael and works of Antiquity, or in the Bibliothèque Impériale (Imperial Library). In the late afternoons he went to the drawing class held at the Manufacture des Gobelins (Gobelins Tapestry Workshop) where drawing was done from a live model and, in the evenings, he reproduced from memory what he had observed during the day.

Then he discovered sculpture. 'I went into the class where we drew from sculpture in the round. Students were modelling from Antique works. For the first time I saw clay, and I had the feeling that I was ascending into heaven. I made separate pieces, arms, heads or feet. Then I tackled the whole figure. In a flash I had an overall conception ... I was in ecstasy!'[11]

He sat the entrance exam to the Ecole des Beaux-Arts on three occasions. Whilst he failed each time, he did not let this discourage him. However, the Rodin family eked out a hard life from the modest pay of Jean-Baptiste Rodin, a clerk in the Police Headquarters in Paris, and so Auguste had to earn a living as early as possible. Under the direction of Baron Haussmann, Paris had taken on the look of a huge construction site full of builders and decorators, and Rodin went from one to the next, working in succession for the ornamenters and artisans Blanche, Bièze and Cruchet. 'The need to live forced me ... to work for everyone, which gave me a de facto apprenticeship. I made earrings with a goldsmith followed by decorative figures on three-metre torsos, and that is how I learned all parts of the trade.'[12]

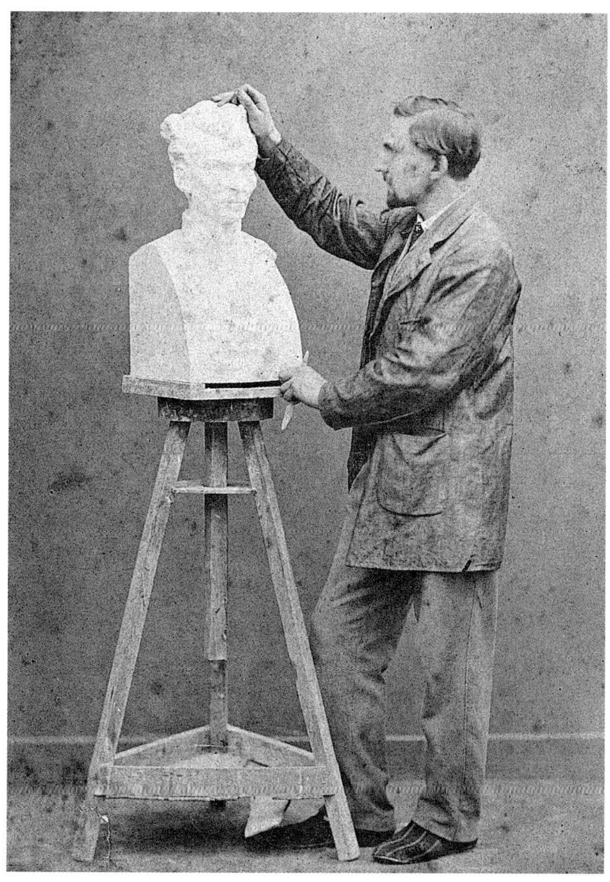

Charles AUBRY *Rodin at Work on the Bust of Father Eymard* 1863
Carbon print 23.0 x 17.5 cm Musée Rodin

These formative years were difficult ones from both a material and emotional point of view. Indeed, they were marked by his sister Maria's entry into a convent and her death in 1862. There was a very deep emotional bond between the brother and sister to the extent that, after Maria's passing, Rodin decided to give up sculpture and take orders with the Monastery of the Most Holy Sacrament.

He spent only a few months there. By the end of 1863 he had taken up his work again, and 1864 was to mark his real entry into adulthood. First of all, he met Rose Beuret. Then he was able to realise one of his most cherished desires, to have his own studio. It was only an uninsulated horse stable in the rue Lebrun in the Gobelins district where the Rodin family was then living, but there Rodin set to work like a man inspired. Few works remain from that period, however, as he was too poor to have his clays cast and, despite the care that he took in covering them in damp cloth, 'under the effect of frost or the heat, whole blocks came asunder, with heads, arms, knees and bits of torso falling off'.[13]

In 1864 Rodin was taken on by Albert-Ernest Carrier-Belleuse (1824–1887), a prominent sculptor of the day. In order to respond to the many commissions he received, Carrier-Belleuse had set himself up in an impressive studio in Montmartre. Being admitted there represented a stage in Rodin's career that provided him with some very modest financial security and, above all, constituted a real recognition of his modelling skills. He took part in decorating various Parisian buildings, in particular one of the most luxurious *hôtels* that went up during the Second Empire (1852–1870), the Marquise of Païva's private residence on the Champs-Elysées.

After France's defeat in the Franco-Prussian War in 1871, Carrier-Belleuse brought Rodin to Belgium, where he spent seven years in Brussels. There, thanks to the material comfort he was able to enjoy, he could devote himself to creating his first great figure, *L'Age d'airain* (*The Age of Bronze*).

TAKING ON THE SALON

During the Second Empire, the Salon was still the main point of contact between artists and the public.[14] It was therefore vital for artists to be accepted there but, in making its decisions, the selection panel maintained a very strict sense of academic tradition. Yet, younger sculptors, who were admirers of the Florentine Renaissance, infused fresh life into it, by rejecting the idealised models of Antiquity and striving instead to convey an impression of real life. Their favourite material was bronze and, in this way, they tried to bridge the gap separating sculpture from the contemporary world.[15] After 1870, and with the French defeat in the Franco-Prussian War, their work reflected the suffering of the French people and their strong desire for revenge.

The bust of *L'Homme au nez cassé* (*The Man with the Broken Nose*) was the first work by Rodin to be accepted into the Salon. This was in 1875, and the artist's delight was all the greater as the mask had in fact been refused for exhibition ten years earlier. It had begun as a portrait of an old resident of the Saint-Marcel district, named Bibi, hence the initial title given to the work, *M.B.* This portrait was probably done at the end of 1863, but the following winter was very harsh, the consequence being that the rue Lebrun studio was impossible to heat and the clay model froze. 'The back of its head cracked and fell off. I was only able to preserve the mask, and sent it to the Salon which refused it.'[16]

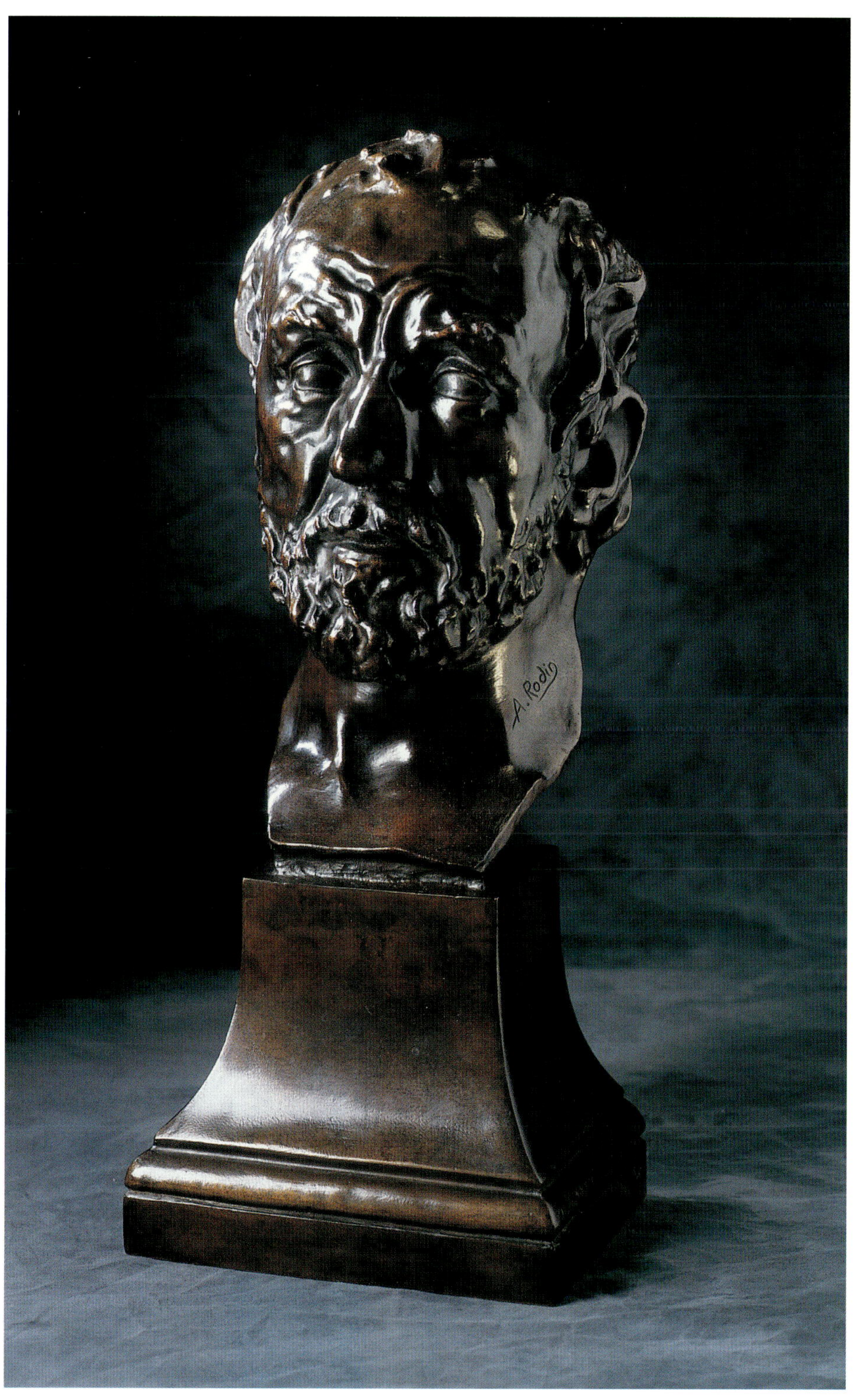

Mask of the Man with the Broken Nose 1863–64 (cat. 2)

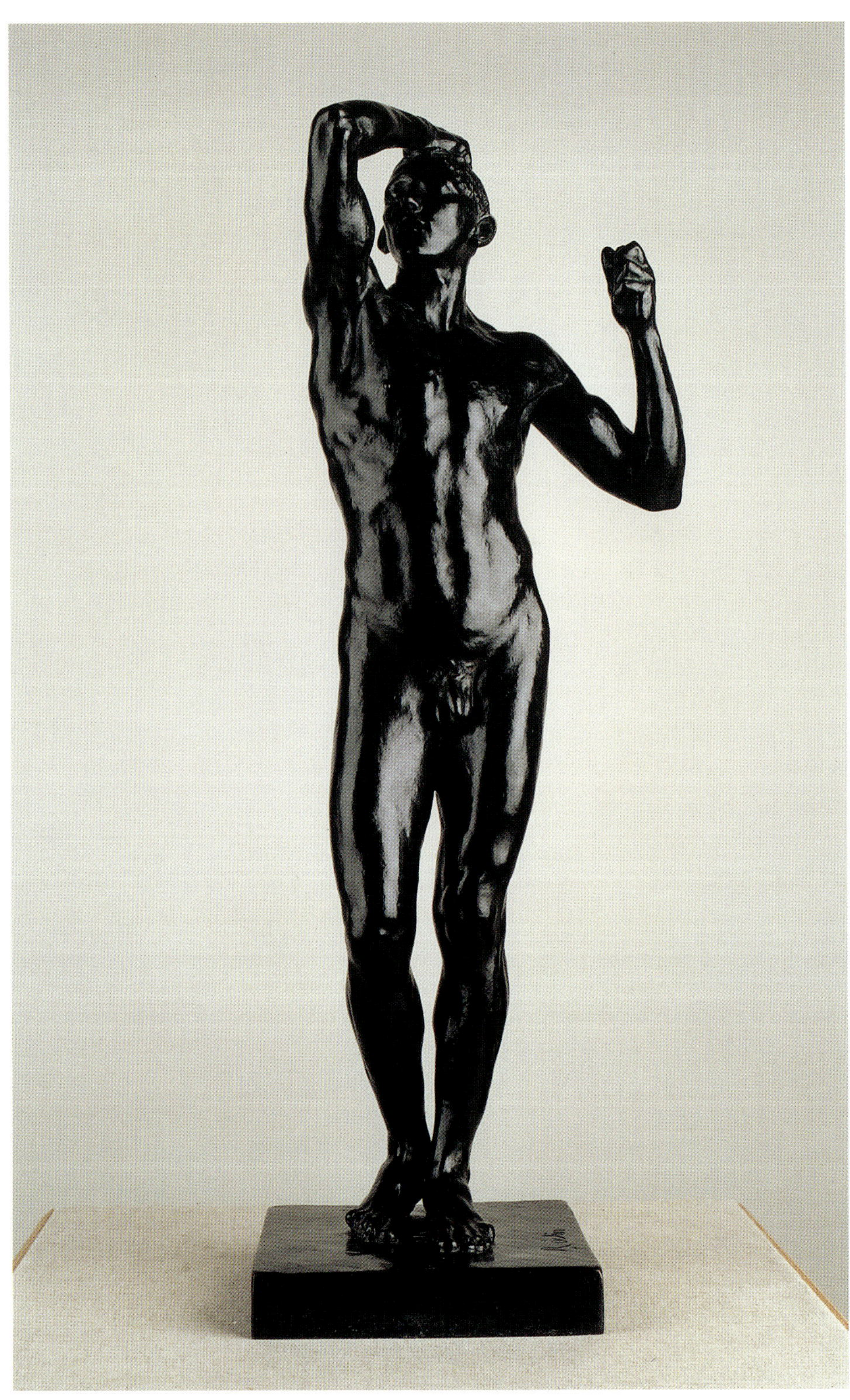

The Age of Bronze (reduction) 1876 (cat. 15)

Official institutions were not yet ready to accept a fragment. Rodin was, however, very attached to this piece. 'This mask', he told Truman Bartlett, 'determined all my future work. It is the first good piece of sculpture that I did.'[17] So he carefully preserved it and later gave it back its initial form as a bust. This was exhibited as a plaster in Brussels in 1872 but, as soon as he could, Rodin had it sculpted in marble.

This time, the work was accepted. It is true that Rodin had finished the back of the head and reworked the hair, whose locks were held in place by a headband. The bust thus took its place in the line of portraits of ancient philosophers, something which could of course only please the Salon panel members. As for the mask, it was exhibited for the first time in 1878, with the simple title of *Portrait of M.B.–*, and Louis Ménard, writing in the review *L'Art*, then noticed its resemblance to the portrait by Daniel de Volterra of Michelangelo, whose unkempt and deeply hollowed-out features were like those of the face modelled by Rodin.

In 1877, Rodin tried his luck again. He was nearing forty, and it was time for him to see his efforts recognised. For eighteen months he had devoted an immense amount of energy to making a figure on which all his hopes rested, which would become *The Age of Bronze*. Exhibited in January 1877 at the Cercle Artistique de Bruxelles (Brussels Art Society), this plaster, which is known to us thanks to priceless photos taken by Marconi and Eugène Druet, was not well received.

In Bartlett's opinion, Rodin's sole purpose was to make a nude study, a good figure that was correctly proportioned and smoothly contoured. After no doubt having tried them, he did away with professional models who offered him only conventional poses. Thanks to the officers at a barracks near where he was living in the rue du Bourgmestre, from October 1875 he had the opportunity of working with Auguste Neyt, a twenty-two year old soldier belonging to the contingent of rural telegraphists. According to Bartlett, Rodin had his model try out different natural poses until one of them completely satisfied him, chosen for its own sake and not because of its relation to any particular subject matter. 'I do not create', he said, 'I see, and it is because I see that I am able to do.'[18]

In the nineteenth century, a sculpture had to have a clearly identifiable subject, be it historical, literary, allegorical or mythological. Once the figure was completed, it had to be given a title. Rodin could not think of one at the time, however, and it seems that the piece was exhibited without a title in the Cercle Artistique de Bruxelles. An admirer of the sculptor, Jean Rousseau, wrote at the time that 'purely concerned with questions of style and execution, like any artist really smitten with his art, the author had forgotten just one thing – to name his plaster cast and reveal its subject.'[19]

In Paris, the figure remained unchanged but it did finally get a title: *The Age of Bronze*, that being the third of mankind's four ages (gold, silver, bronze and iron), as defined by the Greek poet Hesiod (eighth–seventh century BC), whom the poet Leconte de Lisle had translated into French in 1869. It was during the 'age of bronze' that man is thought to have learned to fashion metal so as to make weapons and tools, the consequence of which was the development of warfare and violence. Rodin disregarded these historical elements, in order to give us insight into the internal world of the creature that he is representing: confronted with the brutality of a troubled period, this creature becomes aware both of what he has lost and the talents that enable him to survive. This figure, 'who looks as if he is consumed by suffering and dreams', becomes the image of a painful awakening.[20]

That the subject was not evident, coupled with the impression of life that the work conveyed – this 'very down-to-earth whiff of humanity' (Octave Mirbeau), noticed with such admiration by the majority of critics – lay at the heart of the accusations levelled against the work in Brussels and later in Paris, of being made from a cast taken from a live model.[21] Enlivened by the interplays of light produced by the figure's slight tilt of the hips, the model presents an exactness and acuteness reminiscent of Renaissance bronzes.

In the winter of 1875–1876, while the statue was still being cast, Rodin fulfilled his youthful dream of going to Italy. In Florence, he was especially struck by Michelangelo, whose work, whatever he may have said, he had almost certainly studied in the Louvre. There, he could have seen *The Dying Slave*, whose pose is so close to that of *The Age of Bronze*. But he also stopped and looked at the great bronze artists of the Renaissance, in particular Donatello (*c.*1386–1466). The study of their works could only encourage him along the path previously trod by the Neo-Florentines, who strove to get close to living nature.

Other sculptors became jealous of Rodin's extraodinary modelling ability and this, coupled with the obscurity of the subject matter, resulted in the accusation intended to discredit the work: that the figure was cast from life. At the same time as saying that they believed this accusation to be ridiculous, others criticised *The Age of Bronze* for being 'the slavish imitation of a model devoid of character or beauty'.[22] However, if it is indeed this 'realism' that constitutes the artist's originality, it is a realism whose source he had found in the sculpture of Antiquity.

In March 1877, Rodin returned to Paris with the plaster cast that he was hoping to show at the Salon. The work was indeed accepted but, being presented by an unknown artist, it was badly placed in a dark corner. In addition, the rumour now also spread in Paris about its being cast from life. This was a very bad blow for Rodin, as he was counting on *The Age of Bronze* to bring him recognition as a sculptor and was hoping that the work would be purchased by the State, which was the starting point of any career as he knew full well.

He tried to defend himself against these accusations but did so clumsily, and the request that he sent on 22 May 1877 to the director of the Beaux-Arts, Henri de Chennevières, to purchase the work, was rejected. 'I don't know what to do', he wrote to Rose Beuret in May, 'I have financial commitments all over the place and no money. The future is very bleak, and misery lies before me.'

However, Rodin's modelling talent enabled him to be employed on different construction sites. For example, he sculpted masks for the water tower at the Trocadéro Palace built for the Exposition Universelle of 1878, he went to Nice in August 1879, and later Strasbourg, to do some decorative pieces there, as well as working for the Sèvres porcelain factory between 1879 and 1882.

In February 1879, Chennevières had been replaced as director of the Beaux-Arts by Edmond Turquet, to whom the painter Maurice Hacquette (who also worked for the Sèvres porcelain factory) warmly recommended Rodin. Turquet asked for a new report but, on 5 February 1880, the examining board of the Ecole des Beaux-Arts again concluded that 'whilst this statue might not be duplication by casting in the absolute sense of the word, duplication is involved in such a significant way that it cannot really pass as a work of art'.[23] A few days later, a group of sculptors including Paul Dubois, Alexandre Falguière, Carrier-Belleuse, Henri Chapu, Chaplain, Gabriel-Jules Thomas, Eugène Delaplanche and Charles Moreau, also spoke out on his behalf. In search of work, Alfred Boucher called in at the Laoust studio where he spotted:

> A man with a red beard busily preparing large balls of clay ... to make heads and plump limbs of children from them, with a remarkable assuredness and speed of execution. He asked the name of the sculptor and learned that it was Rodin, Rodin, the so-called fraud ... He went straight off to see Paul Dubois, his teacher and member of the Salon selection panel, and told him about what he had just seen. The author of the *Chanteur Florentin* (*Florentine Singer*) immediately informed his friend Henri Chapu and took him over to Rodin's studio. The sculptor repeated an improvisation from memory in front of his two fellow artists. They immediately concluded that it was out

of the question that *The Age of Bronze* was a fake. They went to get the support of a few other well-known sculptors, including Carrier-Belleuse who had already known Rodin's worth for quite some time. The upshot was that they wrote a collective letter on 23 February 1880 to the Under-Secretary of State, affirming the bona fides of the artist.[24]

Official orders for *The Age of Bronze* followed: the acquisition of the work in plaster, at a cost of 2000 francs on 26 May 1880 and, the same day, a commission for a casting from Thiébaut Frères, for 2200 francs. At that time, the bronze – to which a vine leaf had been added – was exhibited in the Salon, open since 1 May. The purchase and order had thus been announced unofficially, before being made public. In the autumn, *The Age of Bronze* received a gold medal at the Salon in Gand. In 1885, it was put in the Luxembourg Gardens in Paris, where it stayed until 1901 when, with Rodin at the height of his fame, a place was found for it in the rooms of the Museum there. It left the Luxembourg in 1933 for the Louvre, and today it is in the Musée d'Orsay.

Besides two smaller scale copies, a dozen plaster casts and fifty or so bronzes also attest to the popular success of *The Age of Bronze*. Whilst Rodin himself seems to have despised it by the end of the century, the piece subsequently came back in his favour, as shown by the admirable photos that he had Druet, Jean-Francois Limet and Jacques-Ernest Bulloz take of it in the early 1900s. Indeed, one can say that Rodin had an awareness of photography as an art form very early on and, just as each work that came from his hands was capable of becoming the starting point for new compositions, he was very much interested in the transfigurations that a work of art could undergo as the result of a photographer's sensitive treatment.

THE GATES OF HELL

By administrative decree of 16 August 1880, Rodin received a commission for a decorative portico, intended for the projected Musée des Arts Décoratifs (Museum of Decorative Arts), which was to be adorned with bas-reliefs inspired by Dante's *Divine Comedy*. No doubt it was the sculptor himself who suggested the subject, as he was known to be a long-time admirer of Dante, whose writings he always carried around in his pocket. His sudden interest in relief is more surprising. Was it the memory of the doors of the Baptistry in Florence? Or was it rather the influence of Augustin Préault[25] who (discarding what he had learnt from his teacher David d'Angers, according to whom the principal quality of a relief is its readability) had revitalised that form of sculpture by taking its power of expression to the extreme? Préault had died in 1879, and it is possible that Rodin discovered his work through a few articles about him that appeared at the time. For work on this commission, the ruling body of the Ecole des Beaux-Arts had allocated him the atelier[26] of the Dépôt des Marbres in the rue de l'Université. In October 1880, he received the initial instalment of a quarter of the agreed amount, but the first year was especially given over to drawn studies. This was the time of the 'black' drawings, of the groups of the damned sketched in Chinese ink with a great boldness of touch, tinted with brown or purple ink and interspersed with splashes of gouache to anticipate their sculptural effect, or again cut out, pasted onto a sheet of paper, reworked and transferred to a third medium.

To begin with, he had imagined a division into panels like that of Lorenzo Ghiberti's *Gates of Paradise* in the Baptistry in Florence (1425–1452), but by the second maquette[27] he had decided against any partitioning of the panels, following the example of *The Last Judgment* on the altar wall in the Sistine Chapel. It was again perhaps the influence of Michelangelo and, more precisely, the presentation of *The Slaves* in the Louvre, on either side of the *Gates of the Stanga Palace* (as it was reproduced in the *Magasin Pittoresque* in 1877), that spurred him in 1881 to propose completing his own *Gates* with the figures of *Adam* and *Eve* on either side. As for the panels, he discarded two-thirds

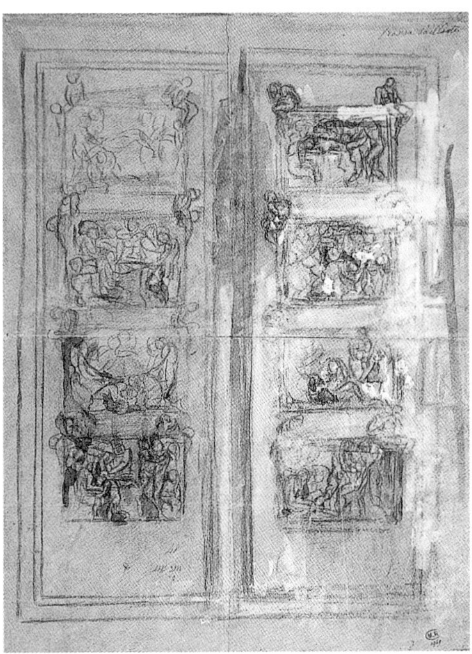

Proposal for the Gates of Hell with Eight Panels c.1880
Charcoal, grey wash and gouache 55.7 x 44.7 cm
Musée Rodin

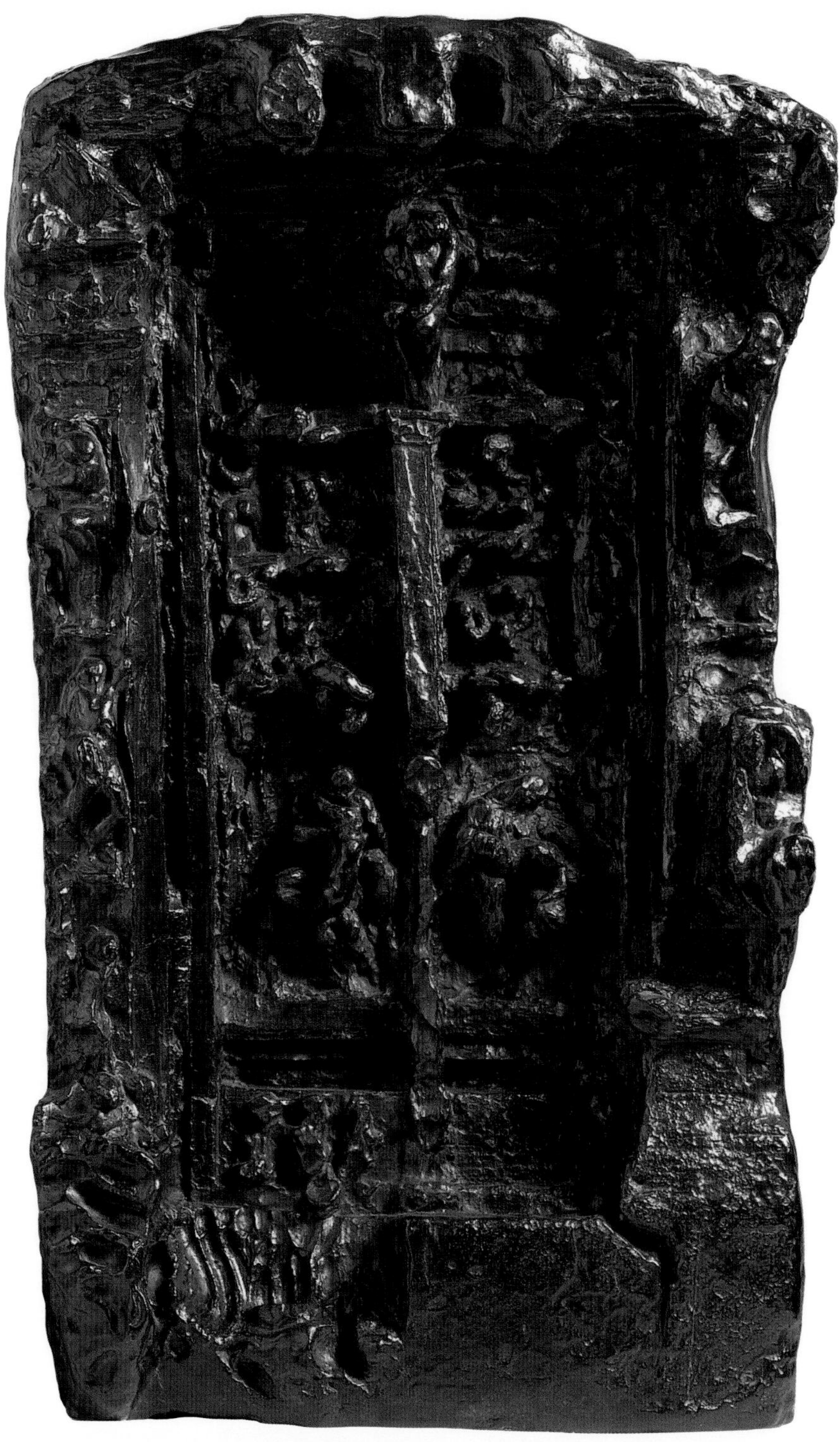

Third Maquette for The Gates of Hell 1880 (cat. 31)

of Dante's poem, being only interested in the darkest part, *Inferno,* and keeping only a few identifiable characters: Paolo and Francesca, Ugolino and his children, the Shades and the Thinker, who is none other than Dante himself, within a swarm of figures of various sizes. These figures and groups, invading the traditional structure in which they sometimes replace the architectural elements, had been created independently of each other. They were tried out on the panels, the latter already represented in 1882 by a wooden frame, before being set aside.

In 1884, Rodin's friend William Ernest Henley, an English art critic, asked him for 'some of those admirable figurines of despairing souls' for the exhibition that he was organising in London, at Grosvenor House (10 March 1884), but it seems that Rodin did not send him anything. By the end of 1884, however, he felt himself to be sufficiently sure of his project to have estimates for the cast drawn up, and an order was placed by decree on 20 August 1885. The model, probably set up in late 1885 or early 1886, did not satisfy him, however, and he modified it time and time again, *The Gates of Hell* thereby evolving in a spontaneous and organic way, without any prior set pattern.

Whilst the order that had been placed for *The Gates* and the importance it had taken on were known in artistic circles, few people had yet seen the work. The general public had to wait until 1885 to have a first inkling of it through a very detailed description that appeared in an article by Octave Mirbeau (1848–1917), one of the artist's inner circle of friends. He had obtained information from Rodin showing how the artist had a very clear idea of the overall composition – and in this context we should remember that in early 1885 *The Gates* had not yet been assembled:

> The subject chosen by the artist is Dante's *Inferno*. It is framed by exquisite architectural mouldings whose style belongs to that vague and charming period that extends from the Gothic to the Renaissance, a period rich in the mysticism of the one and the elegance of the other.
>
> It is amidst the terrifying circles outlined by the Florentine poet, in the inextinguishable flames and perpetually boiling lava, that Rodin gives full flight to his imagination. Apart from its important groups, this vast lyrical composition has more than three hundred figures, all different in both attitude and feeling, each one expressing, in a kind of synthesis, a form of human passion, pain and malediction. In scrutinising these contorted mouths and convulsed fists, these panting breasts and bewildered masks down which flow endless tears, it seems that we can hear the cries of eternal Desolation.

> Below the capital of the gate, in a panel that is slightly hollowed out in the form of an arch, the figure of Dante is jutting out … from the background, surrounded by bas-reliefs representing the arrival in the underworld. His pose is somewhat reminiscent of that of Michelangelo's *Thinker*. The Dante is sitting, his torso thrust forward, his right arm resting on his left leg, giving the body an inexpressible tragic movement. His face, looking as terrible as that of some vengeful god, leans heavily on his hand that is being pushed into his skin at the edge of his pinned-back lips, and his dark eyes stare out into the abyss whence sulphurous vapours arise with the lament of the damned.
>
> The leaves of the portal are divided into two panels, each separated by a group, in a hammer-like formation. On the right side are Ugolino and his sons. On the left Francesca da Rimini, entwined in Paolo's body, provides a most sweet and tender contrast with Ugolino's group, which captures all the horrors of hunger … Above the groups, Rodin has composed bas-reliefs on which stand out three-dimensional figures and scenes in relief, giving an extraordinary perspective to his work. Each side of the gate is crowned by tragic masks, heads of furies and terrible or gracious allegories of the guilty passions. Beneath the groups, more bas-reliefs, from which masks of pain jut out. Along the river of mud, there are galloping centaurs, bearing off bodies of women struggling, rolling and writhing around on the reared rumps of horses. Other centaurs are drawing bows against the wretched creatures wanting to escape, and we can see women, prostitutes, being rapidly carried away, lunging forward headfirst into the inflamed mire.[28]

It was only at the end of 1885 that *The Gates of Hell* was mounted in Rodin's studio. A few in the inner circle were allowed to see it, such as Félicien Rops, Edmond de Goncourt and Félicien Champsaur who, a year after Mirbeau, gave a new description of it, based for the first time on the plaster cast. His text brings little more than one additional element to bear, the mention of three characters 'dominating the whole, seeming to embody the phrase that they show written on the pediment: *Lasciate ogni speranza, voi ch'entrate*: *The Shades*.'[29]

The eighth instalment (the final one before payment of the balance in 1917) was paid on 31 March 1888. It was then expected that Rodin would present *The Gates* at the 1888 Salon or at the Exposition Universelle the following year. He couldn't make up his mind about it, but he did permit more visitors, such as Claude Monet, 'amazed' at what he discovered in the studio, Edmon Bazire, Léon Lequime, Georges Rodenbach and others. In order to imagine what they saw, we need to look at the description given by Gustave Geffroy of a work

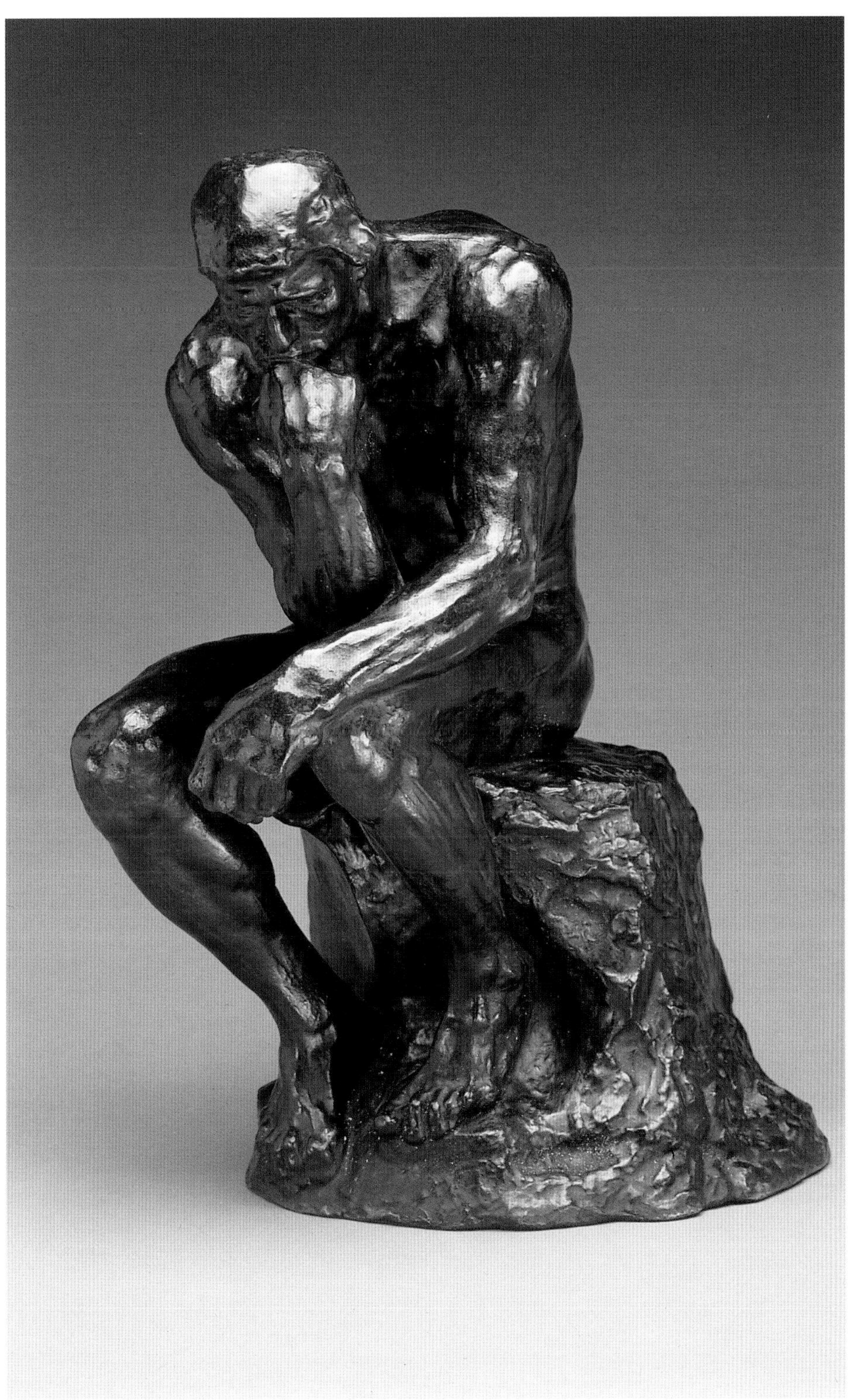

The Thinker (reduction) 1880 (cat. 33)

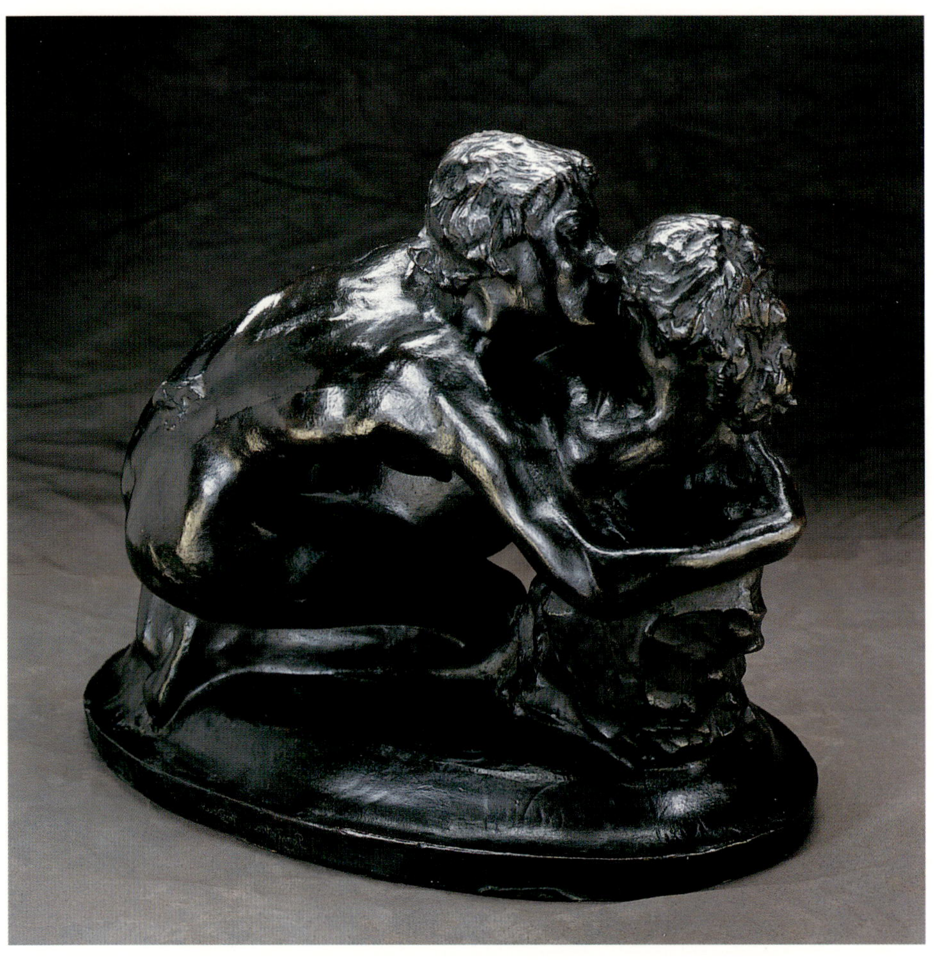

Ovid's Metamorphoses *c*.1885–89 (cat. 42)

at once 'upright and ... spread out. The statues at the top, some of the panel groups, the uprights and the bas-reliefs are all in place. But right throughout the vast hall are scattered statuettes in all shapes and sizes – on the sculptors' stands, the shelves, the divan, the chairs, the ground – their faces raised, arms twisted and legs flexed, all in a jumble, lying down or standing upright, giving the impression of a living cemetery. Behind *The Gates*, six metres high, is a crowd, silent and eloquent, that one should look at individual by individual, as one might, in reading a book, stop at the pages, the indented lines, the sentences, the words ... As *The Gates* is not yet finished, it can not yet be completely described.'[30] However, a series of photographs from the studio of the Dépôt des Marbres taken by Druet between 1896, when he began to work with Rodin, and 1898 when some of them were published, shows a plaster cast in the background that seems clearly identical to the one we know. This would mean that *The Gates* had found its present appearance before 1900, and perhaps as early as 1888–1889 since, after that date, it seems that Rodin, busy working on prestigious commissions (such as *The Kiss*, 1888; *Monument to Victor Hugo*, 1889; *Monument to Balzac*, 1891) had hardly any time now to devote to it.

After 1889, virtually no further mention is made of *The Gates of Hell*, and it was only in 1900, not as part of the Exposition Universelle, but rather the personal exhibition organised by Rodin in Paris in the Pavillon de l'Alma, that the general public finally discovered 'this work about which more and more is said each day but that no-one ever sees'.[31] Yet, when the exhibition opened on 1 June, the visitors who had had the good fortune to see the plaster cast in the studio, discovered a new *Gates* and a very surprising one at that, as the figures had not been put back in place.

It has often been said that if *The Gates of Hell* was presented unfinished, it was because Rodin had lacked the time to fully assemble it. This is barely plausible, however, given that we are talking about an official commission which he had worked on so much and which was finally shown to the public as part of the artist's first personal exhibition in Paris. Moreover, nothing prevented him from putting the small groups in place after the opening of the exhibition, as he did for the *Shades*. The reason for this choice no doubt lies in the changing nature of Rodin's approach. Henceforth, he eliminated everything that seemed superfluous and, as he had just done for the armless *La Voix intérieure* (*The Interior Voice*), he very deliberately stripped from *The Gates* everything that made it too immediately comprehensible. Such an approach was perfectly coherent with the Symbolist aesthetic that the imagination of the spectator or reader participates in creating the meaning of the work of art.

After the closure of the exhibition, *The Gates of Hell* went back to the rue de l'Université where it still was in 1911, but by the following year it was in Meudon. Rodin left his home there, the Villa des Brillants, less and less frequently, and he doubtless felt the desire to have the work close to him, even if it was now clear that he would never finish it. In any event, the 1885 commission for the cast had been cancelled by 1904.

To his secretary René Chéruy, who asked him at the time why he did not consider *The Gates* to be finished, Rodin replied that he was not satisfied with the architectural part, and in particular with the mouldings that were intended not only to frame the doors but also to create a transitional mood. During the years that had followed the commissioning of *The Gates of Hell*, Rodin had amassed over two thousand drawings of architectural details in notebooks. A large number of these drawings focused on the mouldings. Twenty-three plates out of the hundred in his work *Les Cathédrales de France* (*The Cathedrals of France*) were devoted to them, as well as the final chapter of the work: 'The moulding he had in mind essentially represents the whole governing idea of the work.'[32] But he no doubt never found the miraculous profile that would have bestowed a perfect homogeneity on the whole. Thus Gustave Coquiot had no hesitation in saying very clearly in 1913: 'Within just a month, everything could have perhaps been set up. Rodin was unable to devote this month to his *Gates*, and it will most likely remain unfinished'.[33] To which Rodin retorted: 'And do you think that cathedrals are finished?'[34]

The Gates of Hell was the first major work to be commissioned from Rodin, even if it did not really come off in so far as he did not deliver it. The work can be regarded as the summation of his entire life, and it certainly did accompany him all throughout his existence, reflecting his main interests, his admiration for Gothic architecture and the Italian Renaissance, and for Dante and Baudelaire. Above all, it is the best demonstration of the power of expression he gave to the human body.

In actual fact, Rodin had become aware very early on of the force of his small figures and, well before 1889, some of them were made into stand-alone works in their own right. Indeed, as early as 1881, he had exhibited *Adam*, the first piece that came from work related to *The Gates*; in 1883, in the Cercle des Arts Libéraux (Liberal Arts Society) in Paris, one could see the *Cariatide à la pierre* (*Fallen Caryatid with Stone*) and a *Torse de femme nue contorsionnée* (*Torso of a Convoluted Woman*) which was none other than *Eve jeune* (*Young Eve*). At the Galérie Georges Petit in 1886, a series of fragments was shown, three *Etudes du rut humain (Studies of Human Mating)*, one of which was *Je suis belle*

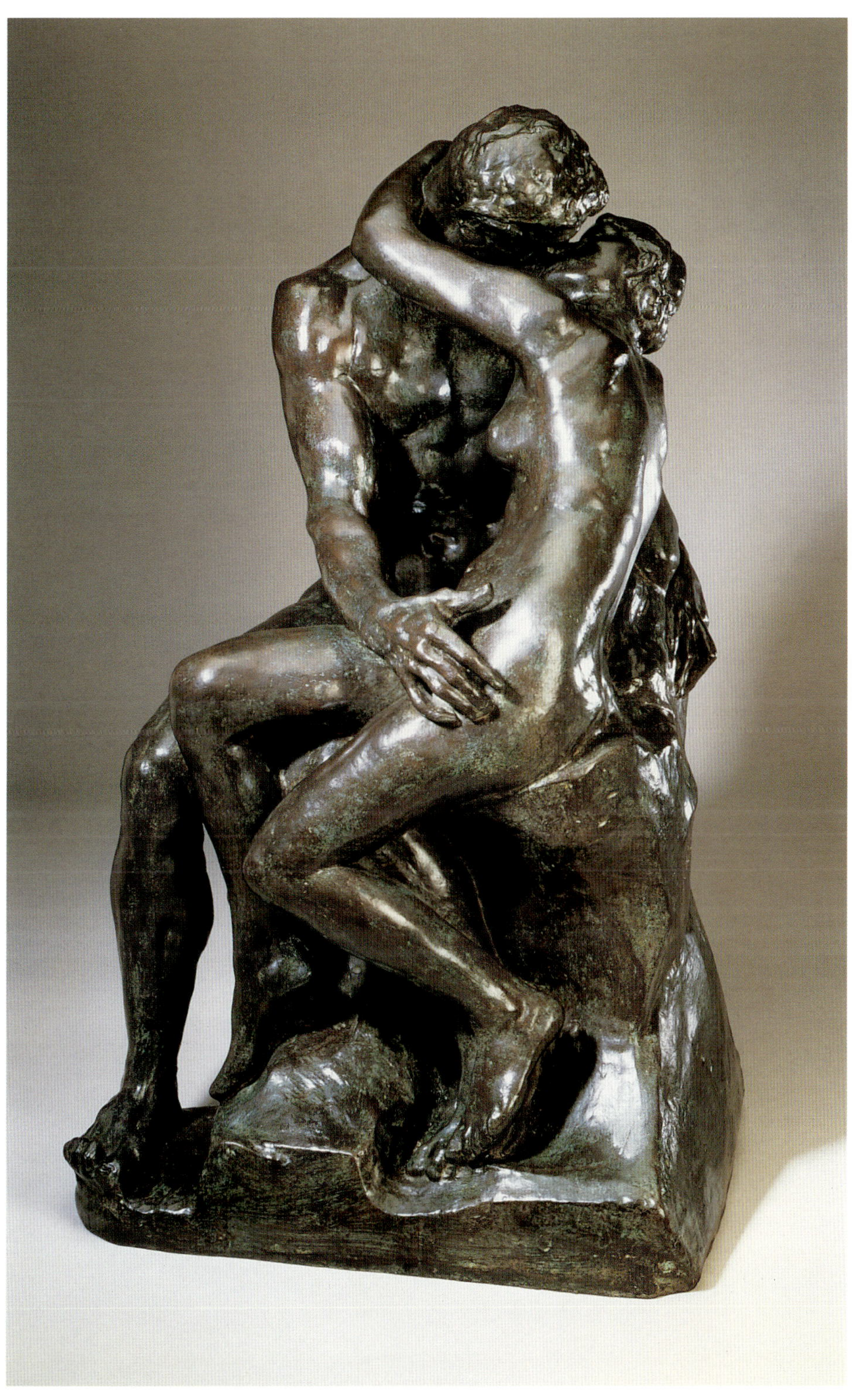

The Kiss c.1881–82 (cat. 37)

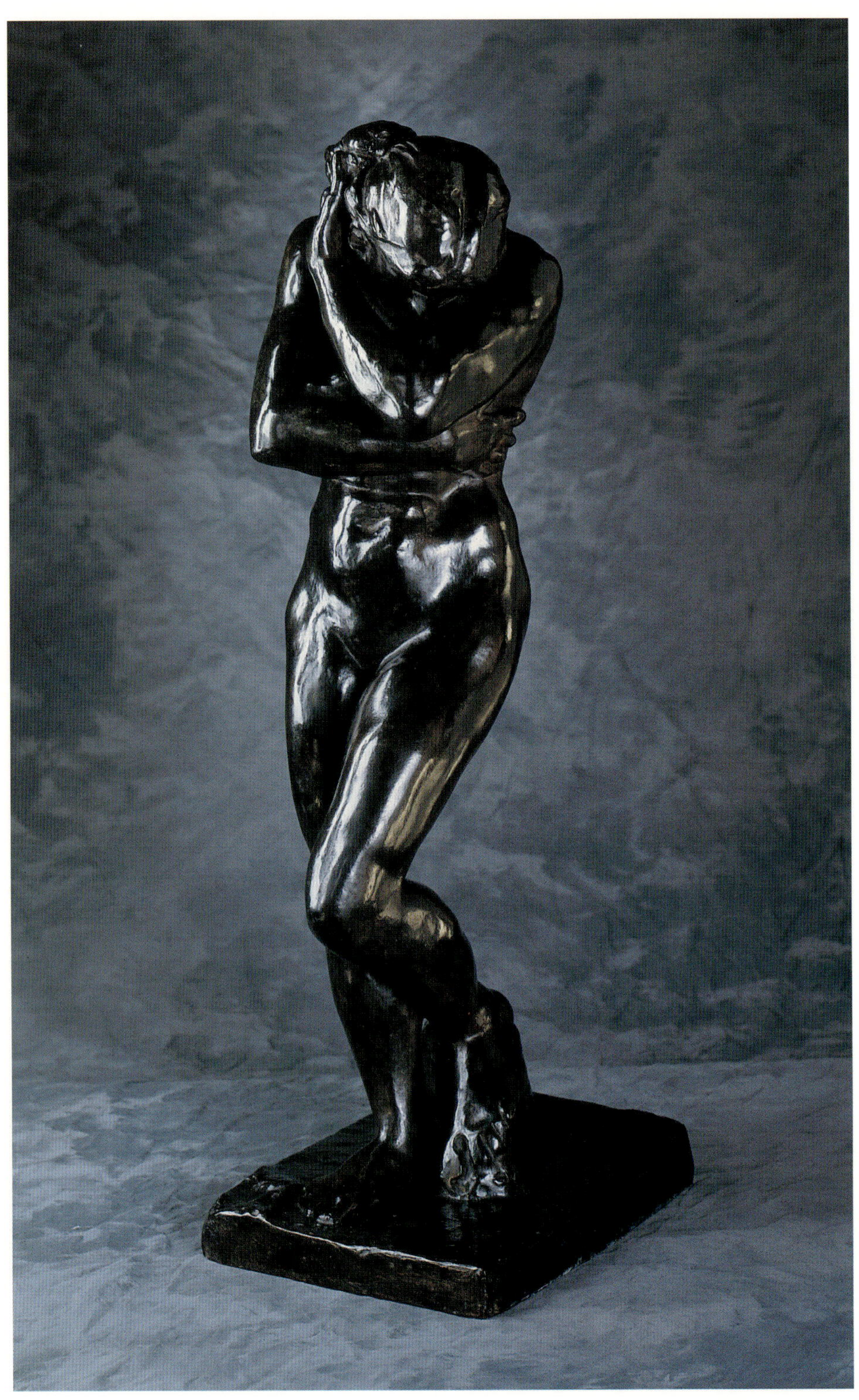

Eve (reduction) 1883 (cat. 41)

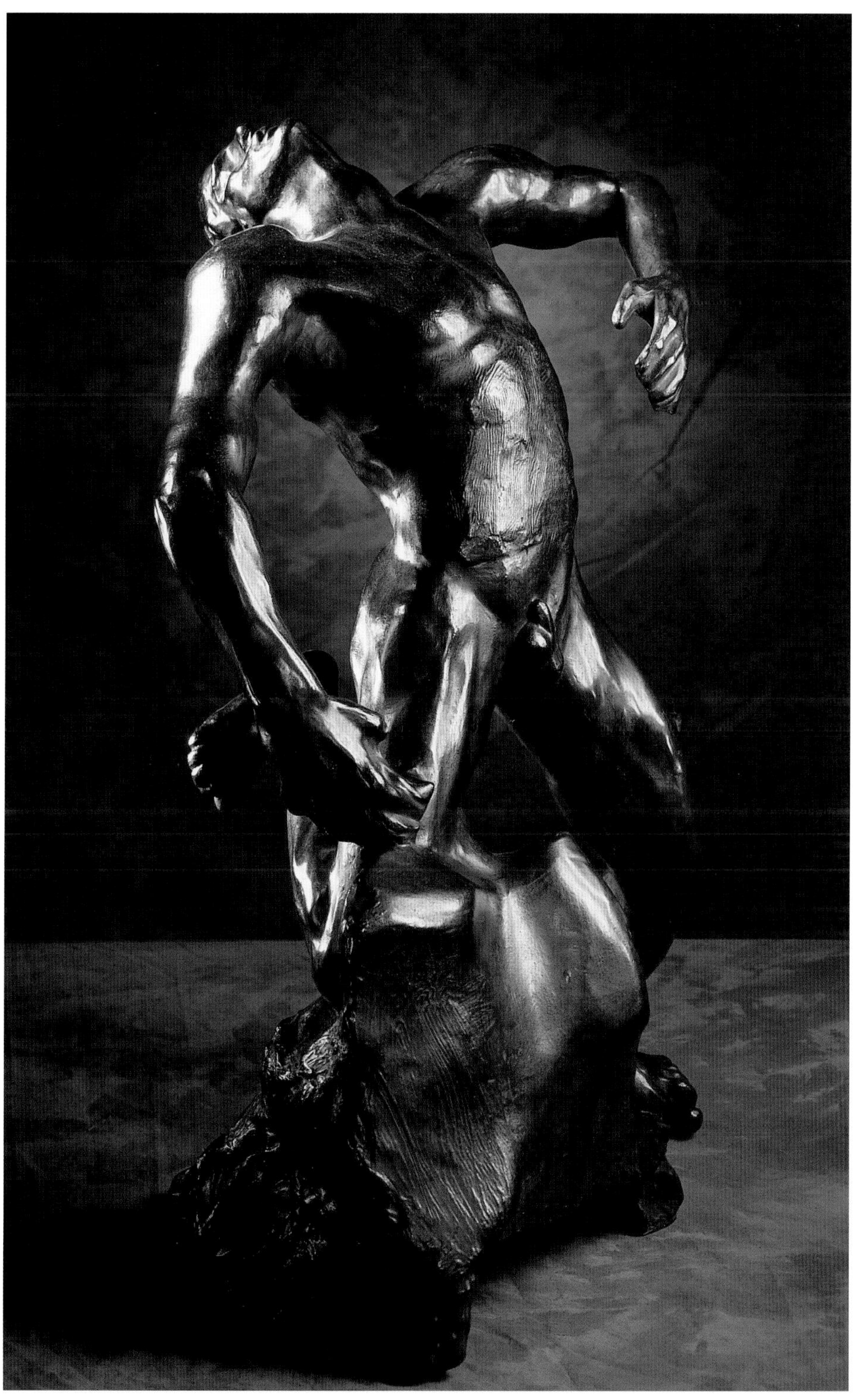

The Falling Man 1882 (cat. 38)

(*I am Beautiful*), and three *Femmes lasses* (*Weary Women*), today known by the title of *La Femme accroupie* (*The Crouching Woman*), *Andromède* (*Andromeda*) and *Fallen Caryatid with Stone*, the latter bearing as an epigraph a verse by Baudelaire whose influence was omnipresent throughout the whole work. In Brussels, in 1887, Rodin showed for the first time *Le Baiser (The Kiss)*, which he had just taken off the door panels, and *Ugolino*; and in 1888, in Copenhagen, *Le Penseur* (*The Thinker*) under the title *Le Poète* (*The Poet*). But it was in 1889, during the *Monet–Rodin* exhibition at the Galérie Georges Petit, that his work was really revealed to a broader public. He there exhibited an important set of fragments from *The Gates*: *Sphinge, Métamorphoses d'Ovide (Ovid's Metamorphoses), Tête coupée de saint Jean-Baptiste (Severed Head of Saint John the Baptist), L'Eternel Printemps (Eternal Spring), Sirènes (Sirens), Fugit Amor (Fugitive Love)*, a mask from *Pleureuse (Weeping Woman), The Thinker* under the name of *Poète-Penseur*, the *Ombres* (*Shades*), then entitled *Grandes figures douloureuses* (*Great Suffering Figures*).

Visitors to the exhibition were astounded by these 'bodily contortions, these unexpected inversions, these unforeseen flexions, the disconcerting originality of all the poses of these figures, bowed and bent, jostled and head over heels ... these couplings [that] no sculptor had previously dared treat'.[35] They could see none of the traditional Salon poses or references that they were familiar with. Thus, deprived of clothes and decor, Paolo and Francesca are no longer identifiable, and it was the public that suggested calling the group *The Kiss*. Rodin makes the body itself significant, having the figures take on new positions, sometimes verging on acrobatics, in order to achieve this. *Le Désespoir* (*Despair*), sitting on the ground, holds a leg up in the air; *The Crouching Woman* turns her head round in an almost impossible contortion, twisting the opposite way to her body. *L'Homme qui tombe* (*The Falling Man*) is arched over backwards. At the bottom of the right pier, on the shoulder of the *Creator* who is curled up to fit the square-shaped base, a crouching figure seems to be whispering ideas in his ear. The long beard of this masculine character may be interpreted as a sort of symbolic self-portrait, a kind of personal signature.

The period of intense creation related to *The Gates of Hell* subsequently allowed Rodin to have many figures at his disposal, whether they were retained in the complete plaster cast or not. It was also at that time, between 1880 and 1885, that he discovered the processes that were later to become an integral part of his way of working, those involving fragments, assemblages and the multifarious. In order to carry out these assemblages, Rodin had no qualms about using the same figure or group on several different occasions. *Fugitive Love* appeared twice in the right door panel, *The Falling Man* is here fastened to the lintel, elsewhere bent over backwards to lift *The Crouching Woman*. This is taken

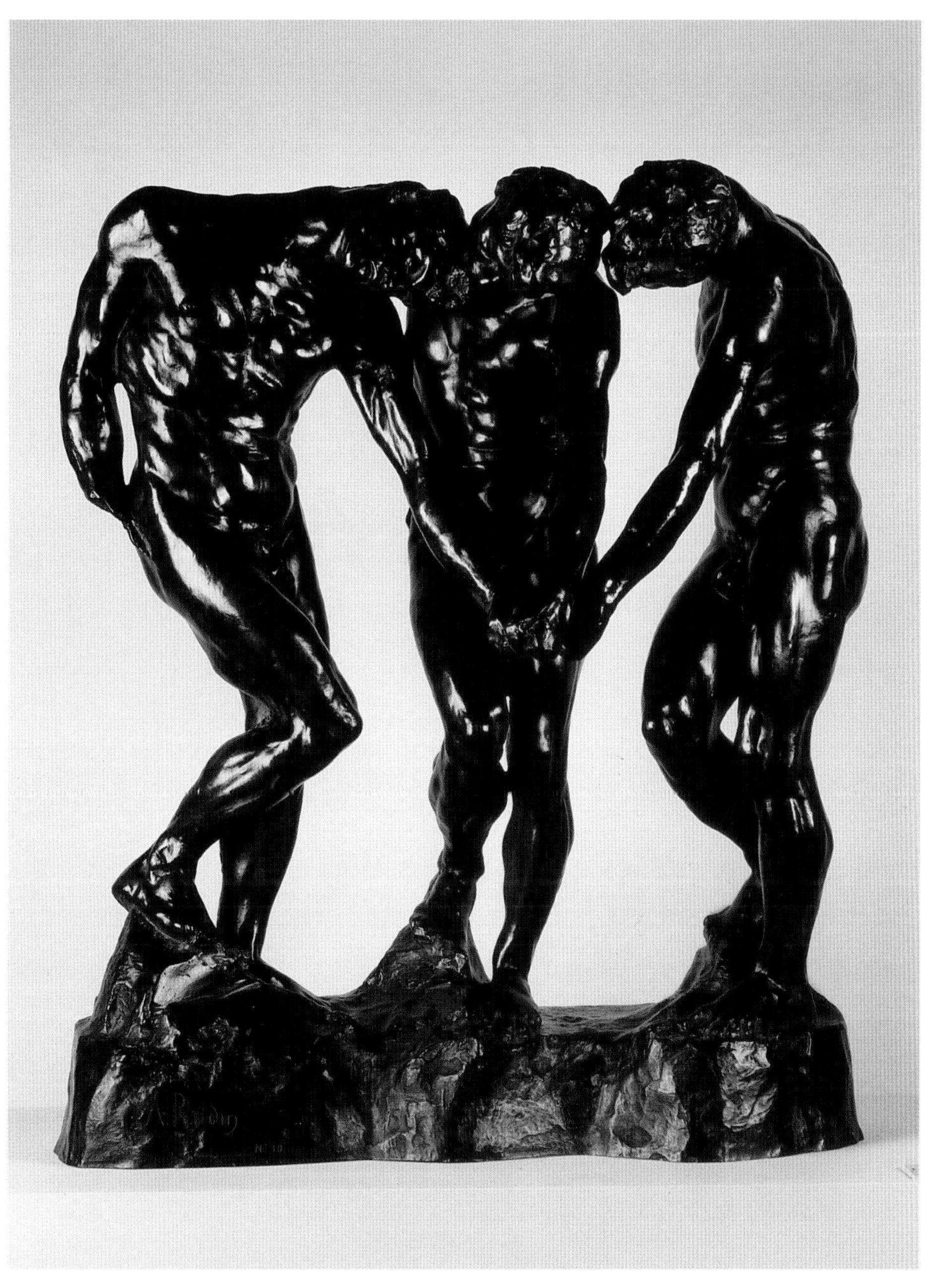

The Three Shades 1880–1904 (cat. 36)

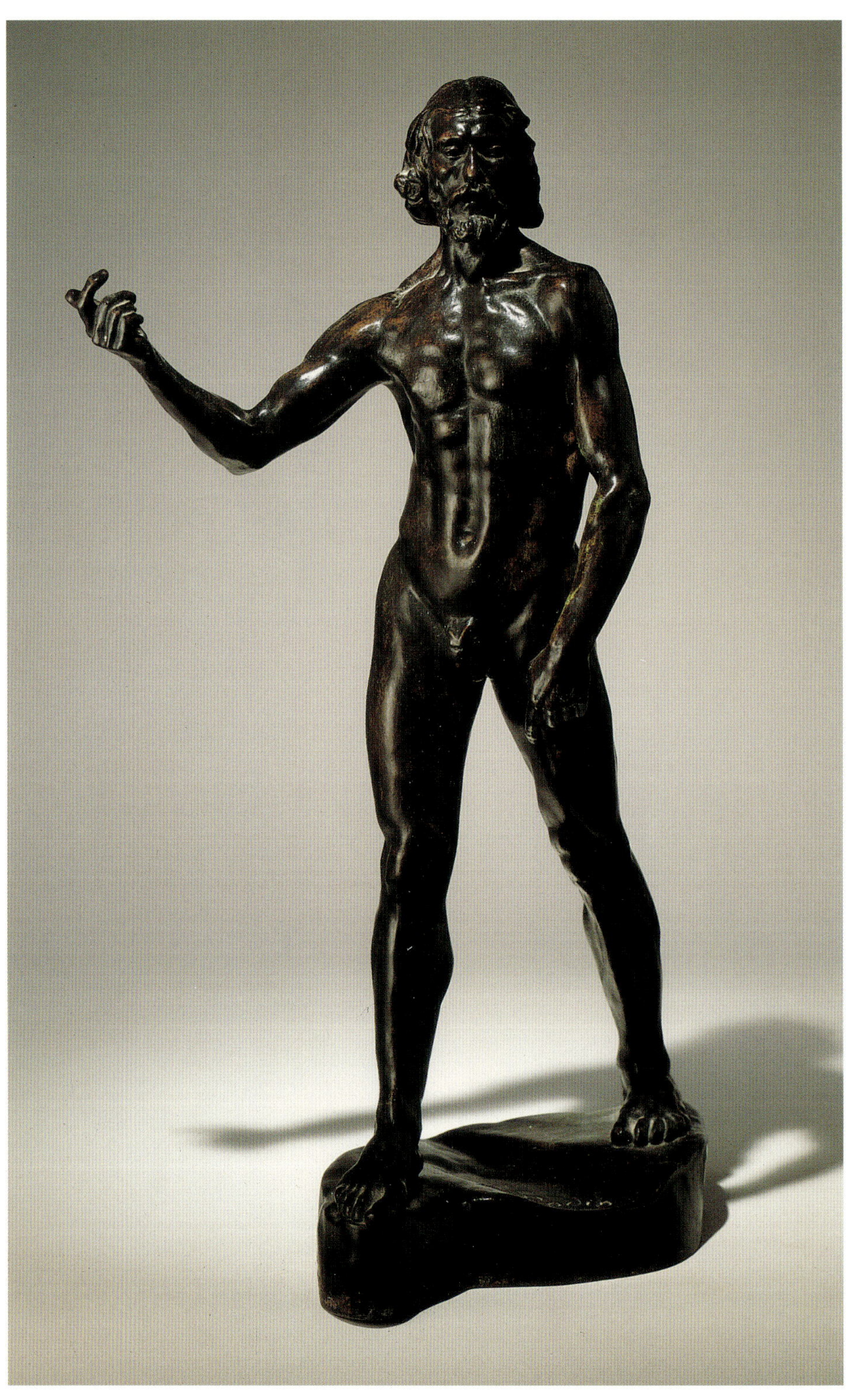

Saint John the Baptist Preaching c.1880 (cat. 17)

to its extreme with the *Les Trois Ombres* (*The Three Shades*), a group based on the same figure which, repeated thrice over, appeared from three different angles. The spaces between the figures become as important as the figures themselves, while the insistent vertical line of the arms, although bereft of hands, leads the viewer towards the Thinker, the Poet, Dante or perhaps Rodin himself contemplating his own work.

VIGOROUS AND DARING

'Just as (contemporary French sculptor) Antoine-Louis Barye revealed the true nature of living creatures by showing their instinctive behaviour, so Rodin reveals moods beneath contorted bodies and desolated poses.' This was how Gustave Geffroy stressed the profound originality of the artist's work in his review (in *La Justice*) of Rodin's set of fragments from *The Gates of Hell,* exhibited at the Galérie Georges Petit in 1886 as part of the Fifth International Exhibition of Painting and Sculpture. At that time, only a gallery like the Petit, which had always striven to encourage modernity, could actually venture to show such audacious works, as witnessed by the appearance there of three *Studies of Human Mating*, one of which was *I am Beautiful*, and three *Weary Women*: *The Crouching Woman*, *Andromeda* and the *Fallen Caryatid with Stone.*

This was not the kind of thing that could be exhibited at the Salon of the Société des Artistes Français (Association of French Artists) where Rodin was now regularly represented, at least in the early part of the decade. After *The Age of Bronze*, he showed *Saint Jean-Baptiste* (*Saint John the Baptist Preaching*) there (in plaster cast in 1880, in bronze in 1881, the bust alone having been presented in 1879), then *Adam* (plaster in 1881) and each year new busts: *Laurens* and *Carrier-Belleuse* in 1882, *Danielli* and *Legros* in 1883, *Hugo* and *Dalou* in 1884, *Proust* in 1885, and finally *Mme V.* (*Mme Vicuña*) in 1888. Characterised by a simple and strong idea, by 'exceptionally broad, vigorous and daring' contours, these figures, the *Saint John the Baptist Preaching* in particular, contrasted with the 'pretty objects of sculpture: neat, elegant and well-mannered' that were exhibited at the Salon. 'Monsieur, you are a spoil-sport', exclaimed Dargenty in 1883. 'When one works like this, one stays at home. You are like an elephant in a china shop. I tell you quite sincerely, Monsieur Rodin, your fully naked men are not presentable ... But, since you are here, we will not have the indecency to kick you out; no, not outside, as such, but as close to the door as possible. And so it is that the *Saint Jean* by M. Rodin, which is assuredly the strongest and most personal work in this Salon, is consigned to very bad company, in the most obscure corner of the whole place.'[36]

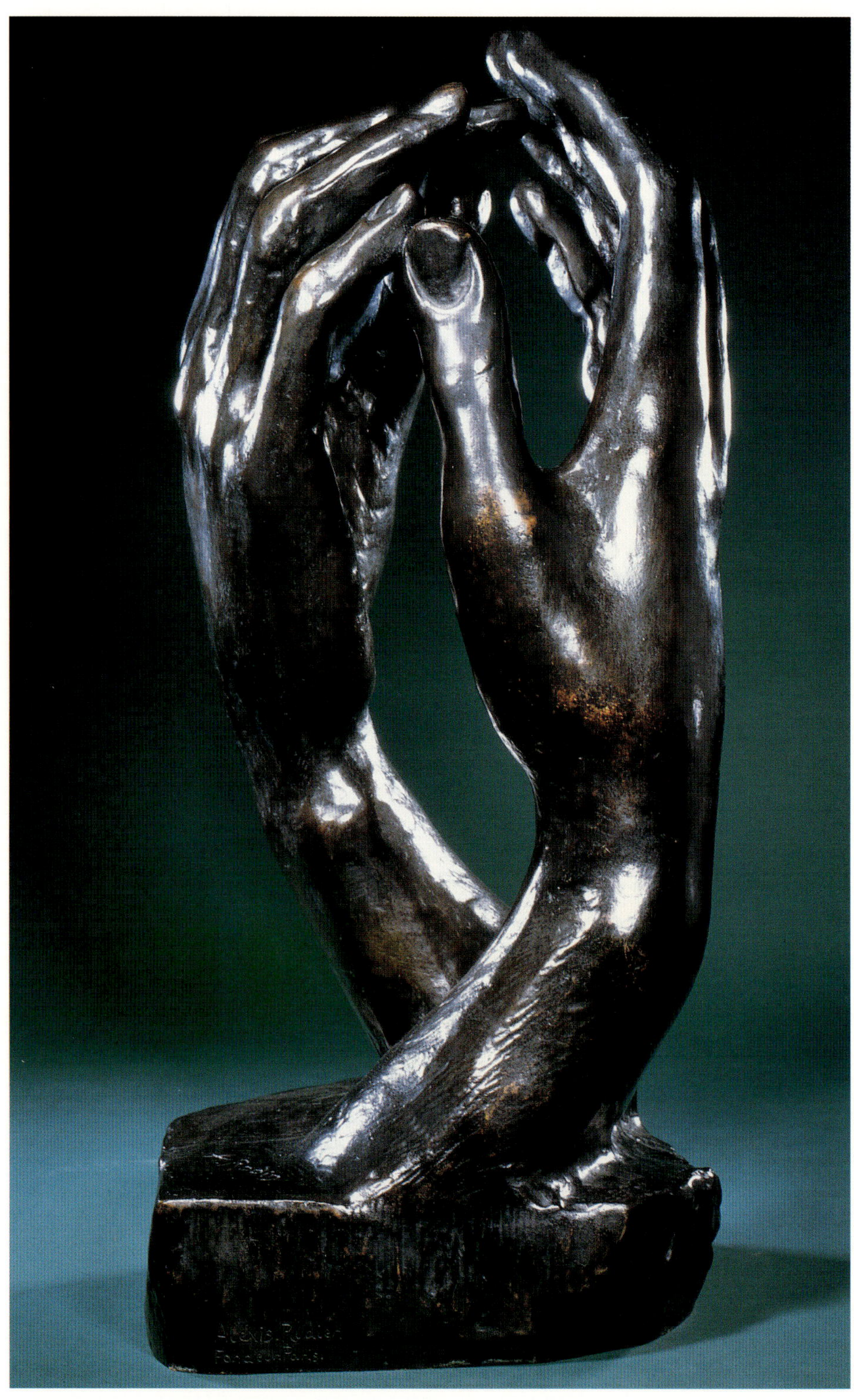

The Cathedral original stone version executed in 1908 (cat. 68)

With his tongue-in-cheek commentary, Dargenty successfully managed to bring to public attention what was new in Rodin's work. The *Saint John the Baptist Preaching* exhibited in 1883 in fact belonged to the State and was to enter the Luxembourg Museum the following year (today it is in the Musée d'Orsay).

Like *The Age of Bronze*, *Saint John the Baptist Preaching* makes reference to the great bronze sculptors of the Florentine Renaissance, in particular to Donatello. With *Adam*, Rodin turned away from the imitation of nature to let himself be imbued with the influence of Michelangelo. *Eve* was once again the scrupulous study of a model. Rodin himself told the story of how he came to abandon the figure, already well on the way to completion, by discovering that the young woman was pregnant and that her body contours were thus changing every day. This great *Eve* was only exhibited in 1899. On the other hand, Rodin presented a small version, a younger, more sleek and sensual *Eve*, whose first copy in marble was acquired by Auguste Vacquerie in 1885, and François Rudier cast the first one in bronze the following year. This *Petite Eve* (*Little Eve*) or *Eve jeune* (*Young Eve*) proved to be a resounding success.

From 1890 on, Rodin exhibited at the new Salon of the Société Nationale des Beaux-Arts (of which he was one of the founding members, along with Meissonier, Puvis de Chavannes, Carolus-Duran, Roll, Besnard and Dalou). The Nationale, as it was called, was a counterbalance to the Société des Artistes Français, which was accused of arch-conservatism from which Rodin, like many others, had suffered. Henceforth, there would no longer be any limitation on the number of entries or medals and if an examining panel, which was felt indispensable, had to be maintained, it would be drawn by lot. Rodin exhibited from the very first Salon of the new Société, and this time he presented figures related to *The Gates of Hell*, if not directly derived from it. It was under these auspices that he began to show the works that meant the most to him: after *La Danaïde (The Danaïd)* in 1890, *The Thinker* in 1895, then in 1896 a very important group that contained several marble pieces including *L'Illusion, sœur d'Icare*, (*Illusion, the Sister of Icarus*), *L'Homme et sa pensée* (*Man and His Thought*) and *L'Eternelle Idole* (*The Eternal Idol*), as well as a plaster cast of *The Interior Voice*, better known by the name of *La Méditation* (*Meditation*). Tinged with symbolism by the writers in Rodin's entourage who gave them their titles, almost all of these works were derived from previous figures, created during the course of the 1880s.

In the 1890s, and again after 1900, Rodin did more and more of these figures, these groups born from the development or the assemblage of previous works, whose subject matter was only defined after their completion. Instead of explaining, Rodin extends the work's meaning into a world which is no longer that of sculpture but rather one of poetry. That is why the titles of the works could change, in accordance with the particular sensibility of each one, whereas their meaning remained for the most part obscure. Auguste Thyssen complained about this to Rodin, asking him for explanatory notes. These were drawn up by Rainer Maria Rilke, who was then Rodin's secretary and who, better than anyone, knew how to analyse *The Danaïd*, *Meditation* or *Balzac*, as he did in the work on Rodin that he published in Leipzig in 1913.

At the Salon de la Société Nationale des Beaux-Arts in 1898, Rodin seemed to take a step backwards with what is perhaps his most famous work: the great marble piece, *The Kiss*. This had been a State commission ten years previously, begun with enthusiasm but soon abandoned, probably the following year when, in June 1889, the sculptor's assistant, Turcan, announced that he would not be able to come back for some time. Rodin then put it to one side and the work was never really finished. He did decide to present it in 1898, but by then he considered it to be an outmoded work. That same year, he exhibited the model of the statue of *Balzac* that had been commissioned by the Société des Gens de Lettres (Society of Authors), and he suspected that this monolith, the whole of whose force of expression is concentrated in the face, would cause a scandal. *The Kiss* would reassure a public used to the academic style of the Ecole des Beaux-Arts. Indeed, he was highly praised for it, two replicas in marble being created after 1900, whilst there was none of the criticism that had been directed against the *Balzac*.

Rodin had eliminated everything from the *Balzac* that seemed to him superfluous or anecdotal. The *Age of Bronze* had, with considerable subtlety and as early as 1877, borne the first fruits of this approach that was reaffirmed in 1896, and again in 1897, with the exhibition at the Salon of *The Interior Voice* (or *Meditation*), finally leading the artist in 1900 to present *The Gates* without the characters.

The Interior Voice had become a figure in its own right at the end of the 1880s, and Rodin drew inspiration from it in his drawings to illustrate, as a commission for Paul Gallimard, the poem 'La Beauté' ('Beauty') from Baudelaire's *Les Fleurs du Mal* (*The Flowers of Evil*). A few years later, he returned to the figure that did not yet have a name and used it in various ways – in *Le Christ et la Madeleine (Christ and Mary Magdalena)*, in *Constellation*, and especially in *Monument to Victor Hugo* on which he was then working. In 1894, he decided to make the allegory of *Les Voix intérieures* (*The Interior Voices*) from this. But, in order to incorporate it into the monument, he had to eliminate the arms that did not fit, cut off a knee and lower the outer part of the right leg. In the process, he

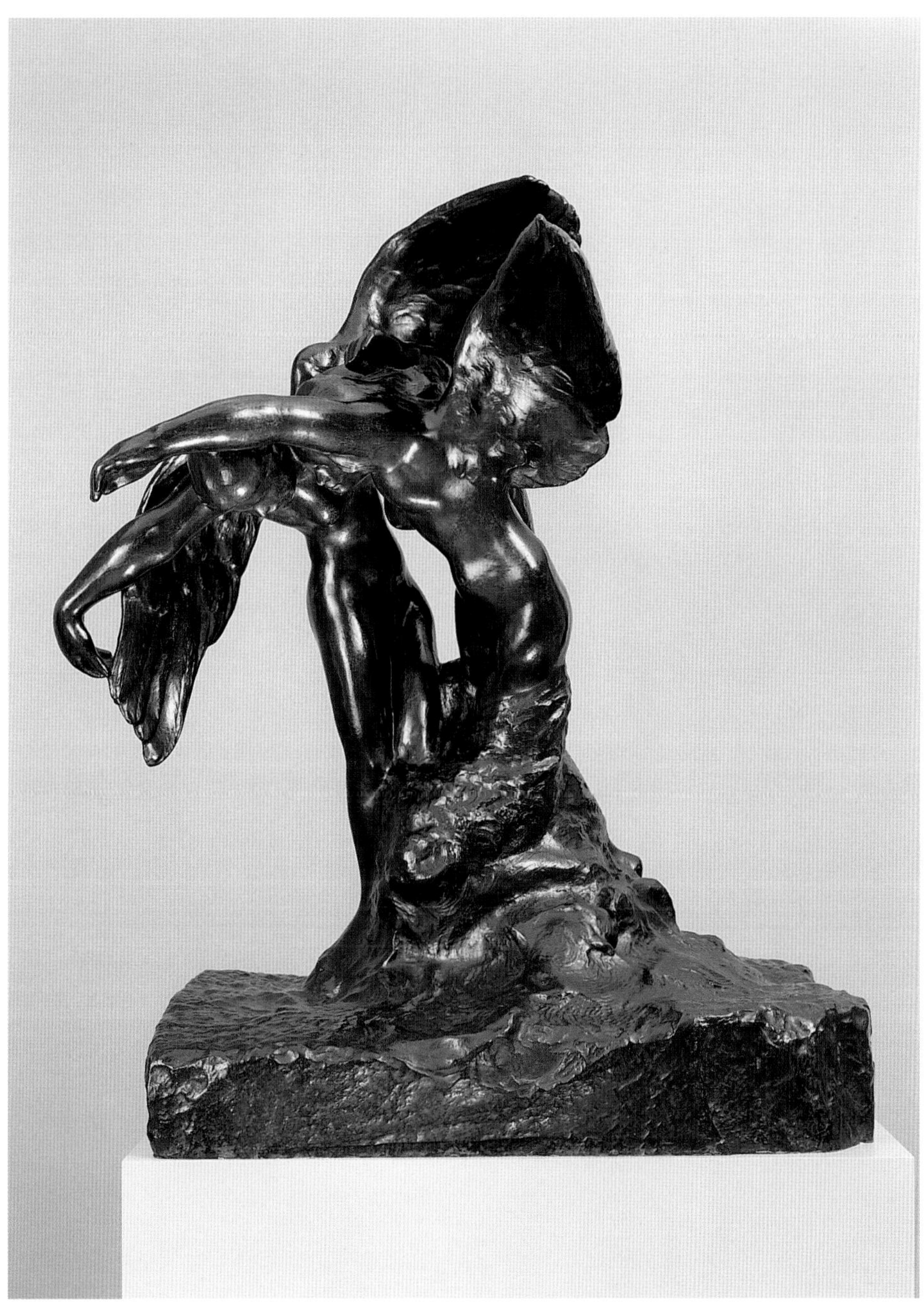

The Benedictions 1894 (cat. 9)

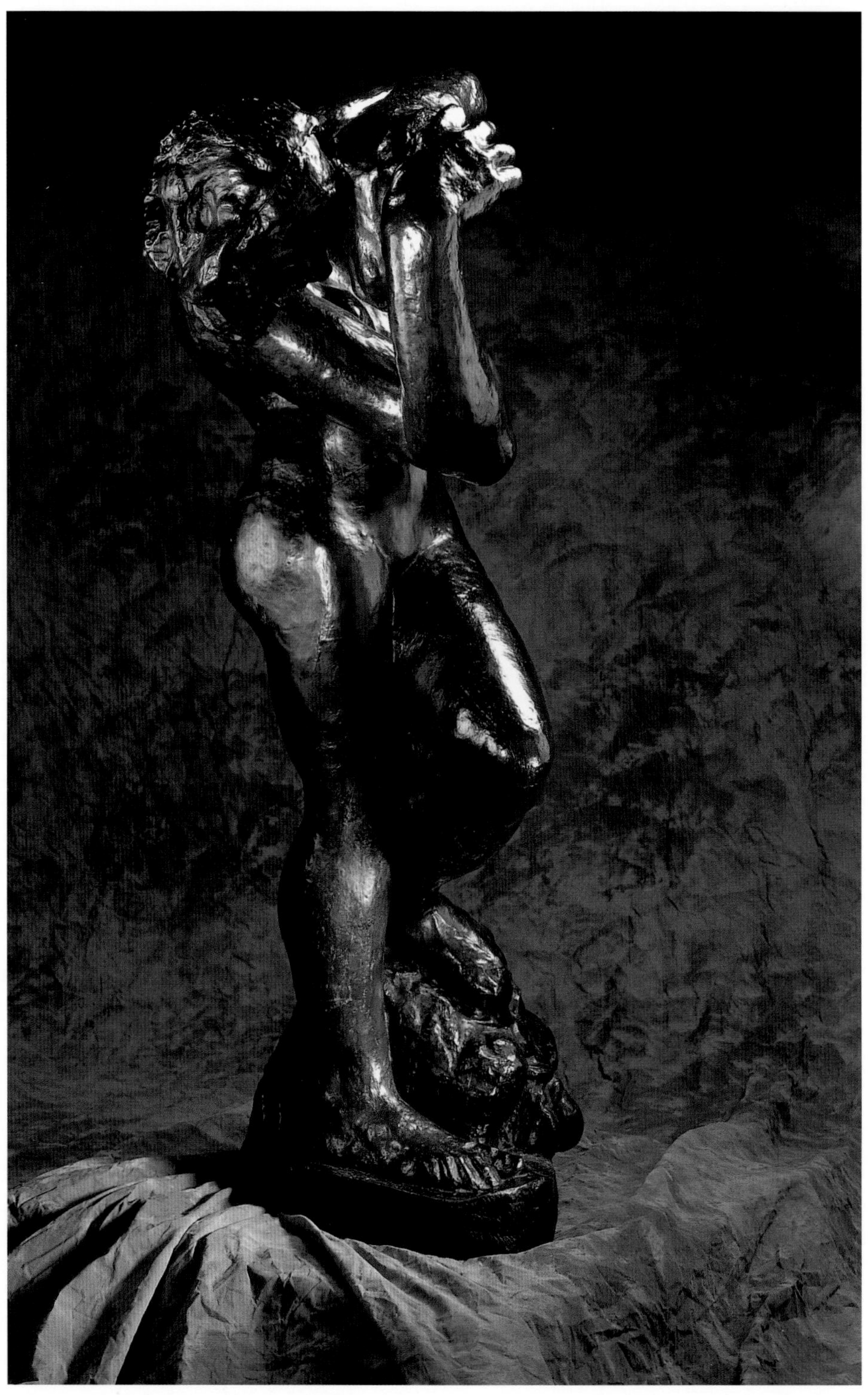

Meditation (with arms) c.1885–1900 (cat. 18)

obtained a fragmentary figure that was enlarged, cast in this form during his lifetime, photographed by Freuler and Druet and exhibited in 1897.

It was Rilke who, thanks to his poetic intuition, gave the best interpretation of this figure, in a famous and often quoted text:

> The arms are missing, as in this case Rodin felt them to be an over facile solution to the task at hand, like something that was not in keeping with the body, which just wanted to curl up within itself without any outside assistance. One may think of the great Italian actress Eleonora Duse who, in one of d'Annunzio's plays, after having been painfully abandoned, tried to clasp without arms and hold without hands. This scene ... gave one the impression that her arms were a luxury, an adornment, the good fortune of the rich and the intemperate that one could simply cast off to become perfectly poor. She did not seem to have sacrificed anything important ... The same applied to Rodin's armless statues – they lacked nothing that was necessary. One stood before them as before a whole, perfectly complete and needing nothing additional.[37]

This was the first time that Rodin so clearly accorded the status of successfully completed work to a figure that was apparently unfinished. He reaffirmed this soon after with *L'Homme qui marche* (*The Walking Man*), often considered to be the very symbol of pure creation finally freed of the weight of the subject. The title of the work no longer bore any historical reference but was merely an observation, here accentuated by the elimination of the head and the arms. The figure was born by putting together a study of the legs of *Saint John the Baptist Preaching* and a torso, probably also linked to *Saint John*, which had been found cracked and damaged after years of neglect, before being reproduced in 1888. The smooth modelling of the legs contrasts with the fractured torso, which accentuates the reference to Antique remains, already conspicuous in 1897 in *Meditation*.

In the final years of his career, Rodin had no qualms about exhibiting fragmentary or unfinished works, whose power of expression was such 'that it sweeps everything before it, injecting blood, muscle and movement into the entire piece'.[38] If the armless *Muse* that was put before the public in 1908 was in reality only one stage of the figure intended for the *Monument à Whistler (Monument to Whistler)*, the splendid *Torse de jeune femme cambré* (*Arched Torso of a Young Woman*) and *La Prière* (*The Prayer*), both exhibited in 1910, are on the contrary finished works in the eyes of their maker. The admiration that Rodin had always felt for Antiquity but which, for more than a quarter of a century, had been supplanted by the influence of Michelangelo, now became predominant.

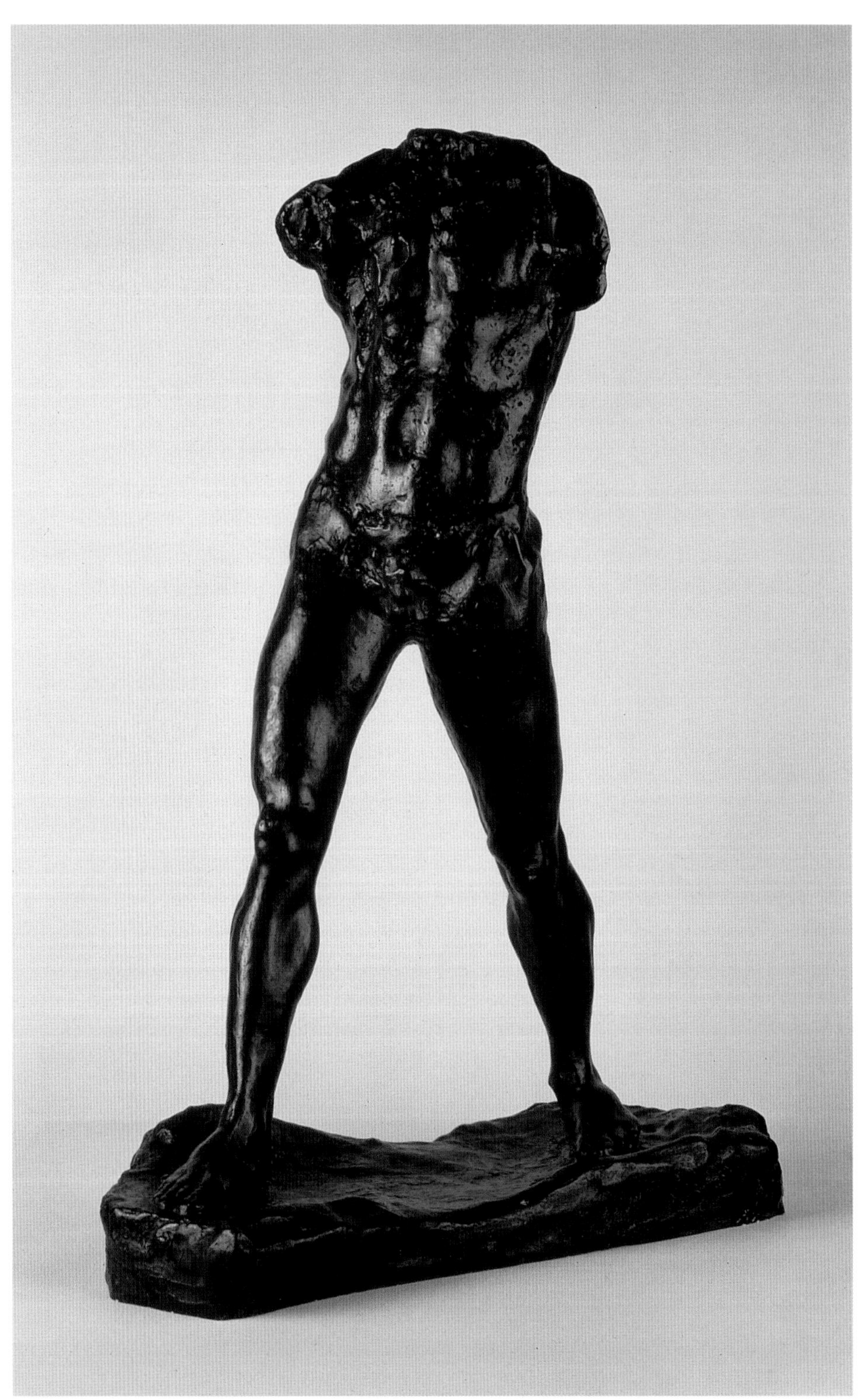

The Walking Man c.1889 (cat. 19)

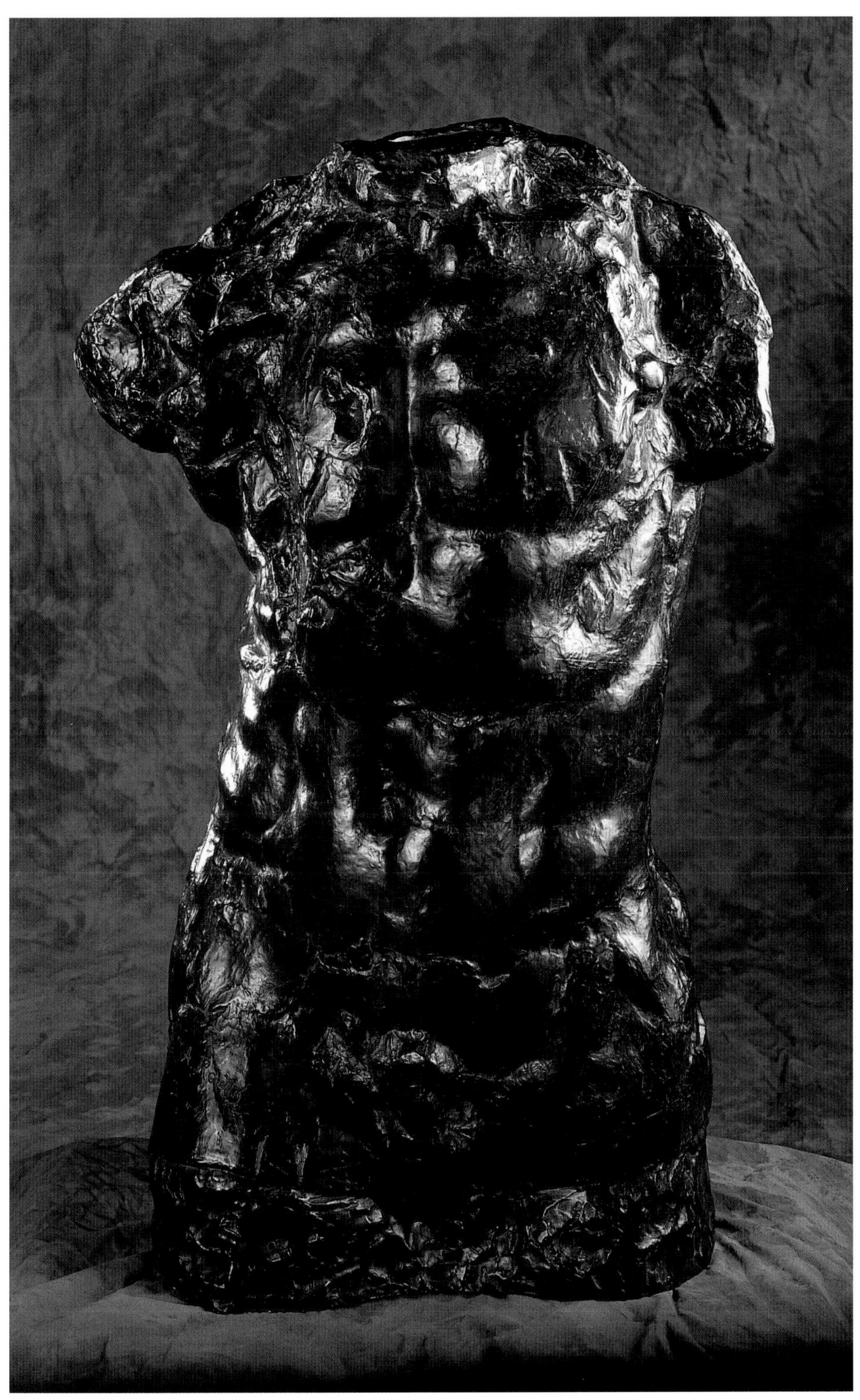

Monumental Torso of the Walking Man c.1905 (cat. 24)

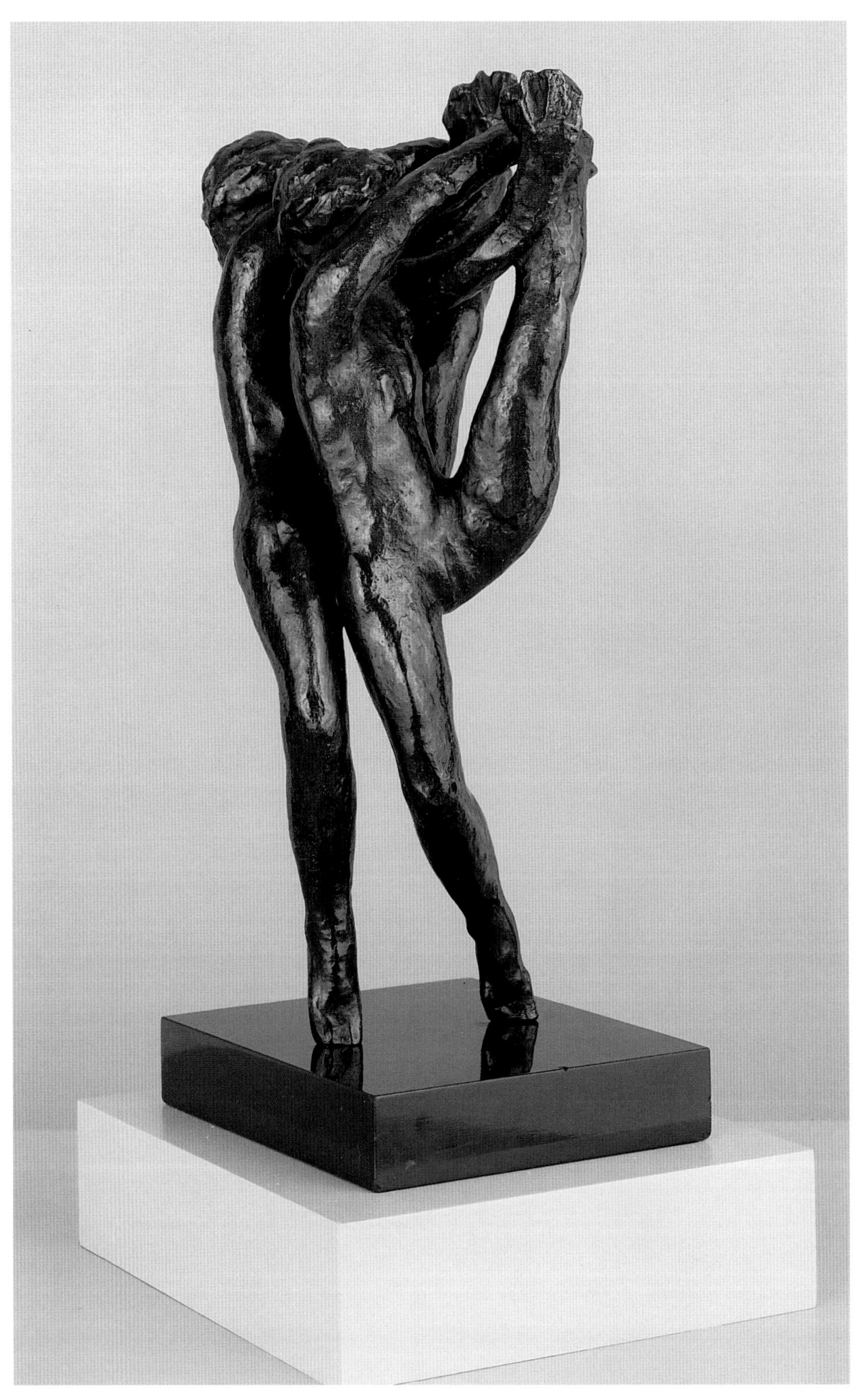

Dance Movement, pas de deux (type B) c.1910–11 (cat. 26)

In comparison with more ancient figures, the *Muse*, like the *Arched Torso of a Young Woman*, is of a striking simplicity in both form and expression, as far removed from the nude quivering with life of *The Age of Bronze* as from the passionate and pained bodies designed for *The Gates of Hell*. Rodin told his secretary Frederick Lawton that, after having sought for movement more than anything else, he had now come to think that the very essence of sculpture was expressed through the modelling: 'That is what made the greatness of the Greeks. There is a peace of mind, a marvellous feeling of rest and calm in their sculpture. Not the tranquillity of the academic style which is nothing more than the absence of nature, the absence of life, but the repose of strength, the repose of conscious power, the impression of flesh controlled by the spirit'.[39]

Rodin, who had probably met Aristide Maillol as early as 1902, took a friendly interest in him, helping him at the start of his career as a sculptor and closely following the creation of the great *Femme assise* (*Seated Woman*), later entitled *Méditerranée* (*Mediterranean*), that Maillol exhibited at the Salon in the autumn of 1905.

Without going as far as to imagine that Rodin was carried along by his young friend towards the new classicism of the period 1905–1910, it is undeniable that through their formal completeness, the *Arched Torso of a Young Woman* and *The Prayer* bear a certain relation to Maillol's works. But the younger sculptor was only interested in form, in which he sought perfection. Rodin went further than that, as it was the profound meaning of a work that really interested him beyond its formal characteristics, and so he eliminated from the figure everything that might take the viewer's attention away from it.

Emile Antoine Bourdelle (1861–1929), who at the time was undergoing a similar development which took him from the limits of expressionism to a classically-inspired discipline, was the person with the best insight into this:

> These simple figures, these fragments, human trunks or ensemble pieces which, without any heroics, are dependent neither on anecdote nor literary narrative – these finally manage to bring together in magnificent cohesion all the genius of the great sculptor ... Standing before these pieces of pure sculpture, of sculpture alone, it is impossible to capture them in words ... This is the fate of great works, to be so simple in appearance, on the outside, that, as they do not inspire any stories, the mass of humanity passes by without seeing them.[40]

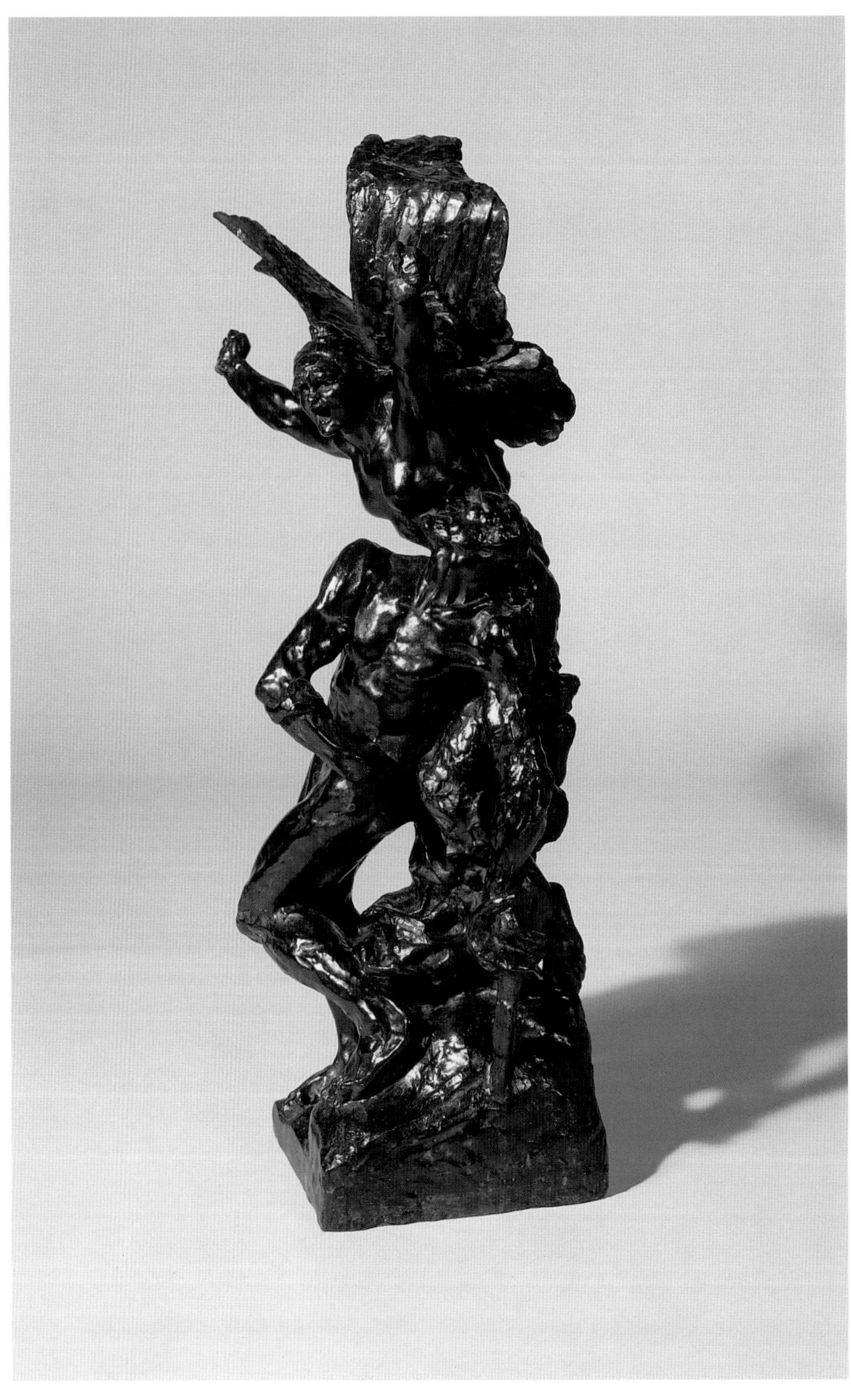

The Call to Arms 1879 (cat. 3)

PUBLIC MONUMENTS

Throughout his career, Rodin devoted an important part of his working life to producing public monuments. For him, as for his contemporaries, monuments were, just like the figures exhibited at the Salon, a means of making contact with the public, a commission being the only way of carrying out large-scale works using costly materials.

Rodin's first known work of this kind was the project he conceived for the competition for a monument to the defence of Paris that was to be erected in the suburb of Courbevoie. In *La Défense (The Call to Arms)*, the winged figure (which can be read as representing the Spirit of Liberty or the Motherland) is wearing the Phrygian cap, the symbol of freedom for the French, and has her mouth exaggeratedly open in a howling rage, her arms taut and fists tightly clenched. A dying soldier sinks in front of her with a hollowed-out mask and broken body. This group appears as a homage to the artist's favourite masters: Michelangelo, whom he admired above all, and François Rude (1784–1855).[41] In it one can find both the memory of the *Pieta* of the Florence Duomo and a gesticulating expressionism straight out of *La Marseillaise*. This is, however, above all a monument expressing the horror of war and the desire for revenge, far removed from the ideas of sacrifice and courage exalted by most monuments erected after the defeat of France in the Franco-Prussian War of 1870.

In 1881, then again in 1884, Rodin unsuccessfully participated in competitions for the monuments to *Lazare Carnot* (the famous French mathematician, revolutionary and military strategist) and *General Margueritte* (who had distinguished himself during the Franco-Prussian War), before finally receiving from the City of Calais his first important commission. This was the monument to *Les Bourgeois de Calais* (*The Burghers of Calais),* the six volunteers who, according to Froissart's *Chroniques* (*Chronicles*), clad in nightshirts and with a rope around their necks – the apparel of the condemned – gave the keys of their city to the King of England, Edward III, who had taken it after after eleven months of siege (1347). Various proposals for monuments (from the sculptors David d'Angers and Clésinger, among others) celebrating the abnegation and heroism of Eustache de Saint-Pierre, the most famous of these Burghers, had come to light in Calais after 1840. None had gone ahead but, as Omer Dewavrin, the Mayor of Calais, put it to the Municipal Council on 16 September 1884, the idea was 'to erect at a place and time to be determined ... a monument to Eustache de Saint-Pierre and his companions ... with the help of a national subscription'.[42] A few days later, the monument planning committee appointed P.A. Isaac, originally from Calais but now living in Paris, as its representative

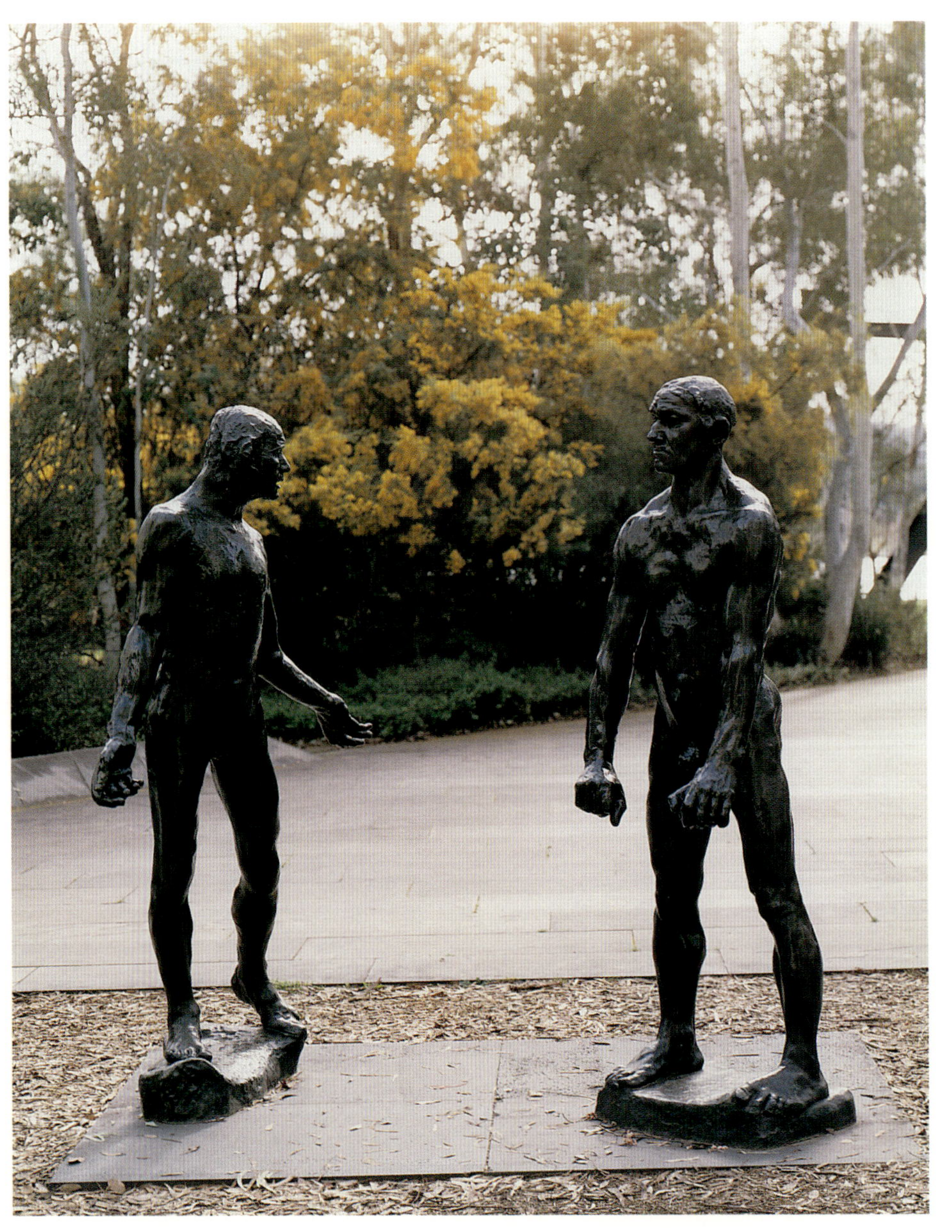

Nude studies for *Jean de Fiennes* c.1885–86 and *Jean d'Aire* 1885–86 (cat. 122 and 120)

responsible for making enquiries into possible sculptors. A month later, he recommended to Dewavrin that 'we should approach a man whose past record would give us a guarantee of getting a real work of art. Monsieur A. Rodin … is the person whose robust talent would be most suitable for the subject at hand.'[43] Isaac, who had probably made contact with Rodin through the painter Jean-Paul Laurens, went on to list all the commissions that the sculptor had received and all the honours bestowed on him.

Other sculptors had also been sought. However, by November Rodin had submitted an outline that he came to present in person in Calais. The upshot was that, thanks to Dewavrin's support, he received a firm commitment for the monument in January 1885. This was a monument that appeared quite exceptional in that, instead of a single character or at the very least a principal one, he proposed a group of six figures all put on the same level, with each giving a different view of their agony. In July he made the maquette public, unleashing a wave of criticism. The committee did not appreciate finding in the gestures and attitudes of the Burghers an expression of suffering that made them appear like criminals on the way to punishment rather than as heroic

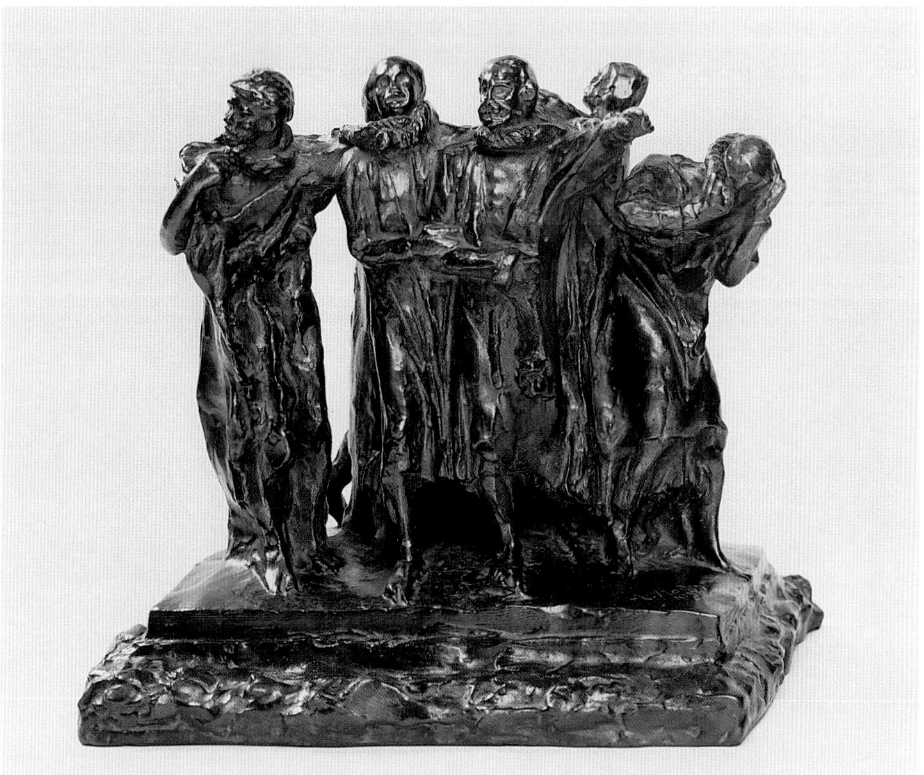

First Maquette for the Burghers of Calais 1884 (cat. 118)

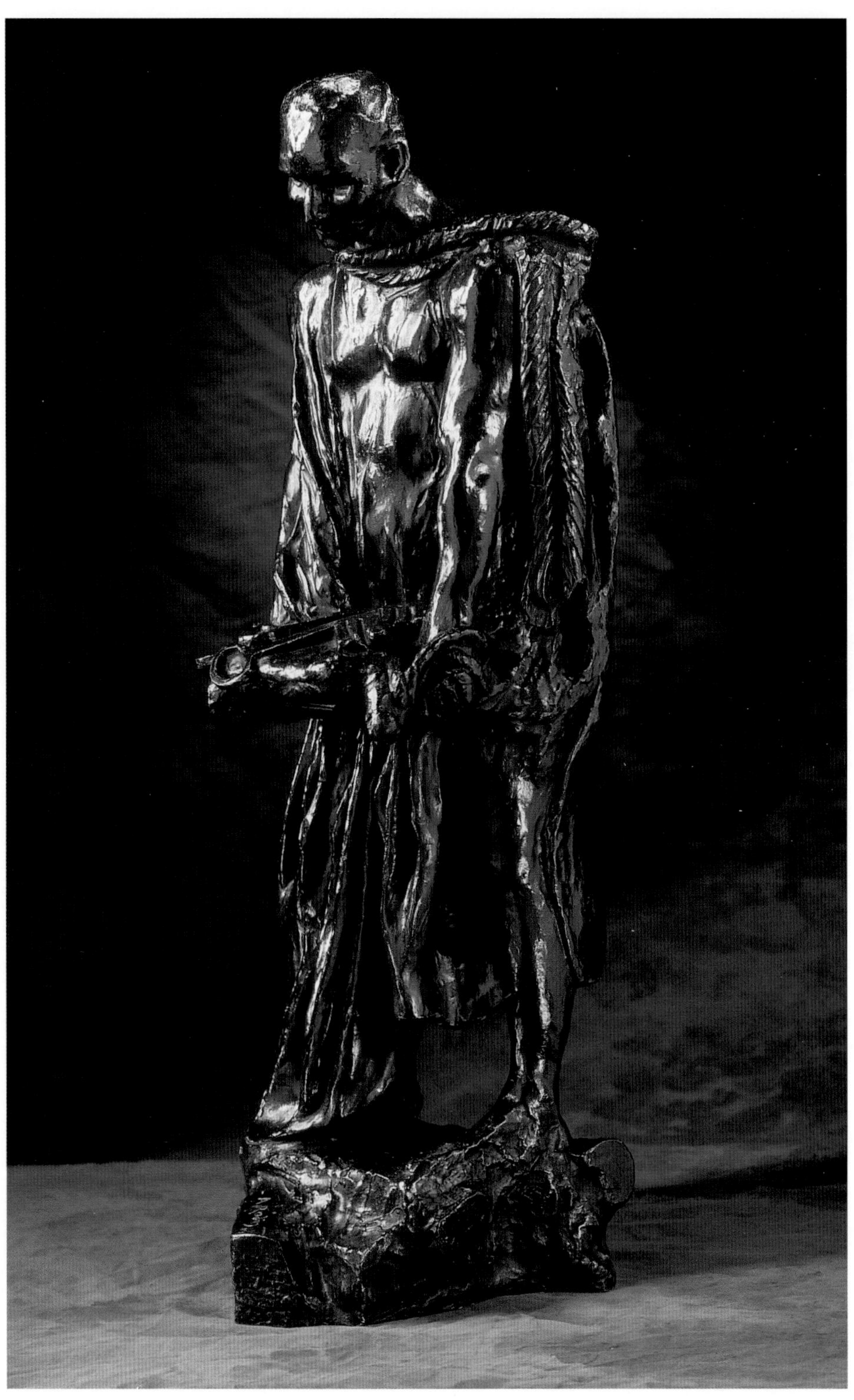

Second Maquette for Jean d'Aire 1885–86 (cat. 52)

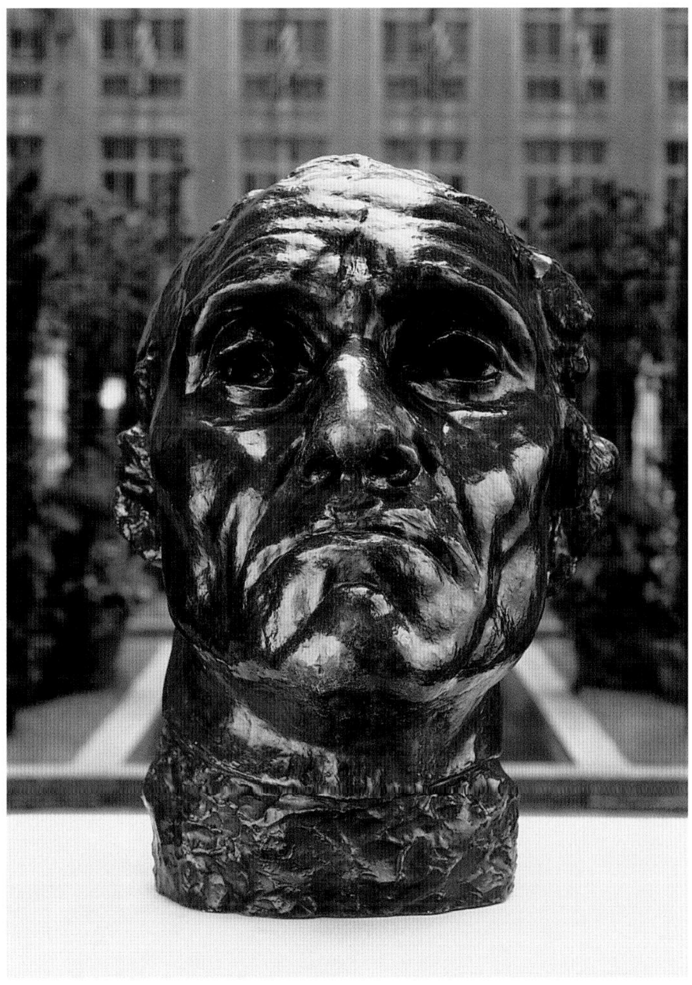

Monumental Head of Jean d'Aire c.1884–86 enlarged 1909–10 (cat. 49)

martyrs. Rodin was also criticised for having put the six characters all on the same plane, thereby giving the group the look of a 'cube whose effect was most ungracious', instead of having carried out the traditional pyramidal form of composition.

Rodin and the committee were therefore not in agreement. Indeed, the fact that the monument was completed at all was most probably due to the bankruptcy of the Sagot Bank in February–March 1886. The money, raised by subscription and deposited with the Bank, then disappeared, depriving the committee of its means of applying pressure. Rodin, who had just started work on the figures, thus found himself freed of the constraints that were being exerted on him, and free also to pursue, as he saw fit, a monument whose completion could no longer be taken for granted. The group, whose final size was moulded directly

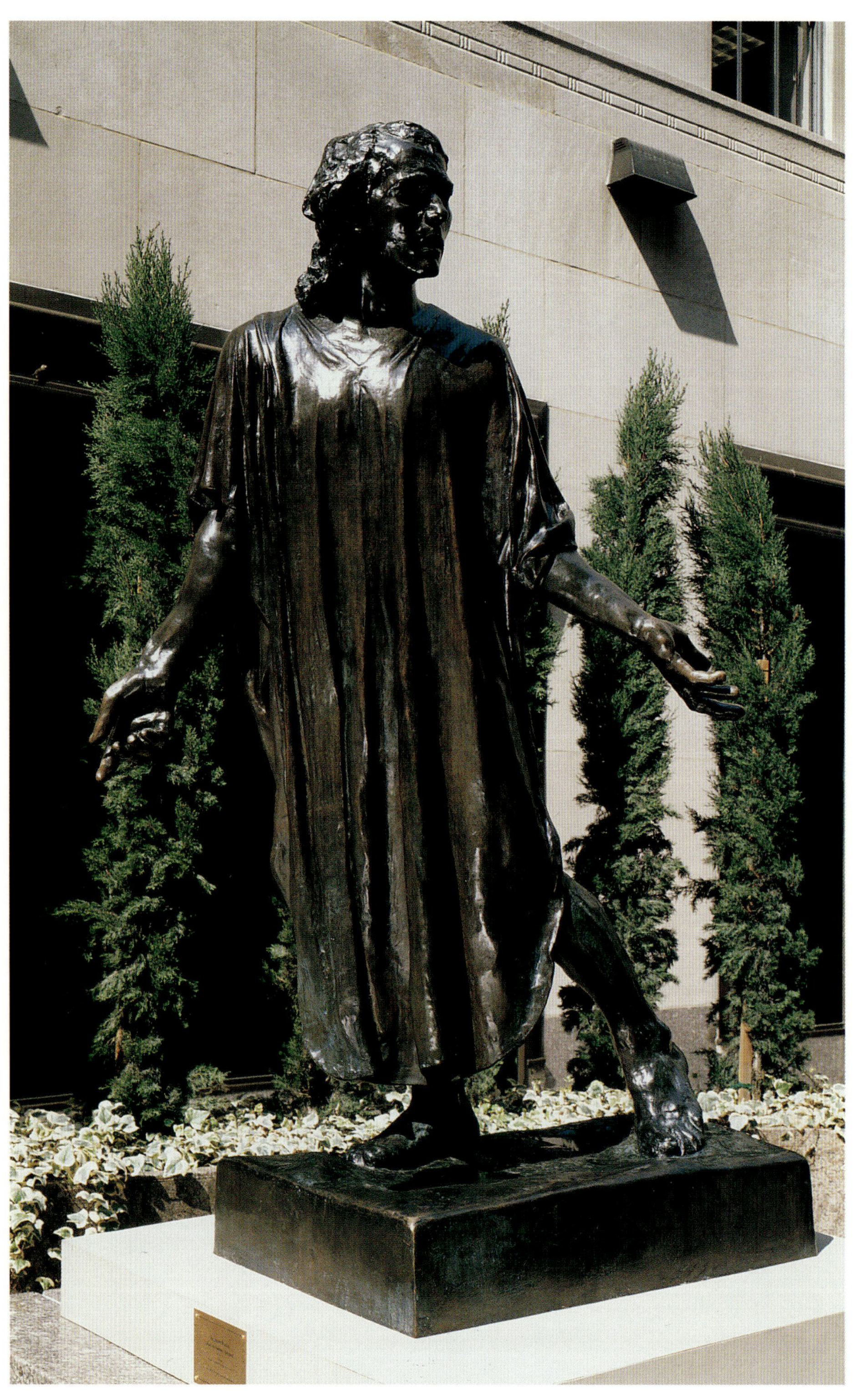

Jean de Fiennes 1885–86 (cat. 54)

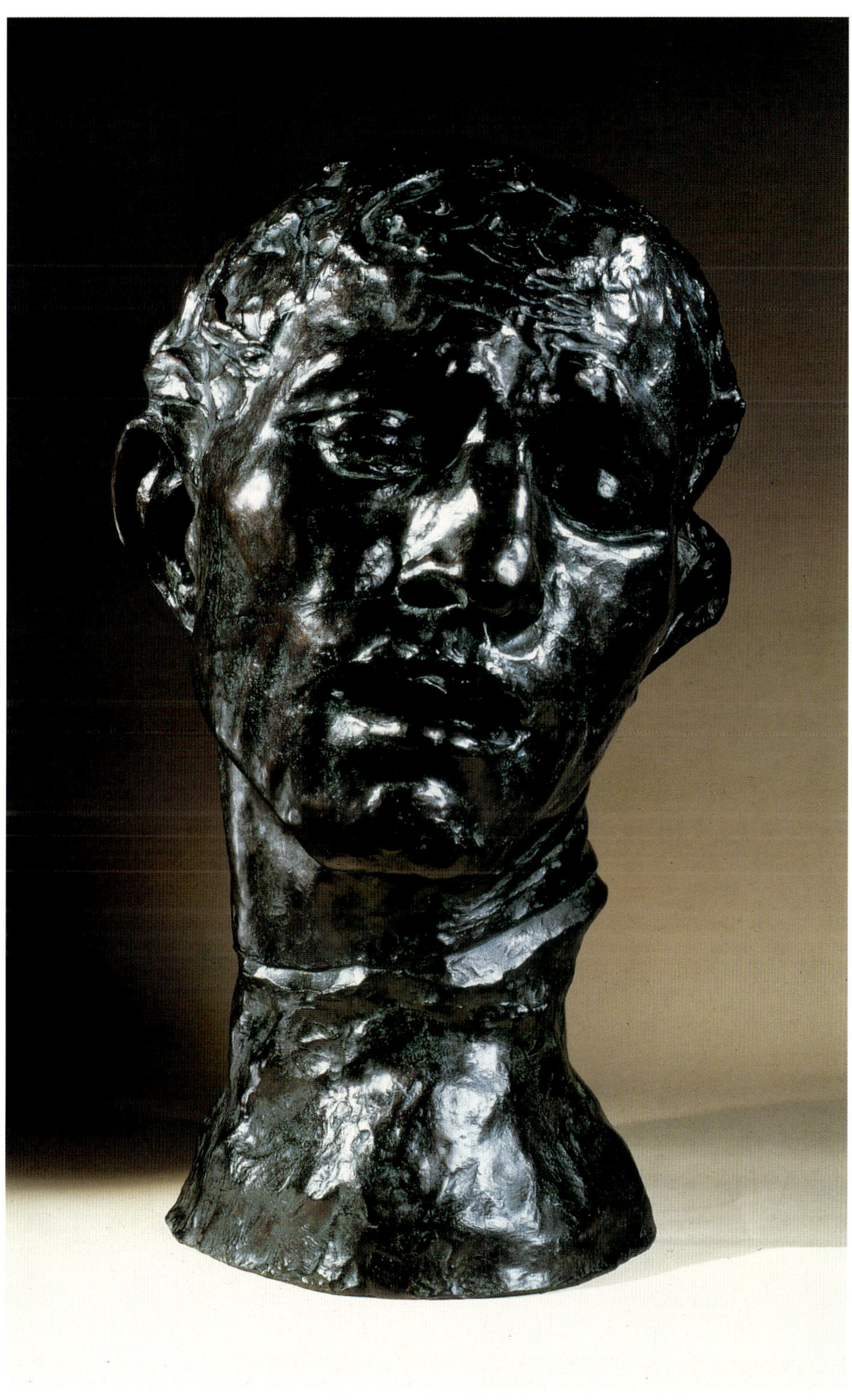

Monumental Head of Pierre de Wiessant c.1884–1909 (cat. 50)

in his boulevard de Vaugirard studio – first of all naked (1886) as, like his predecessors, Rodin always studied the nude figure before clothing it – was presented in 1889 as part of the *Monet-Rodin* exhibition at the Galérie Georges Petit. In the autumn of 1894, Leblanc-Barbedienne was chosen to do the casting.

A new dispute then broke out about where the monument was to be placed. Rodin hoped that there would be an uninterrupted view of the work, in order to emphasise the individual nature of the characters, which counted as much as their common spirit of sacrifice in the overall composition of the piece. But he seems to have hesitated for a long time between a triumphal presentation on a raised plinth accentuating the heroism of the Burghers, and a very low plinth, situated in the heart of the city, in accordance with Froissart's text: 'the Burghers leaving the market square'. He doubtless had the latter in mind as early as 1885, but he did not express his preference until December 1893 when he said that this would mean 'the group became more accessible and made the public enter all the more into the sight of the misery and the sacrifice of the drama'.[44] The committee preferred a traditional pedestal, and the monument was inaugurated in Calais on 3 June 1895 on a raised plinth, surrounded by a neo-gothic grille, but Rodin reiterated his opinion on several occasions and finally got his way in 1911 in London.

Alongside *The Burghers of Calais*, he had also produced the monuments to *Bastien-Lepage* (Damvilliers, 1886–1889) and *Claude Lorrain* (Nancy, 1886–1892). Both of these presented the subject at work: Jules Bastien-Lepage, the naturalist painter carried off by illness at the age of thirty-six, stands frozen before his canvas. Claude Lorrain is walking towards the landscape that he is going to paint, but turns to face the first rays of sunshine that strike him, giving him a surprisingly unstable look. The most interesting part is, however, the pedestal adorned with horses that seem to emerge from the block like those pulling the sun-chariot rising from the ocean in the morning. This project only managed to beat its competitors thanks to the support of Roger Marx and Emile Gallé, both from Nancy and both admirers of Rodin, and it continued to be the object of attacks by critics even after the monument's inauguration in June 1892.

The final decade of the century was taken up with the production of projects to which Rodin devoted boundless energy – the monuments to *Victor Hugo* (1889– after 1900) and *Balzac* (1891–1898). As with *The Burghers of Calais*, he wished to engage in neither description nor story-telling, but rather to have the viewer enter into the most private life of the character concerned. Rodin's interest was in the inner life of people, and he sought to express this power and richness rather than remind us of the external circumstances of their lives.

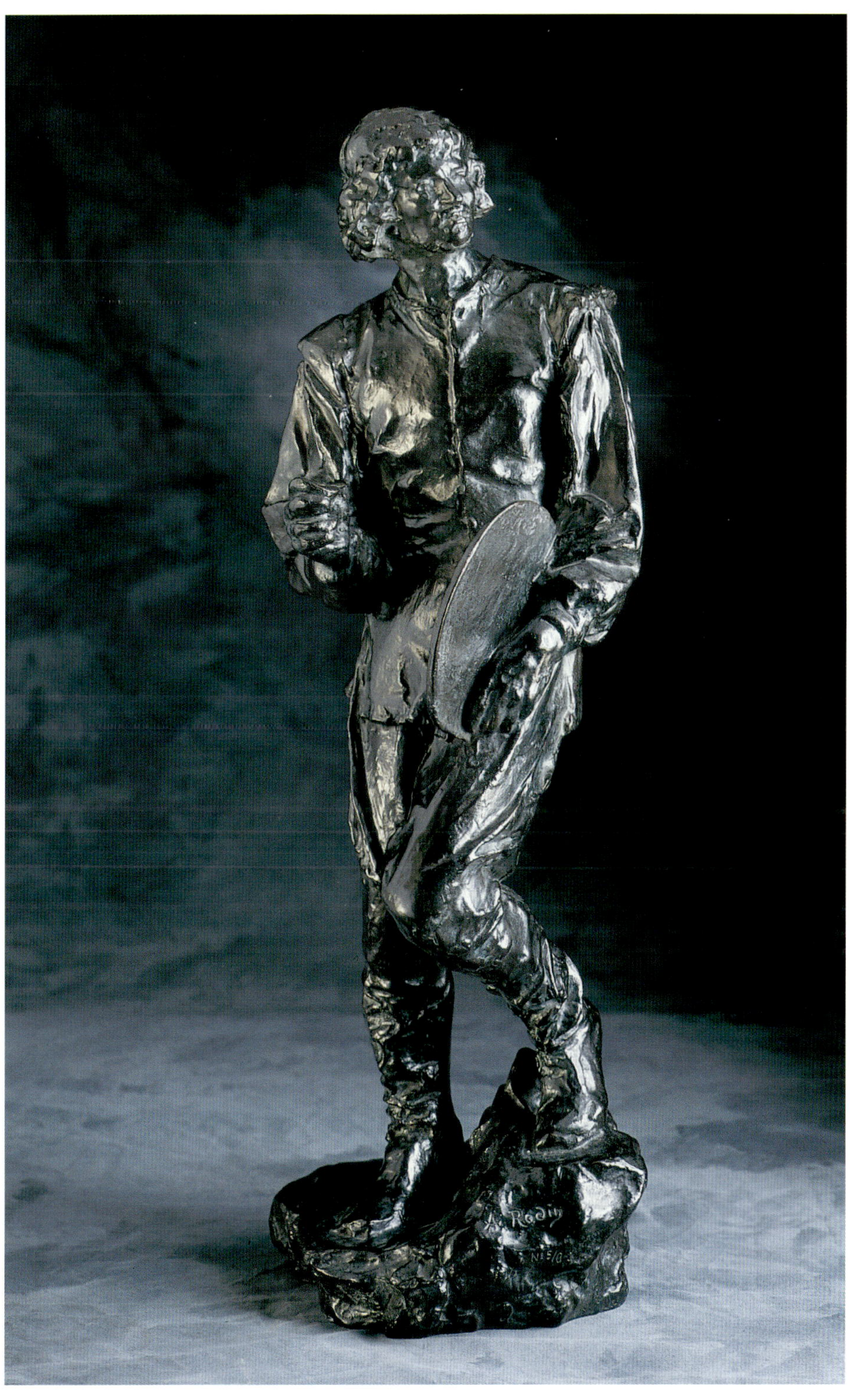

Study for the Monument to Claude Lorrain 1889 (cat. 7)

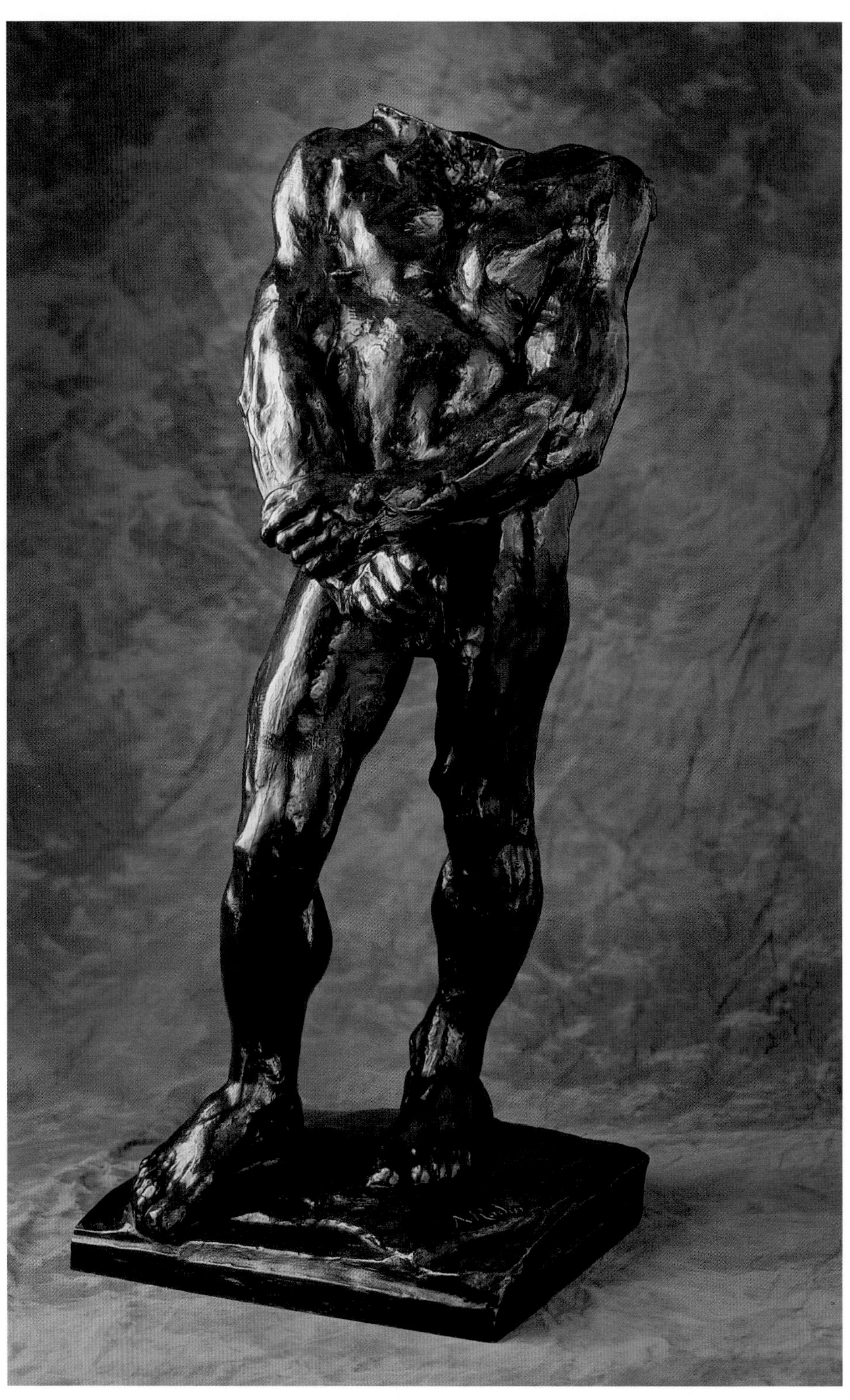

Nude Study of Balzac as an Athlete (type F) 1896 (cat. 61)

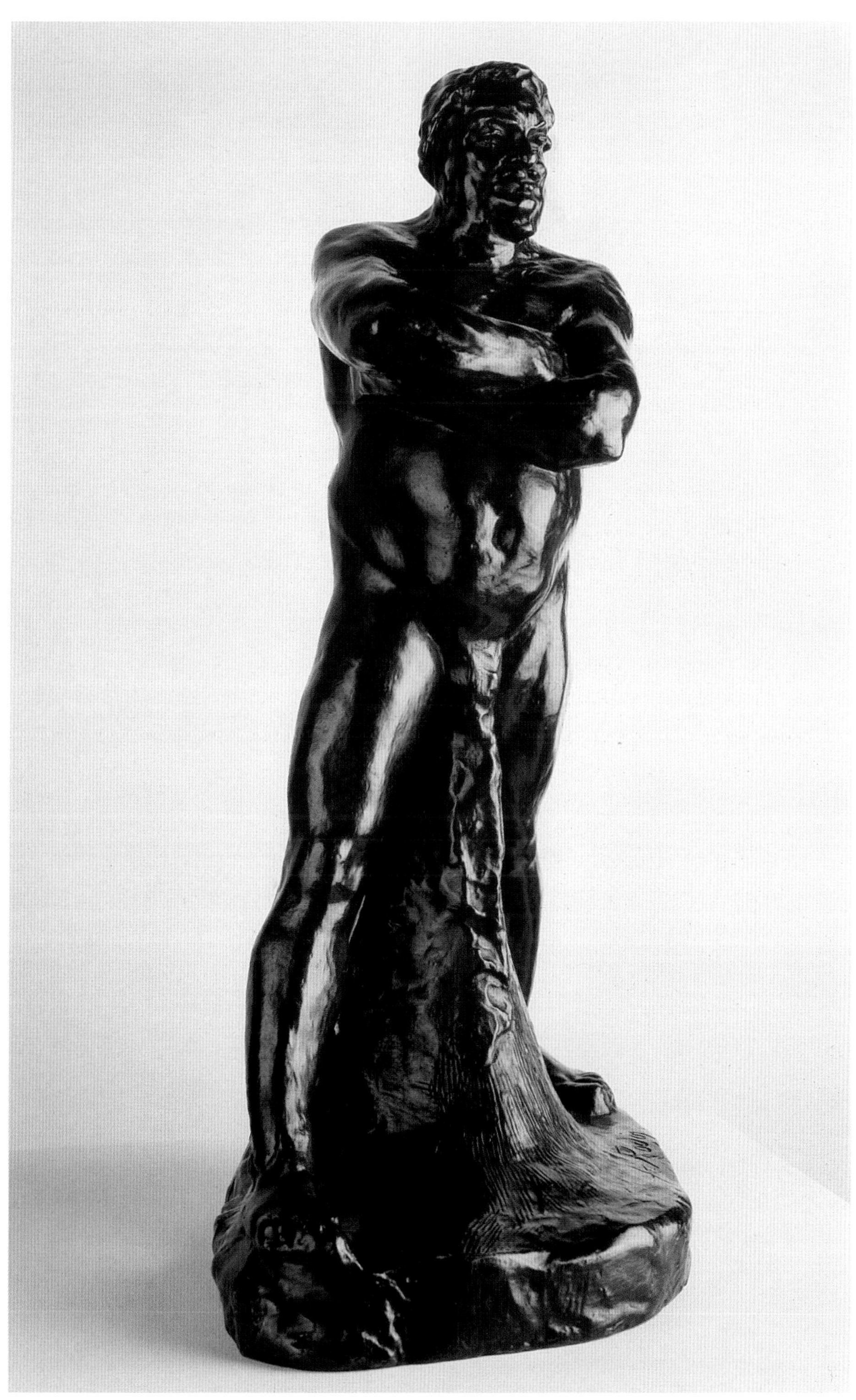

Nude Study for Balzac (reduction, type C) probably 1892 (cat. 57)

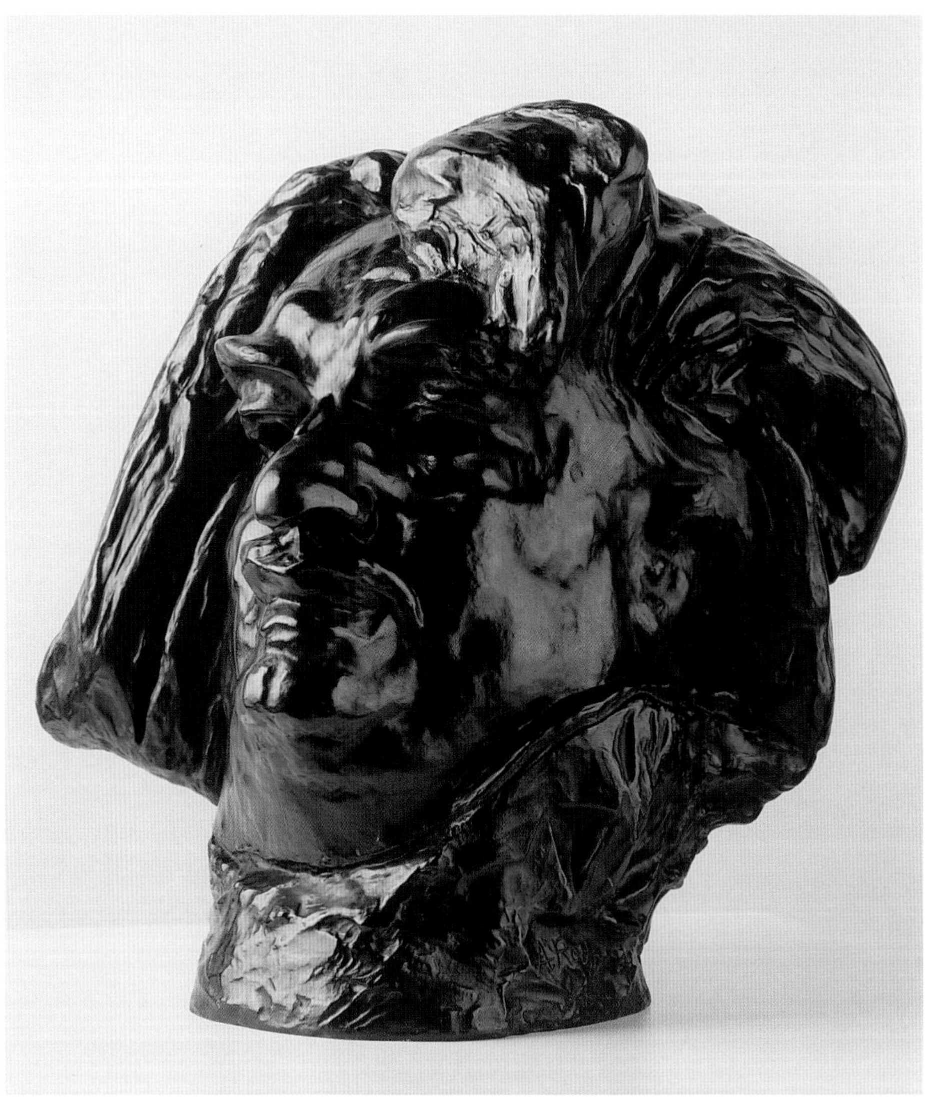

Monumental Head of Balzac (enlargement) 1897 (cat. 62)

He began by reading everything that he could find on Balzac, including personal accounts and documents on the novelist. He wisely started out with contemporary portraits in order to carry out the so-called *Balzac jeune* (*Young Balzac*) bust, but he also thought a great deal about Balzac's stature, his physiognomy and clothing, going as far as draping the empty space with the famous *robe de chambre* (dressing gown) that the writer would put on to work. Once he had completed this preliminary task of documentation, itself worthy of a realist novelist, Rodin retained only those aspects that could serve his idea, such as Balzac's corpulence and dressing gown and, after an extraordinary maquette in which an enormous belly appears through a slit in the gown, he produced a figure that is both an allegory of the novelist's creative power and a portrait of him that is, above all, what one may call 'moral'. Exhibited at the 1898 Salon, the resulting bold image caused a public outcry, 'less a statue than a sort of strange monolith, a millennial menhir, one of those rocks where the whims of prehistory's volcanic explosions by chance fixed a human face forever'.[45]

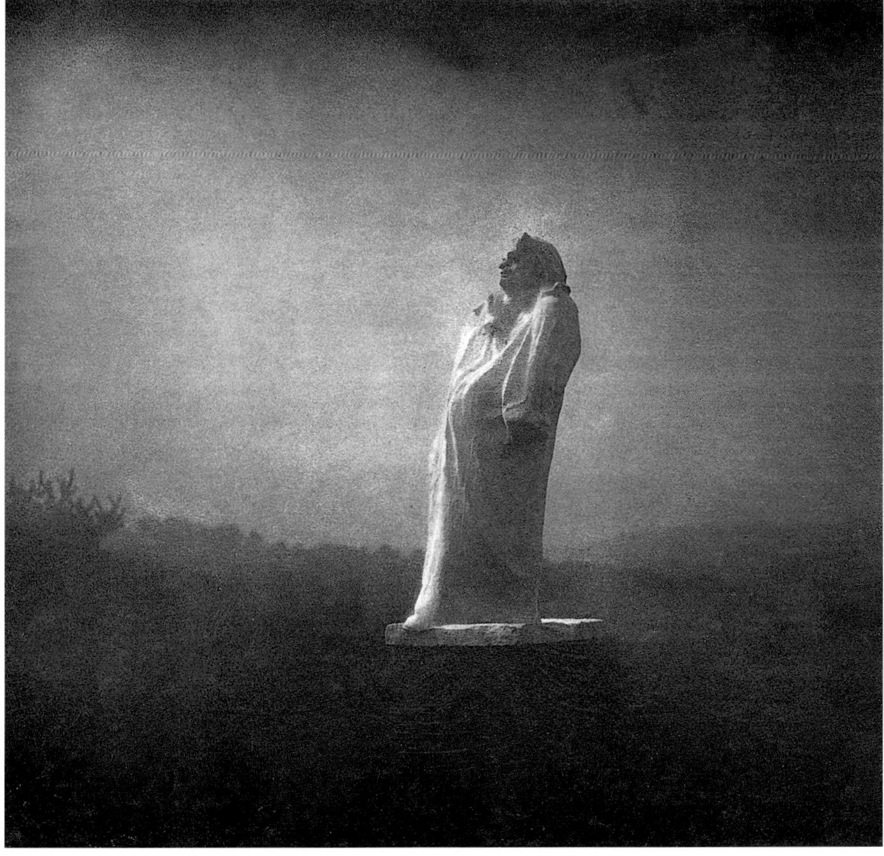

Edward STEICHEN *Balzac, 'Towards the Light at Midnight'* 1908
Gum dichromate 19.3 x 21.2 cm Musée Rodin

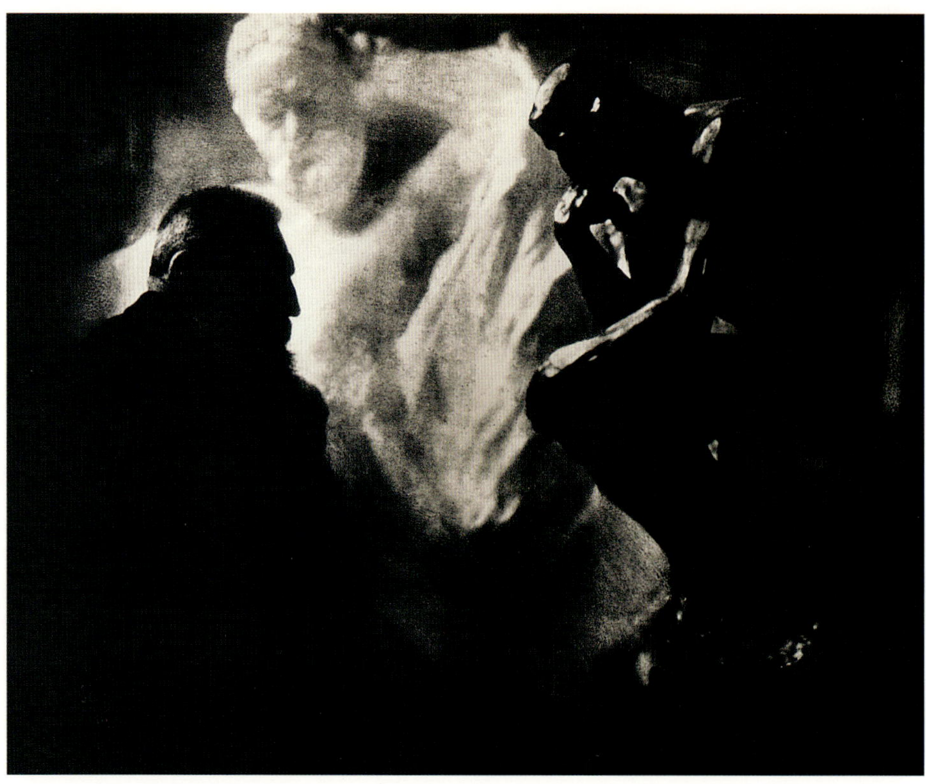

Edward STEICHEN *Portrait of Rodin with The Thinker and The Monument to Victor Hugo* 1902 (cat. 77)

France was at that time in the grip of the Dreyfus affair.[46] The novelist Emile Zola, who was a supporter of Rodin, had just become the unofficial leader of the Dreyfusard party, with the publication of his famous article 'J'accuse' ('I accuse') in the *Aurore* newspaper on 13 January 1898. Going beyond the problem of how the public monument was to be perceived, the struggle between defenders and opponents of the *Balzac* took on a political character. The Société des Gens de Lettres, frightened, rejected the statue and had Falguière (1831–1900) make an effigy whose banality aroused the public's scorn, Falguière having 'borrowed [from Rodin] the powerful neck, the breadth of chest, the drapery, the head of hair, the chin and the pupils of his Balzac ... the whole operation consisted in plonking the character thus pared down on a park bench'.[47]

As for Rodin's great plaster cast, it was taken to Meudon where, a few years later, Edward Steichen was to take some admirable photos of it by moonlight. Worried by the political turn of events that the scandal surrounding the statue had taken on, Rodin had rejected the idea of a subscription to have it cast in bronze and, while a first cast had been purchased in 1924 by the Museum of Fine Arts in Antwerp, he was going to have to wait forty years for his *Balzac* to take its place in Paris, on 1 July 1939, at the junction of the boulevard Raspail and the boulevard Montparnasse. Rodin had, however, claimed in 1908 that this statue 'would be recognised one day ... This work that has been mocked and scoffed at by people, because they couldn't destroy it, is the culmination of my whole life and the very pivot of my aesthetics.'[48]

Following this failure and, with the exception of the one to Domingo Sarmiento, the President of the Argentine Republic, Rodin completed no further monuments. Indeed, while he was as enthusiastic as ever for new projects, he let himself get gradually depressed by the difficulties that he inevitably encountered, to the extent that he ended up putting unfinished work to one side as he waited for the idea that would allow him to see it through.

The most important of the great projects that never came to fruition was the *Monument to Victor Hugo*. In 1883, the journalist Edmond Bazire, who had organised Victor Hugo's eightieth birthday celebrations, had persuaded the poet to let Rodin do a bust of him. Hugo did not want to sit for the bust, so his entourage had arranged everything to help the sculptor who, standing now to the left, now to the right of the poet, stealthily made his drawings during mealtimes, then rushed out to the veranda where, thanks to the visual memory that he had acquired at the 'Petite Ecole', he modelled what he had just seen. Finished in early 1884, the bust was exhibited at the Salon that same year, with the dedication 'A l'illustre Maître' ('To the Illustrious Master').

In February 1889, Gustave Larroumet, the new director of the Ecole des Beaux-Arts, drew up a plan for the interior decoration of the Paris Panthéon which, in 1885, had finally been deconsecrated and was now to be dedicated to honouring the great men of France. A *Monument à la Révolution* (*Monument to the Revolution*) was commissioned from Falguière (but never completed), while on 16 September 1889, Rodin and Jean-Antoine Injalbert (1845–1933) received an order for the monuments to *Victor Hugo* and *Mirabeau*. Rodin immediately set to work and, on 10 July 1890, presented a plan showing Victor Hugo sitting down, accompanied by his Muses. This plan was unanimously rejected as being unsuitable for the Panthéon, the committee in charge of the works having judged that it lacked clarity and that its outline was confused.[49] However, thanks to Larroumet, the commission was maintained for a museum or garden.

Hence, from that time on, Rodin worked in parallel on two projects for the *Monument à Victor Hugo* (*Monument to Victor Hugo*), one showing the poet

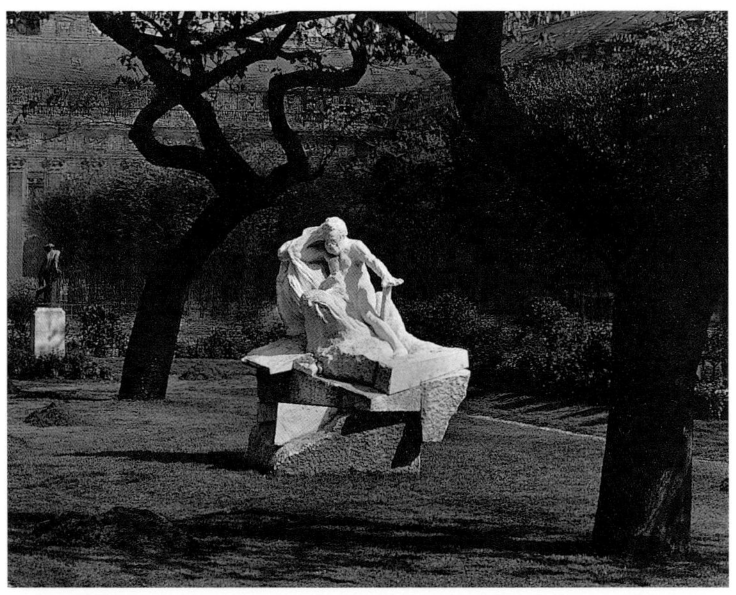

Adolphe BRAUN *The Monument to Victor Hugo at the Palais-Royal* after 1909
Carbon photograph 21.5 x 27.5 cm Musée Rodin

sitting down and the other, intended for the Panthéon, showing him standing up. For the Luxembourg Gardens monument, at least three maquettes were made one after the other, the large version being exhibited in 1897. The poet, at first dressed, quickly found his definitive form: naked, with a garment draped over his legs, his head resting on his right hand – the head none other than the one that had been created in 1883 – his left arm outstretched like that of Michelangelo's God-creator on the ceiling of the Sistine Chapel. Working on the Muses was more difficult. Rodin had first of all thought of using the *Sirènes* (*The Sirens*) from the left panel of *The Gates of Hell*, but they were soon replaced by three new female nudes, also from *The Gates*, yet only more or less directly, as one of them had already been completed and modified and turned into a single figure, *Meditation*. This was the only one kept in the final maquette (1895), the other two giving way to a single figure, the *Muse tragique* (*Tragic Muse*).

In that form the monument was enlarged and, although unfinished – *Meditation*, then known as *The Interior Voice*, did not have any arms, while *Tragic Muse* was fastened onto scaffolding – was shown at the 1897 Salon de la Société Nationale, and subsequently at the Rodin Exhibition in 1900. Both Muses had been begun, but Rodin was not really satisfied with them, or thought them at least to be superfluous. First of all, he cut *Tragic Muse* from a photograph by Freuler then, in 1906, announced that he was discontinuing both of them. So it was a marble Hugo alone that, in 1909, was put on a remarkable plinth made out of irregular blocks, in the gardens of the Palais-Royal. As to the complete monument, it was only much later cast in bronze, at the request of the City of Paris, and erected in 1964 at the far end of the Avenue Victor-Hugo, not far from the small *hôtel* in which the poet died.

The *Victor Hugo* was Rodin's second work to be put in a public space in Paris – *The Thinker* had in fact already been inaugurated on 21 April 1906 in front of the Panthéon. *The Thinker* had been 'offered to the people of Paris', thanks to a subscription launched by Gabriel Mourey, as a tribute to Rodin to make up for the ignominy of the rejection of his *Balzac*. *Victor Hugo* was supposed to occupy a huge space in the Panthéon, so there had to be a number of allegories. That is why Hugo stands upright in the new project, the so-called *Apothéose de Victor Hugo* (*Apotheosis of Victor Hugo*). On the Guernsey shore, he listens to the Sirens while Iris, a messenger of the gods, comes to crown him. In the first maquette (1891) he was dressed, like Mirabeau, but Rodin returned to the eighteenth-century theory of the representation of great men, considering that dress interfered with the aura of a genius by placing him too much within a given period and context. So he decided finally to represent the poet naked. The head is the same as in the plan showing Hugo sitting, as is the left arm, although it now hangs down the side of the body instead of being held out

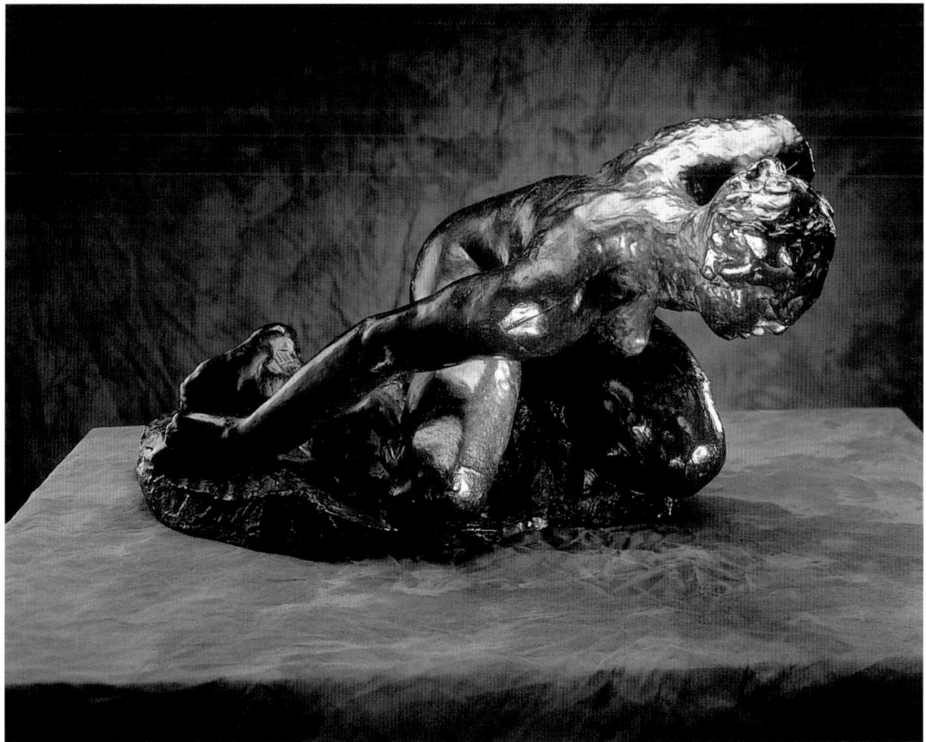

Tragic Muse 1894–96 (cat. 21)

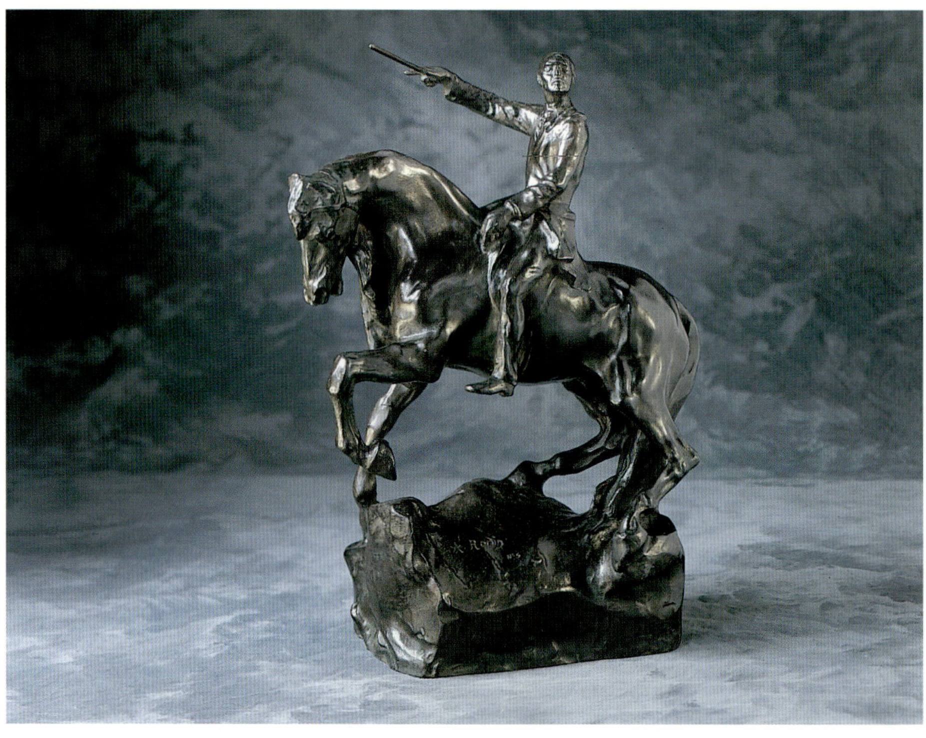

Maquette for General Lynch 1886 (cat. 6)

horizontally, before becoming slightly bent in the last maquette. It was in this state, with both legs firmly planted on the ground, whereas Hugo had formerly been leaning nonchalantly against the rock, that Lebossé enlarged the figure in 1901–1902. The very image of 'strength in action', the upright Hugo takes on its full meaning when we relate it to *The Walking Man*. Whereas the latter embodies a triumphant gait, the former, leaning slightly forward, with a powerful head, is clearly the effigy befitting Hugo the poet and writer, but also the politician who chose exile rather than remain in the France of Napoleon III, who took control after the *coup d'etat* of 2 December 1852.

Not letting himself be put off by the difficulties that he had already encountered with the *Balzac* and the *Victor Hugo*, Rodin undertook to create further monuments: to the painters *Puvis de Chavannes* (1899) and *Whistler* (1905). The latter, the last monument to be commissioned from the sculptor, was intended for London, but its realisation was disrupted by the War and, after the death of the artist, the commission was finally revoked in 1919. The London committee was in fact baffled by Rodin's approach. Taking up where he had left off in the previous monuments, he was not interested in including anywhere the actual figure of the subject. Instead he devoted his entire energy to an allegorical figure, posed by a young English woman, the painter Gwen John (1876–1939),

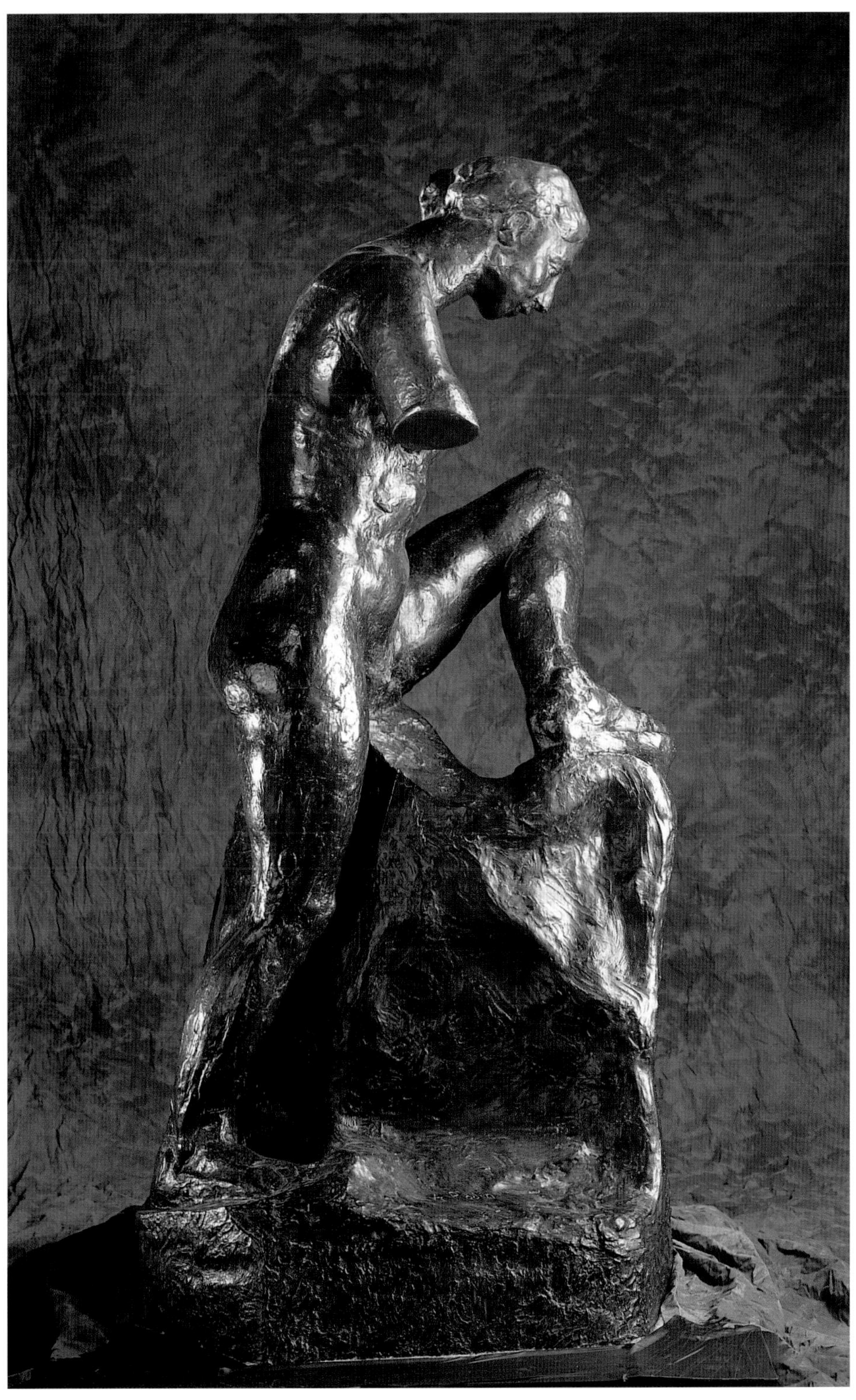

Whistler's Muse 1907 (cat. 12)

that was supposed to evoke the difficulties experienced by Whistler throughout his career. In its most daring version, *The Muse* (studies for the monument are also known as *Whistler's Muse*) is bearing a funeral casket in which one can recognise the cast of a small antique altar belonging to Rodin's private collection but, like *Meditation*, it had remained without arms for a long time as the sculptor did not know how to arrange them. This state of the work has only come down to us thanks to a series of photographs taken by Bulloz in 1908. Appearing there as a reincarnation of the *Venus de Milo*, *The Muse* attests to the distance covered by Rodin since *The Burghers of Calais*.

In the early twentieth century, the function of the public monument was above all didactic. Rodin, however, had defied the traditional descriptive norms and attempted to express the *essence* of those he portrayed. His process condemned him to being incomprehensible to many, and this in turn had a paralysing effect on him. But the sculptors of the next generation were to carry on his work, as Maillol did, for example, with his monuments to Blanqui, Cézanne and Debussy, in all of which he substituted an allegorical figure for a mere portrait of the man. Rodin had changed the course of sculpture.

Translated from the French by Peter Brown

1 J. Cladel, *Aristide Maillol. Sa vie, son œuvre, ses idées*, Paris: Grasset, 1937, p. 149.
2 C. Mauclair, 'Auguste Rodin. Son œuvre, son milieu, son influence', *Revue Universelle*, 17 August 1901.
3 R.M. Rilke, *Auguste Rodin*, Paris: Emile-Paul Frères, 1928, p. 188.
4 P. Gsell, 'Propos de Rodin sur l'art et les artistes', *La Revue*, 1 November 1907, p. 96.
5 C. Mauclair, op.cit.
6 R.M. Rilke, op.cit., pp. 165, 166.
7 A. Rodin, 'La tête Warren', *Le Musée*, 1904, p. 298.
8 See note 7, p. 13, for a description of the Commune.
9 A. Fontainas, *Mes Souvenirs du Symbolisme*, Paris: Nouvelle revue critique, 1928, Brussels: Editions Labor, 1991, p. 69.
10 W. Rothenstein, *Men and Memories. Recollections*, London: Faber and Faber, 1931, vol. I, p. 321.
11 Ibid.
12 Ibid.
13 Ibid., 'Le premier atelier', p. 116.
14 See note 5, p. 13, for a description of the Salon.
15 Sculpture became a large-scale enterprise at the end of the nineteenth century. Developing cities and the expanding middle class created unprecedented demand for multiple copies of popular sculpture, often cast in bronze.
16 Ibid., pp. 115, 116.
17 T. Bartlett, *The American Architect*, 19 January 1889.
18 F. Lawton, *The Life and Work of Auguste Rodin*, London: Fischer Unwin, 1906, p. 58.
19 J. Rousseau, *L'Echo du Parlement Belge*, 11 April 1877.
20 C. Frémine, *Le Rappel*, 28 November 1883.

21 Rodin often used clay to make a small or preliminary model – most famously with *The Gates of Hell* and *The Burghers of Calais* – and this maquette could then be used in preparation for the final sculpture or for presentation to a client for approval. Rodin's clay or wax piece was cast in plaster – when he was accused of casting his sculpture 'from life' his critics were alleging that the work was not made from his clay or wax maquette, but direct from the human body. When the final form was established, carvers used a pointing machine to work up Rodin's plaster models in marble, or patinators and founders were employed to produce the bronzes. Between 1894 and 1917 the Collas pointing method was used to make numerous enlargements and reductions.

22 Ch. Tardieu, 'Le Salon de Paris', *L'Art*, vol. 10, 1877 (3), p. 108.

23 5 February 1880, French National Archives, F21/4338.

24 J. Cladel, op.cit., p. 119.

25 The sculptor Augustin Préault (1810–1879), with his refusal to define forms and with his emphasis on emotion, death and the nature of existence, had established himself as a romantic par excellence with his statement: 'Je ne suis pas pour le fini, je suis pour l'infini' (I am for what is infinite, not what is finished').(C. Mathieu, *The Musée d'Orsay*, Paris: Editions de la Réunion des Musées Nationaux, 1987, p. 40)

26 Ateliers were essentially artists' studios with a stock of casts and models for life-drawing and painting. Although artists had always learned to paint in artists' studios, previously this had been during the process of helping on a commission.

27 See note 21 above for a description of Rodin's working process using maquettes.

28 O. Mirbeau, *La France*, 18 February 1885.

29 F. Champsaur, *Le Figaro*, 16 January 1886. (Translation: 'Abandon all hope, ye who enter here.')

30 G. Geffroy, 'Le statuaire Rodin', *Les Arts et les Lettres*, September 1889, p. 295.

31 J. Wilfrid, *L'Alsacien-Lorrain*, 9 July 1895.

32 A. Rodin, *Les Cathédrales de France*, Paris: Colin, 1914, p. 158.

33 G. Coquiot, *Le Vrai Rodin*, Paris: Taillandier, 1913, p. 126.

34 J. Cladel, op.cit., p. 141.

35 O. Maus, 'Claude Monet –Auguste Rodin', *L'Art Moderne*, 1889, p. 211.

36 G. Dargenty, 'Le Salon national', *L'Art*, vol. 35, 1883 (4), p. 37.

37 R. M. Rilke, op.cit., pp. 51–53.

38 E. Verhaeren, 'Chronique de l'exposition', *Mercure de France*, May 1900. Reprinted in E. Verhaeren, *Ecrits sur l'Art*, Brussels: Labor, 1997, p. 784.

39 F. Lawton, *François-Auguste Rodin*, New York: Mitchell Kennerley, 1908, p. 127.

40 A. Bourdelle, 'Rodin et la sculpture', *Revue des Etudes Franco-Russes*, September 1909, p. 381.

41 François Rude was the leading French sculptor in the early 1800s. His major work, *La Marseillaise*, was on the Arc de Triomphe in Paris (1833–1836).

42 Record of Proceedings, Calais Municipal Council, session of 26th September 1884, Calais, Municipal Archives.

43 P.A. Isaac to the Mayor of Calais, 17 October 1884, ibid.

44 A. Rodin to O. Dewavrin, 8 December 1893, ibid.

45 G. Rodenbach, *L'Elite*, Paris: E. Fasquelle, 1899, p. 290.

46 Alfred Dreyfus (1859–1935), a French army officer, was convicted of treason in 1894 and 1899. He was Jewish and his convictors were accused of anti-Semitism. The conviction was set aside in 1906.

47 Ch. Chincolle, *La Petite République*, 15 November 1898.

48 A. Rodin, *Le Matin*, 13 July 1908.

49 French National Archives, F21/4758.

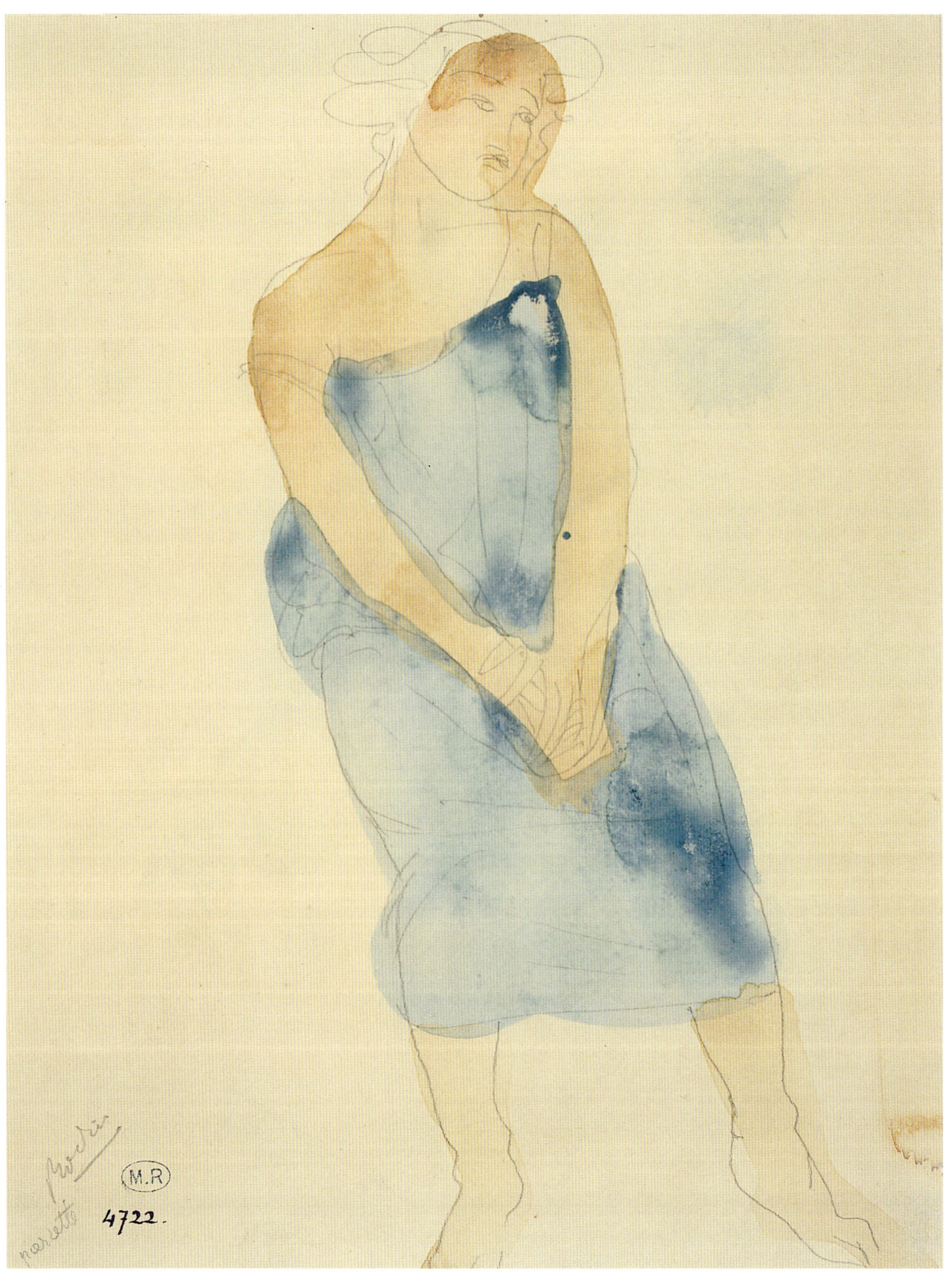

Pierrette *c.*1900 (cat. 100)

RODIN'S DRAWINGS

Claudie Judrin

Contrary to the received view that a sculptor's drawings are made with his sculpture already in mind, Rodin kept his various activities separate, finding a certain respite as he went from one to the other. Consequently, it would be a mistake to try to lump them both together. There may be exceptions, but we should never lose sight of the fact that we are most definitely dealing with drawings by a sculptor seeking to translate the three-dimensional world into two dimensions.

YOUTH

Childhood and the teenage years are always the most important and yet the most uneasy period in an artist's life, when opinions and attitudes are unconsciously formed amidst the turbulence of adolescence. During this period, more than any other, it is hard to discuss life as one is living it so intensely, and it is only much later that one can take a clear look at one's past. Rodin proved that he was no exception when, in 1910 at the age of seventy, he consented to talk about his youth.

Drawing comes first, as Rodin confided to a journalist: 'I have been drawing all my life. I began my life by drawing.' Similarly, he disclosed to Gustave Coquiot: 'Quite young, as far back as I can remember, I was drawing. A greengrocer where my mother used to shop wrapped his prunes in paper bags made from the pages of illustrated books and even engravings. I copied them down and they became my first models.'

In response to the passionate interest in drawing that their son showed right from the time he was sent to live with his uncle in Beauvais, Rodin's parents enrolled him in Paris at the 'Petite Ecole' in the rue de l'Ecole-de-Médecine, where his teachers were the painters Jean-Hilaire Belloc and later Horace Lecoq de Boisbaudran. Rodin learned two things from them: one was to exercise his visual memory and the other to work from a living model. He complemented this instruction by attending classes at the Medical School, the Gobelins Tapestry Workshop, the Jardin des Plantes (the Botanic Gardens and the Natural History Museum) and of course through his studies at the Louvre and the Bibliothèque Impériale (Imperial Library).

Copying was a standard part of an artist's apprenticeship and drawing from memory was something that Rodin was to practise to great advantage throughout his life. In addition, he started his quest to collect everything that aroused his curiosity, such as engravings, drawings and paintings of the seventeenth and eighteenth centuries, scenes of the Orient, plasters from Antiquity, Greek bowls and anatomical illustrations.

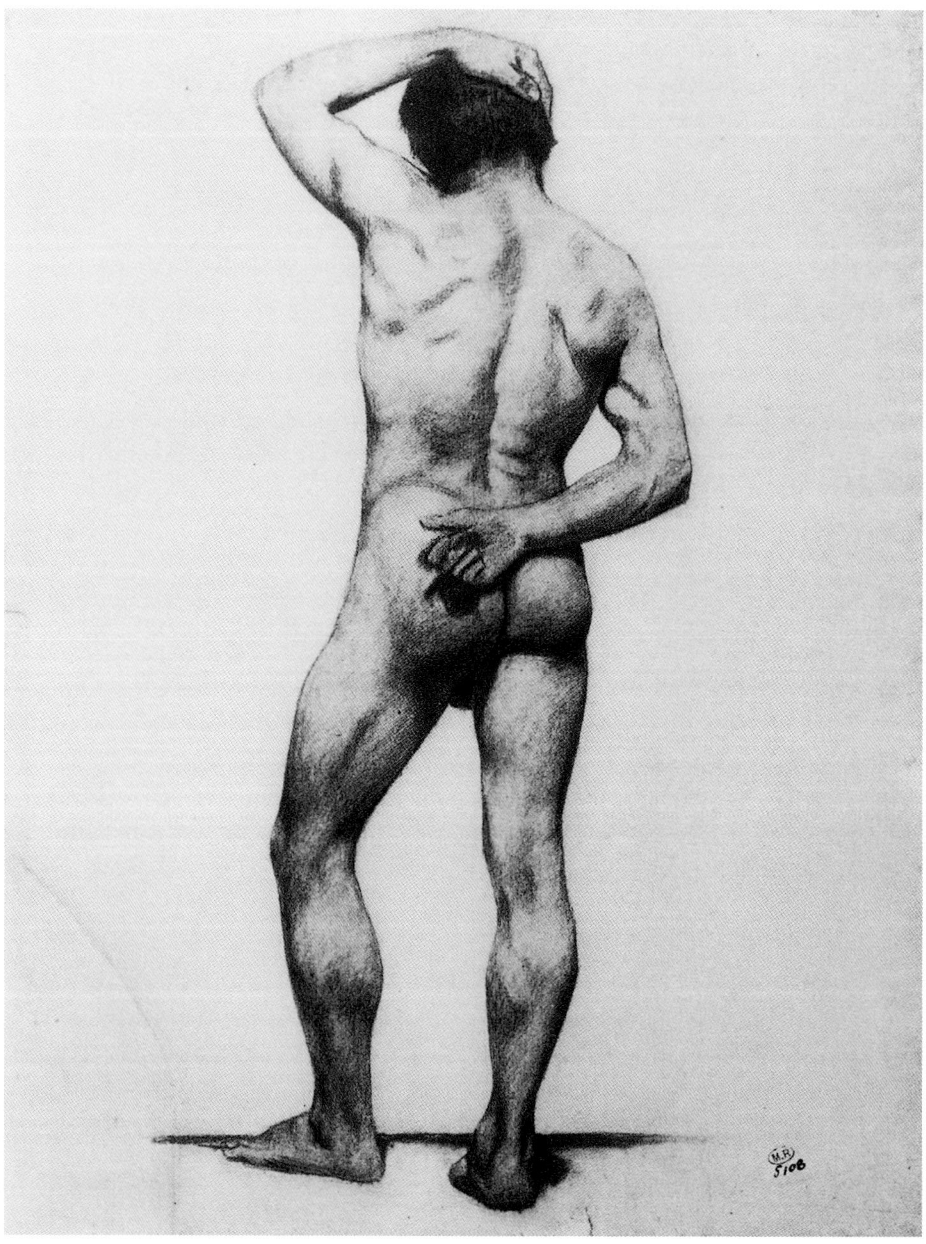

Male Nude From the Back, a Hand on his Head (no date) Charcoal 60.6 x 40.0 cm Musée Rodin

MICHELANGELO AND DANTE

In 1875, Rodin left for Italy in search of Michelangelo (1475–1564). In front of the great Florentine's works, Rodin felt that 'the great magician … passed on some of his secrets to him' and there began a strange alchemy in which Rodin both drew inspiration from Michelangelo's works and appropriated them for himself. This resulted in a huge number of sketches that were not quite copies of Michelangelo, but not yet works by Rodin either. The singular feature of these works still lay in the montage and collage of several sheets of sketches in a very particular order and in the obvious touching up of drawings done at various later stages. Many of these works have disappeared, taking with them what they could have taught us about the *modus operandi* of the artist who, in referring to the Michelangelos in the Medici Sacristy in Florence, gave the following account in a letter to his companion Rose Beuret: 'I have done some sketches in the evening at home, not from his works, but from all the scaffolding and systems that I am constructing in my imagination to be able to understand him.' Thanks to Michelangelo's influence, Rodin was encouraged to let his own fertile imagination fly, and develop a readiness to reappraise and modify his work. As the last great nineteenth-century humanist, Rodin was influenced by two of Italy's creative geniuses – first Michelangelo, and then Dante.

Did his reading of Dante's *Divine Comedy* date back to the 'Petite Ecole' or was it after his trip to the land of the great Florentine? It is tempting to turn Dante's work, as Léon Maillard does, into Rodin's bedside reading on his return from Italy. The artist himself used to say that he 'spent a whole year with Dante, living only from and with him, drawing the eight circles of his *Inferno*'. He admired not only the visionary and the writer in him, but also 'the sculptor'. If we merely had Rodin's sculptures, we could have doubts about his precise knowledge of the text. However, an analysis of the annotations in the margin of the drawings reveals a rigorous commentary at work. He enters into Dante's dream at the same time as giving free rein to his own imagination. We can sense that he steeped himself in this mythology, which was so intimately bound up with the world of Antiquity, a passion for which would make Rodin one of its eminent collectors.

Rodin used many of Dante's real and imaginary characters as source material for his drawings: the poet Virgil who served as a mentor to Dante in his descent into the underworld, Caron, Minos, Paolo Malatesta and Francesca da Rimini, Cerbera, the avaricious and the lustful, the heretics, the centaurs, the blasphemers, Icarus, Medea, Buoso and the thieves, Count Guido da Montefeltro, the sectarians including Mohammed, and finally the traitors embodied by

Count Ugolino della Gherardesca. Condemned to death by starvation in February 1288 in a tower near Pisa (known as the Hunger Tower), Ugolino fascinated Rodin who followed his week-long torture step by step, ending with the dramatic moment when Ugolino crawls over and devours the dead bodies of his sons. Like any artist with a tendency towards Romanticism, Rodin showed himself to be infinitely more sensitive to hell than to either purgatory or paradise.

Intended as research studies, the drawings are highly fragile, done on cheap, low-grade recycled paper, sheets from registers and notebooks of various sorts treated without any particular care by their creator, who was intent on following the whims of his imagination. Often sketched on both back and front, stuck on a variety of surfaces, and touched up with gouache and brown ink wash that coroded the paper, these works of the 1880s remain priceless documents for us today.

Some of these drawings have come down to us through the so-called Goupil Album (1897), as if Rodin, conscious of the general public's inability to understand this kind of study at that time, was already preserving these drawings for posterity.

HUGO AND BAUDELAIRE

During his 'black' period (1880–1890), Rodin found further inspiration in the work of two of his other favourite poets and kindred spirits, Victor Hugo and Charles Baudelaire. From 1883, the date of his first meeting with Hugo and the first preparatory sketches for the bust of the poet, until 1897, when *Monument à Victor Hugo* (*The Monument to Victor Hugo*) was exhibited at the Salon, the poet was forever in his thoughts. This started with minor studies, grudgingly granted by the great man, right up to the engravings and through to the plans for monumental tombs following his death in 1885. The sculptor had the good fortune to know Hugo personally, even if this was towards the end of the poet's life when, tired and indifferent, he was no longer in a position to appreciate Rodin's real worth.

Rodin never met Baudelaire, but we can say that the sculptor's Christian vision is a response to Baudelaire's Dantesque one. Baudelaire's book of verse *Les Fleurs du Mal (The Flowers of Evil)* is like an echo of *The Divine Comedy*. We know that Rodin was imbued with literature to the point of quoting lines of verse from memory, although inaccurately, down the sides of drawings. He conceived the idea of illustrating *The Flowers of Evil*, and the writer and architect

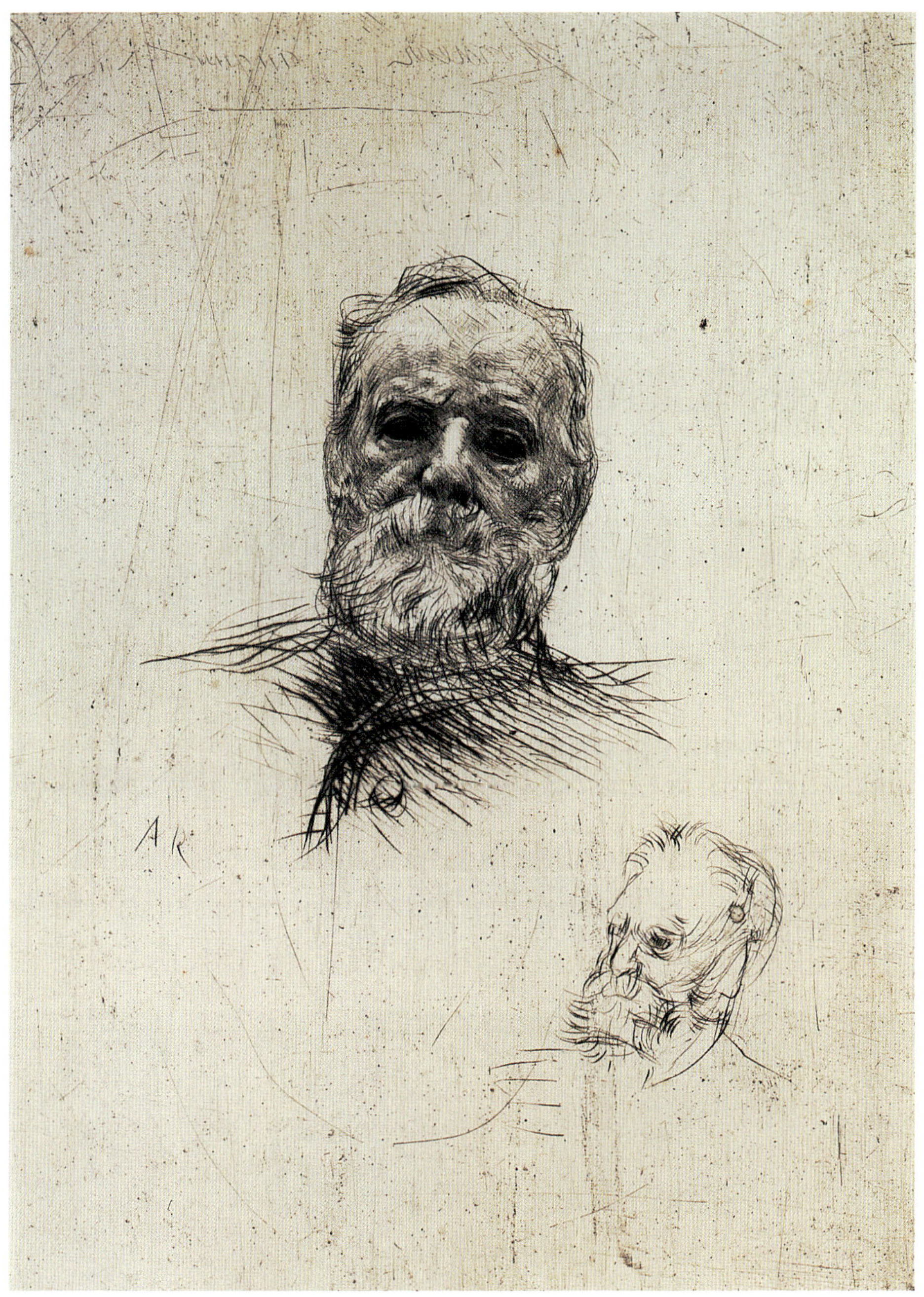

Victor Hugo (frontal view) 1886 (cat. 74)

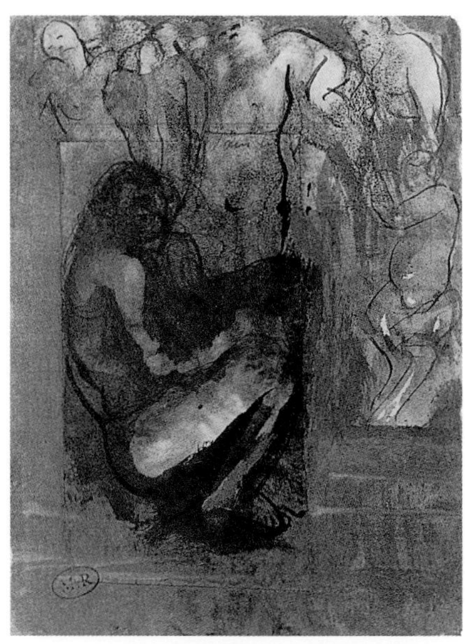

In the Sea c.1880 Graphite, pen and inks
18.1 x 13.6 cm Musée Rodin

Frantz Jourdain acted as go-between for publisher Paul Gallimard who had agreed to commission it. Rodin was hoping for great success as a result of this project but was deeply disappointed when it was not displayed to the public, or printed, but retained as an original copy in private possession. His drawings were not made available in facsimile until 1918, a year after his death, with the printing of 200 copies, followed by 1,500 copies in 1940, 3,000 copies in 1968 and finally several thousand copies in 1983. This disappointment was compounded by the fact that Rodin had some trouble getting paid, raising the possibility that he did not throw himself wholeheartedly into the project during the three months, between October 1887 and the end of January 1888, which he seems to have devoted to it. He went back to some earlier works, drawing from sculptures as he had done with some of his engravings and came up with a few wash-tints, transferring Baudelaire's verse to the margins.

Dante, Hugo and Baudelaire were linked together in Rodin's mind and he interpreted them in similar fashion, firstly doing a pencil sketch that was later over-worked in pen, then often adding brown ink tinting sometimes also enhanced by gouache. In 1897, Rodin entered a new phase as a draughtsman by allowing a collection of 142 drawings to be published in the Goupil Album by the firm of Goupil, Boussod, Manzi, Joyant and Co., underwritten by Maurice Fenaille's patronage. In it, Rodin unveiled the mystery of his most intimate studies, which had never been shown to a wider public. Octave Mirbeau (1848–1917) wrote a preface to the work stating that 'these drawings would alone suffice to secure the artist's reputation'.

ARCHITECTURE

On his way to Italy Rodin had visited, and been dazzled by, Rheims Cathedral and afterwards undertook a tour of monuments that only ceased with the publication of his book *Les Cathédrales de France (The Cathedrals of France)* in March 1914, on the eve of the First World War. Going on a pilgrimage to find source material became a habit, and was a pleasurable necessity with the commissioning of *La Porte de l'Enfer (The Gates of Hell)*, when he had to turn himself into an architect. 'I am becoming an architect. I have to, as it is in this way that I will make up for what I am lacking for my *Gates*'. The result was a series of notebook sketches testifying to a keen attention to detail, especially to architectural mouldings. In around two thousand drawings we see a succession of pillars, arches, buttresses and mouldings that were to remain anonymous, removed from their context. The moulding has a special place since, 'whoever sees and understand it, can see the monument ... The mouldings are sweet symphonies'.

Contrary to what the title of the book *The Cathedrals of France* would lead us to believe, the facsimile reproductions of the drawings on 100 of the album's plates actually deal more with churches that do not have the status of *chefs-d'œuvre*. We can see Rodin is affected as much by Romanesque as by Gothic or Renaissance art. In the manner of the 'black' drawings (1880–1890), the techniques chosen are those of pencil, pen, brown ink wash and gouache.

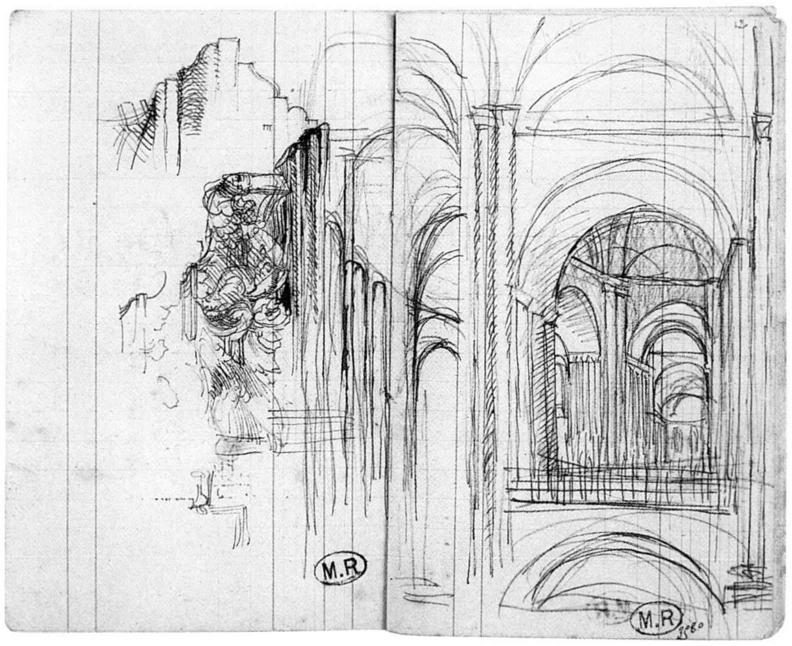

Interior of Saint-Croix Church in Quimperlé 1901? Graphite and sepia ink Musée Rodin

TRANSITIONAL DRAWINGS

After 1890, Rodin's approach to drawing changed. Up to now (apart from during his apprenticeship) he had not really used models; he had neither the means nor the desire to have them pose. For Rodin, drawings that were dependent on a knowledge of literary references were cut off from reality and any artist who forgot this soon lost his way and reached a sort of impasse. A short time later, Rodin confessed:

> This [life-drawing] didn't just come to me all of a sudden, I started very gently. I was afraid, and then gradually, standing before Nature, I began to understand it better and, in order to love it, reject my prejudices. I made up my mind to try ... I was rather happy ... Studying works from Antiquity also gave me heart, as did sculpture of the Middle Ages, which is as beautiful as Greek art. I did everything to bring my soul into harmony with those creatures ...

From then on, the word 'Nature' was always part of his language. Rodin was influenced, among other things, by Japan. He was able to look closely at *estampes* (Japanese prints) in 1887 in the home of the writer Edmond de Goncourt. By 1895, Rodin had the time and the means, since acquiring the Villa des Brillants at Meudon, to study more closely the work of all the artists he was collecting and whose example he followed when he felt the need.

He used only women as his models. He would ask them to move about freely without taking up any particular pose, something that was very unusual in studios at that time. Rodin's beginnings were modest and even timorous. When drawing women dressing and undressing, he would completely change his palette. From being sombre and full of ink wash, his drawings took on clear and sometimes bright tints such as pink or yellow. The format of the page scarcely changed at all but its quality was in general that of writing paper. For a dozen years, his sketches still lacked breadth and assurance. The drawings were, it seems, little shown or exhibited, being used by the artist purely for his experimental research. With the exception of a few sketches in the margins of articles, the only notable and coloured testimony from this rather brief period is the title-page of the first edition (1899) of Octave Mirbeau's novel *Le Jardin des Supplices* (*The Torture Garden*).

OCTAVE MIRBEAU

Mirbeau, a close friend, was the writer whom Rodin knew best. He was the first person to defend the sculptor and draughtsman, as attested by a journalist's quip that 'Rodin is great and Mirbeau is his prophet'. Indeed, there were many signs of friendship between the two men: a bust, a pen portrait on the copy of *Sébastien Roch* belonging to Goncourt, Mirbeau's preface for the Goupil Album and Rodin's illustration for the two successive editions of the novel *The Torture Garden*. The publisher Ambroise Vollard drew up a contract on 10 February 1899 for twenty-odd stone lithographs by Auguste Clot (1858–1936) after Rodin's drawings, as only good-quality engravings could faithfully reproduce the new compositions and capture the subtle nuances of watercolours.

THE NUDE AND THE CLOTHED MODEL

Of the thousands of drawings held in the Rodin Museum, around three-quarters have a female figure as their model. They were not designed as preparatory studies for his sculptures – a common view of those unfamiliar with his working methods – nor were they of any well-known and truly exceptional models, but of the everyday and eternal woman, whom Rodin looked at with a new and ever-curious eye. Standard academic poses, which were a regular feature of studios in the late nineteenth century, were eliminated from his vocabulary. This was a real revolution, the birth of modern drawing. Rodin would ask the model not to become set in any predetermined, and hence stiff, attitude. 'Don't pretend to be doing your hair. Really do your hair'.

Rodin let Nature take over. The challenge now lay with the artist, as he could no longer work at a leisurely pace – his swift pencil strokes had to match his eyes' alertness. Such dexterity requires constant practice, something that his contemporaries were fully aware of when they noticed that Rodin did not take his eyes off his model. The consequence was that, contrary to the draughtsmen of his day, he did not have his gaze glued to his sheet of paper. Such capacity for improvisation was hitherto unknown and was to be taken up by those who followed, such as Henri Matisse and Pablo Picasso. In the first instance, however, it gave rise to a certain lack of understanding on the part of the general public which, without any points of reference, called it a scandal and proclaimed Rodin's work unfinished.

Rodin's audacity now knew no bounds. The body was left free to express itself and the manner of doing so unrestricted. Everything became possible: perspectives, views from above, foreshortenings, contortions, sectional views, use of lines that an eraser would have previously effaced, diagonals,

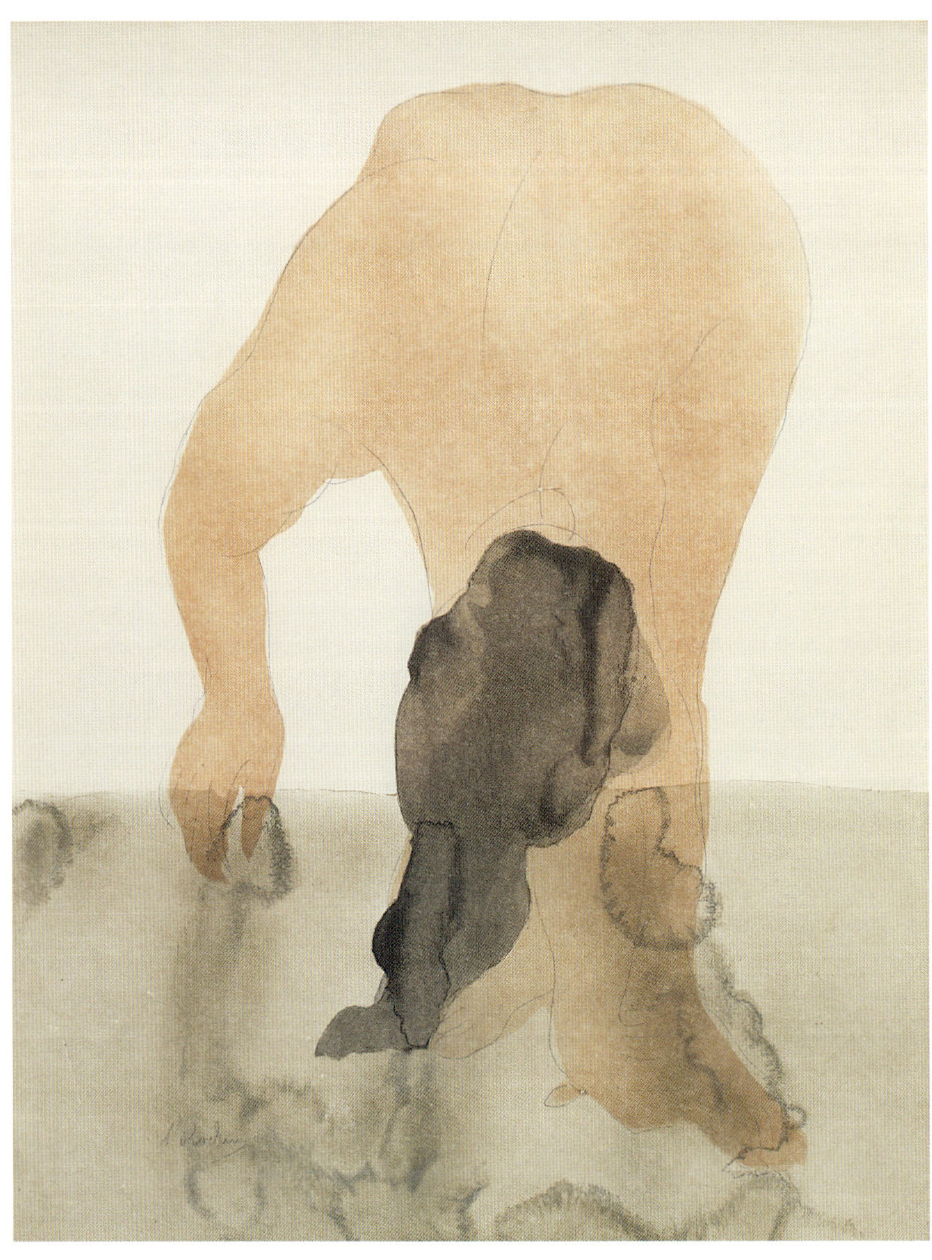

'She seemed to be returning from a long and agonising sleep ...' from *Le Jardin des Supplices (The Torture Garden)* (cat. 127)

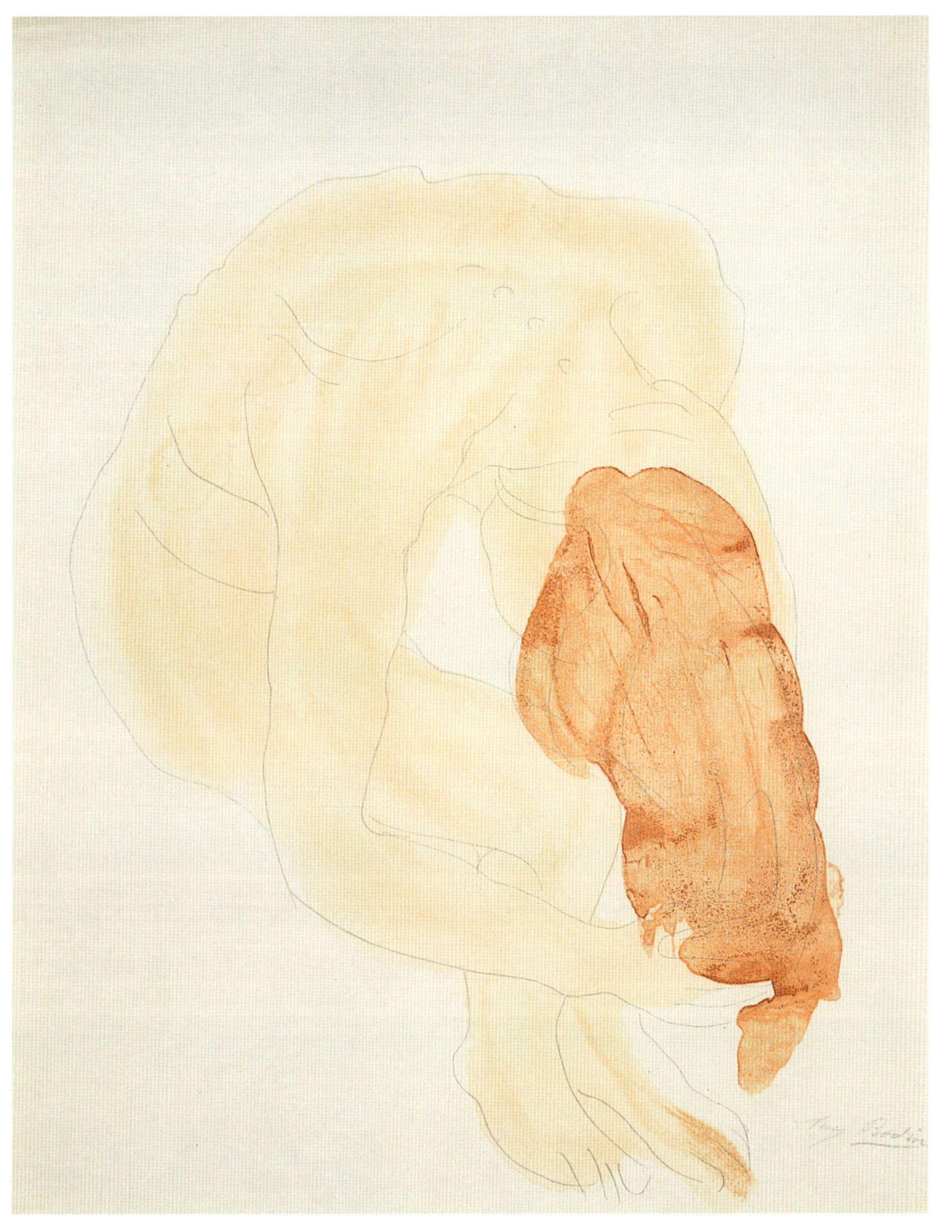

'The second has abundant hair which gleams and flows in long silky garlands.' from *Le Jardin des Supplices (The Torture Garden)* (cat. 127)

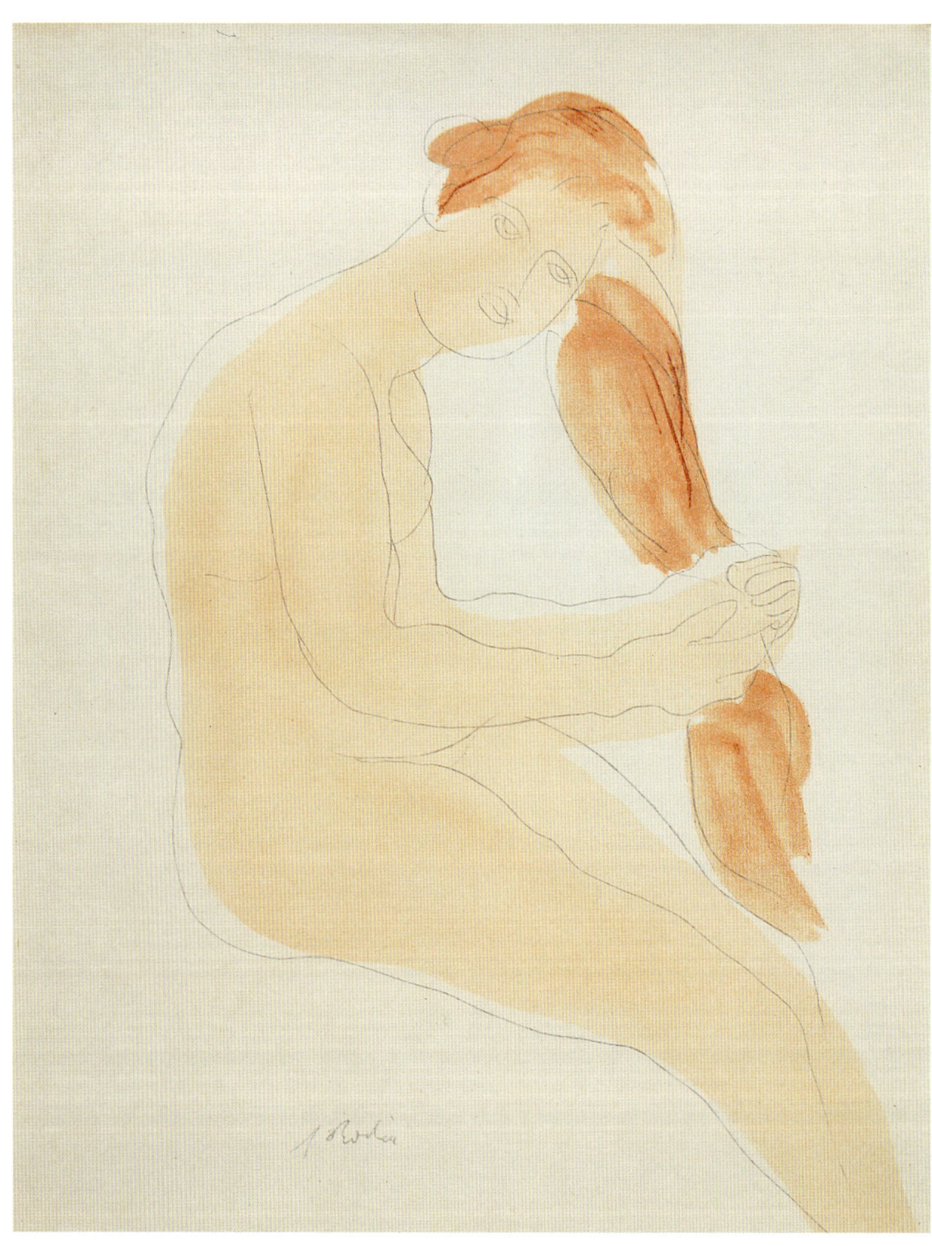

'With slow and charming gestures, Clara smoothed her russet-gold hair.' from *Le Jardin des Supplices (The Torture Garden)* (cat. 127)

and asymmetries. There was no need at all to put down on paper the outline of a chair, or bed or room, or even the ground on which the model stood, contrary to what was being taught in all the schools. With his carefully considered placement of the figure on the page, and his innate sense of space around the body, Rodin became a great innovator, discovering a new visual language. This is something that we have trouble appreciating today, as we are so accustomed to the simplified line. In fact, one could say that modern art has its source in Rodin's perfected form of incompleteness.

A drawing by Rodin can be looked at in several ways. On the first level we have a nude woman, mostly without any recognisable face. Then the artist gave the piece a symbolic title – either mythological, literary, cosmic or religious – that conferred a universal character. He sometimes proposed a number of different readings of his drawings by annotating them with the word 'down' pointing to alternative angles other than that of the model's real pose.

DECOUPAGES

This instinctive desire to have his drawing 'stand out' resulted in Rodin attempting a certain amount of experimentation all through his life. Just as he annotated his drawings with the word 'down' to suggest a way of looking at it other than that indicated by the pose, he also carried out experiments in his compositions with the help of cut-out silhouettes that he manipulated like puppets. He practised on paper the technique of *marcottage*, that is, as he did with his sculpture, reassembling diverse fragments of previously created works to form new compositions. We, who are very used to the collages of the Cubists and the Surrealists, and to the cut-out gouaches of Matisse and contemporary artists, often forget that part of their inspiration for this kind of work came from Rodin.

THE CAMBODIAN WOMEN

At the end of his life, Rodin turned his attention to dance, as if his mastery of drawing was now such that he felt able to tackle that most ephemeral and difficult of things, movement itself.

It was the Far East that gave him a taste for this, thanks to the great Expositions Universelles of the final quarter of the nineteenth century in Paris. In 1889, he admired the Javanese dancers, whose ancient and flowing form he talked about to Edmond de Goncourt, as recorded in the latter's *Journal*. However, for Rodin the real Asian sensation was the ballet troupe of the Cambodian king Sisowath,

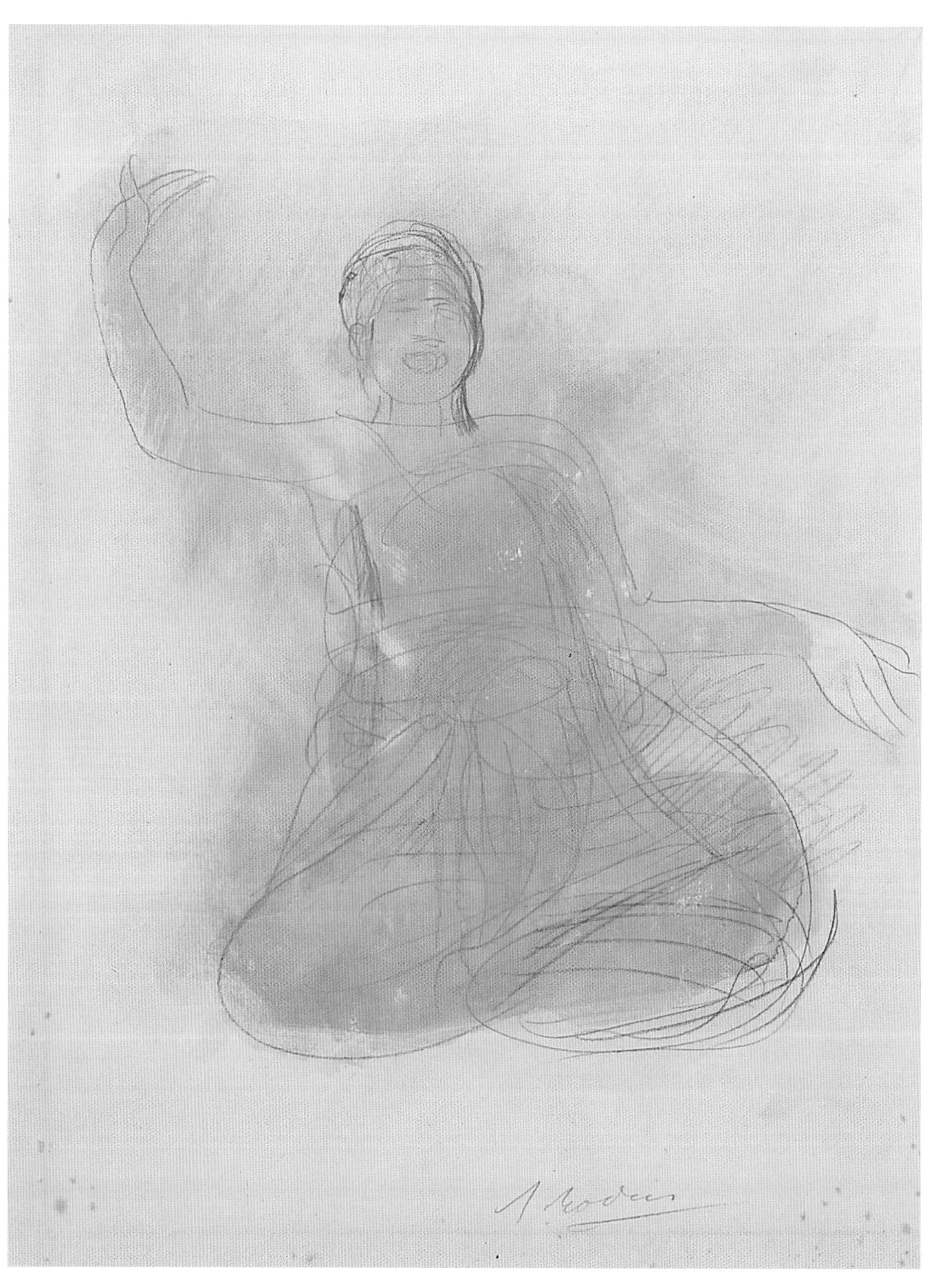

The Cambodian Dancer 1906 (cat. 126)

who performed at the Exposition Coloniale (Colonial Exhibition) in Marseilles in July 1906. After seeing the dancers for the first time at the *Théâtre de Verdure* in the Pré-Catalan in Paris, he tried to get them to pose for him before they left the French capital. Their stay was too short for his liking and Rodin caught the train taking them down to Marseilles in order to make the most of the presence of the young models right up until their embarkation. 'I gazed on them in rapture ... What emptiness they have left in me! When they went away, I was in the shade and the cold, feeling that they were taking away the beauty of the world ... I followed them to Marseilles. I would have followed them as far as Cairo!'

The result of his being struck by the dancers in this way was a series of absolutely delightful watercolours. Between 1898 and 1910, Rodin successfully used a watercolour technique where the applied colour did not conform to his outline drawing, enabling him to convey a sense of volume and space and even movement. The general public was immediately won over by these attractive watercolours, and they proved popular in exhibition, albeit at the cost of their fragility. Rodin realised their worth and agreed to lend them, firstly to the Bernheim Gallery in Paris in 1907 for the first exhibition devoted purely to his drawings (which finally seemed to receive full acceptance as works of art in their own right), then to museums abroad: in Vienna, Budapest, Prague, Brussels, Leipzig and so on. The Austrian poet Rainer Maria Rilke described to his wife Clara Westhoff the excitement that he felt in front of these refined exotic drawings. But if Rilke had a way with words, Rodin himself felt humble and lacking the means of expression, claiming that 'the Cambodian women are beyond the beauty that we can, at least that I have been able to, grasp'.

Less attracted by more traditional ballet current in the West, and especially in France, which he judged to be too set and conventional, Rodin devoted his final research to dancing that was full of invention and daring, such as that performed by Isadora Duncan and Alda Moreno. His penchant for a pure pencil line reappeared, but it was set off by perfectly executed stump drawing, done with the thumb, in an infinite variety of shades of grey, as if a tribute to the smoke-like qualities of the work of his friend Eugène Carrière.

Rodin was a draughtsman of immense capacity, as shown by the fact that there are nearly eight thousand works in the Rodin Museum alone, as well as a great innovator, given that the great artists who were to follow, like Matisse and Picasso, bear his imprint, if not direct influence. In short, with his drawings Rodin commands attention well beyond the realm of sculpture in which the general public tends to confine him. It is now also time for his engravings and his role as a collector to receive the recognition that is their due.

Translated from the French by Peter Brown

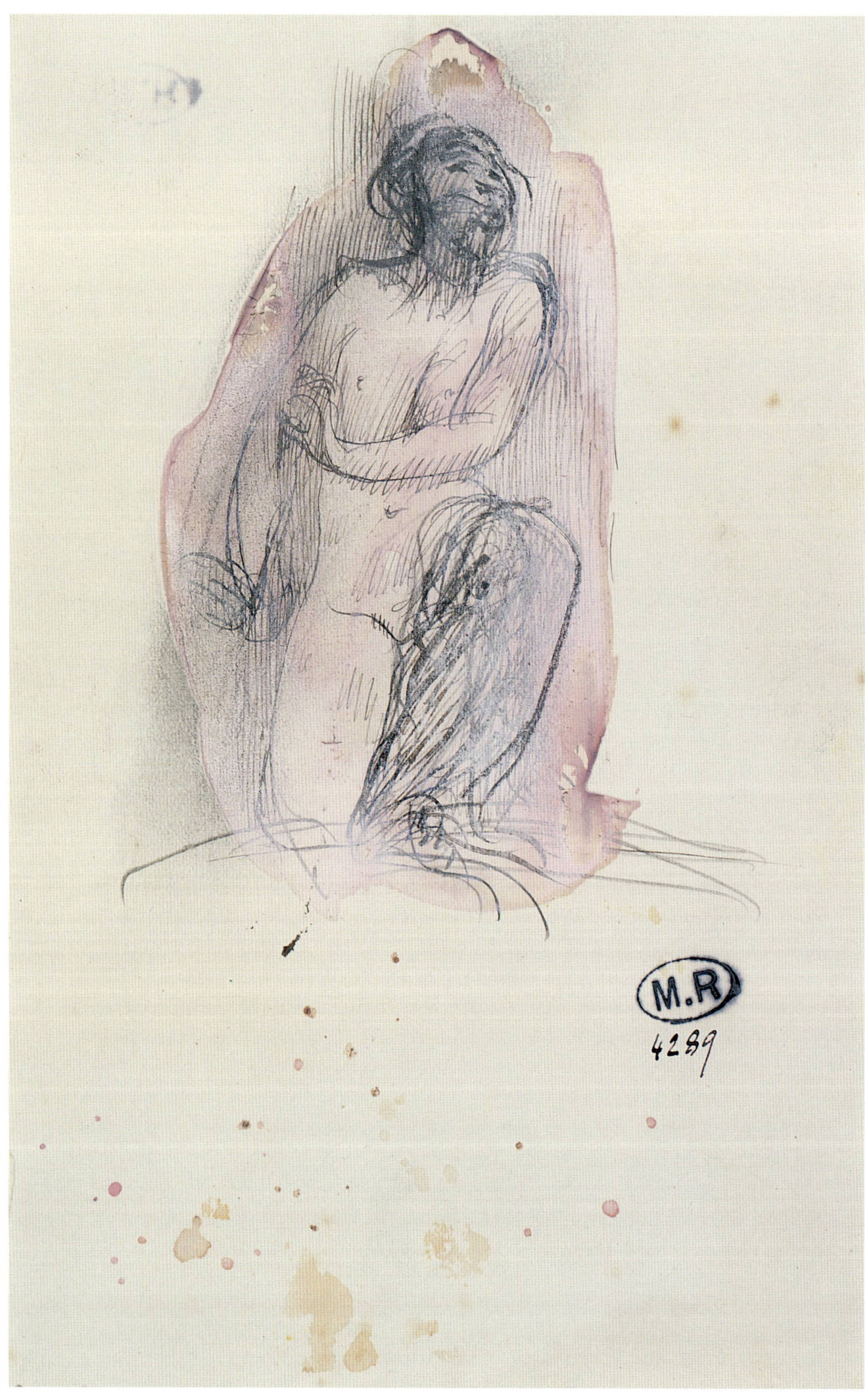

Kneeling Female Nude c.1890 (cat. 80)

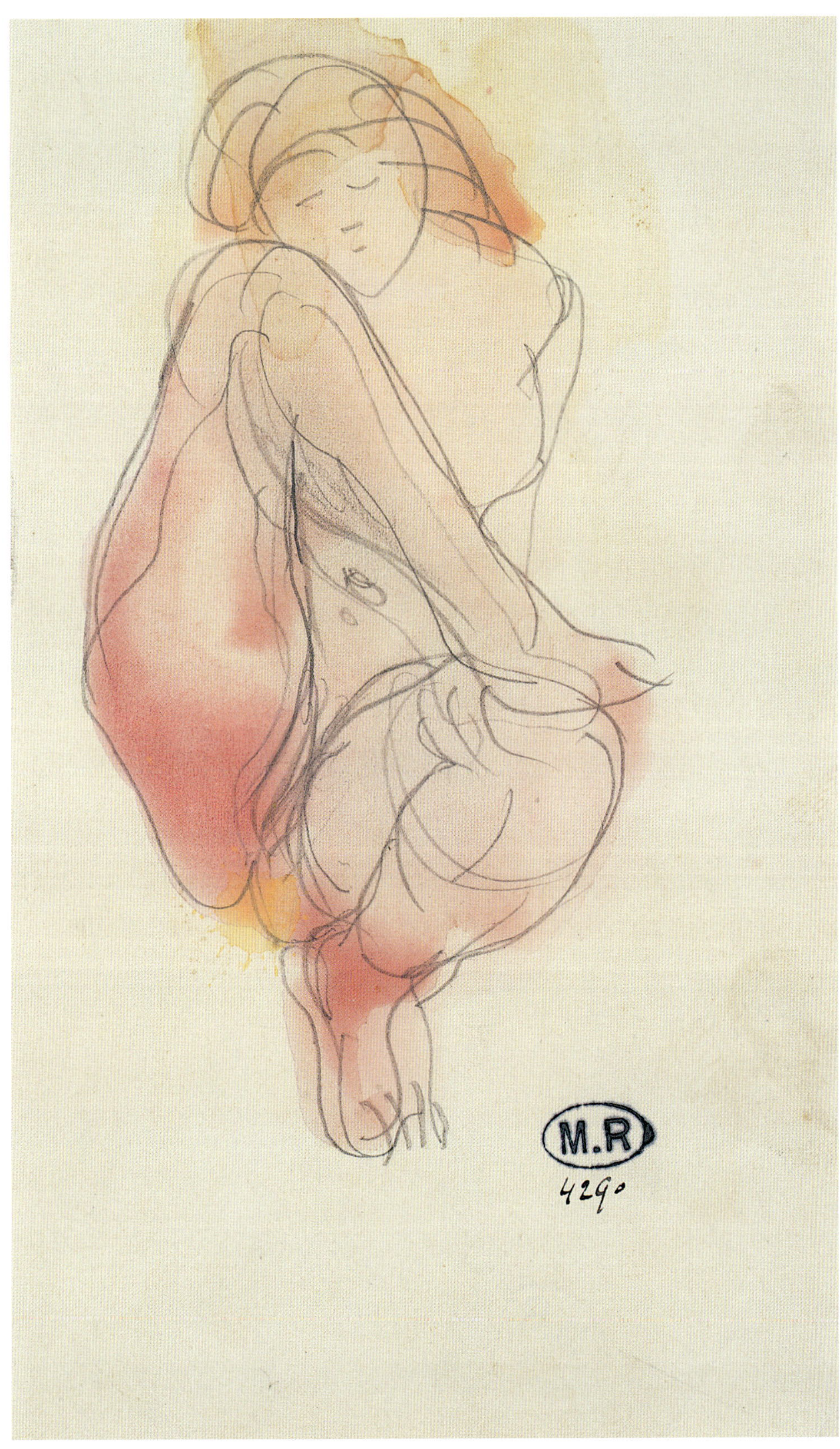

Seated Female Nude c.1890 (cat. 81)

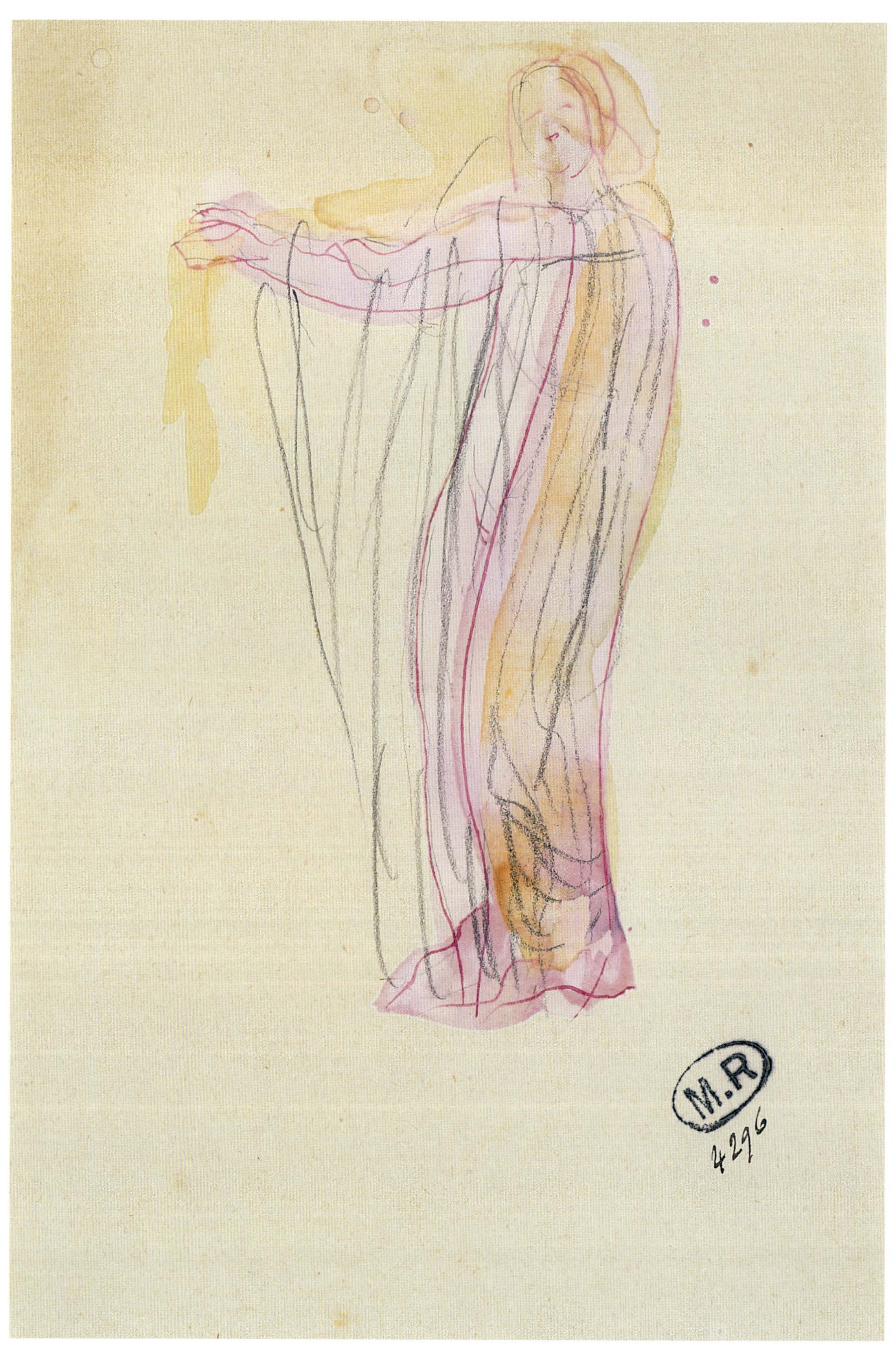

Draped Female Nude c.1890 (cat. 82)

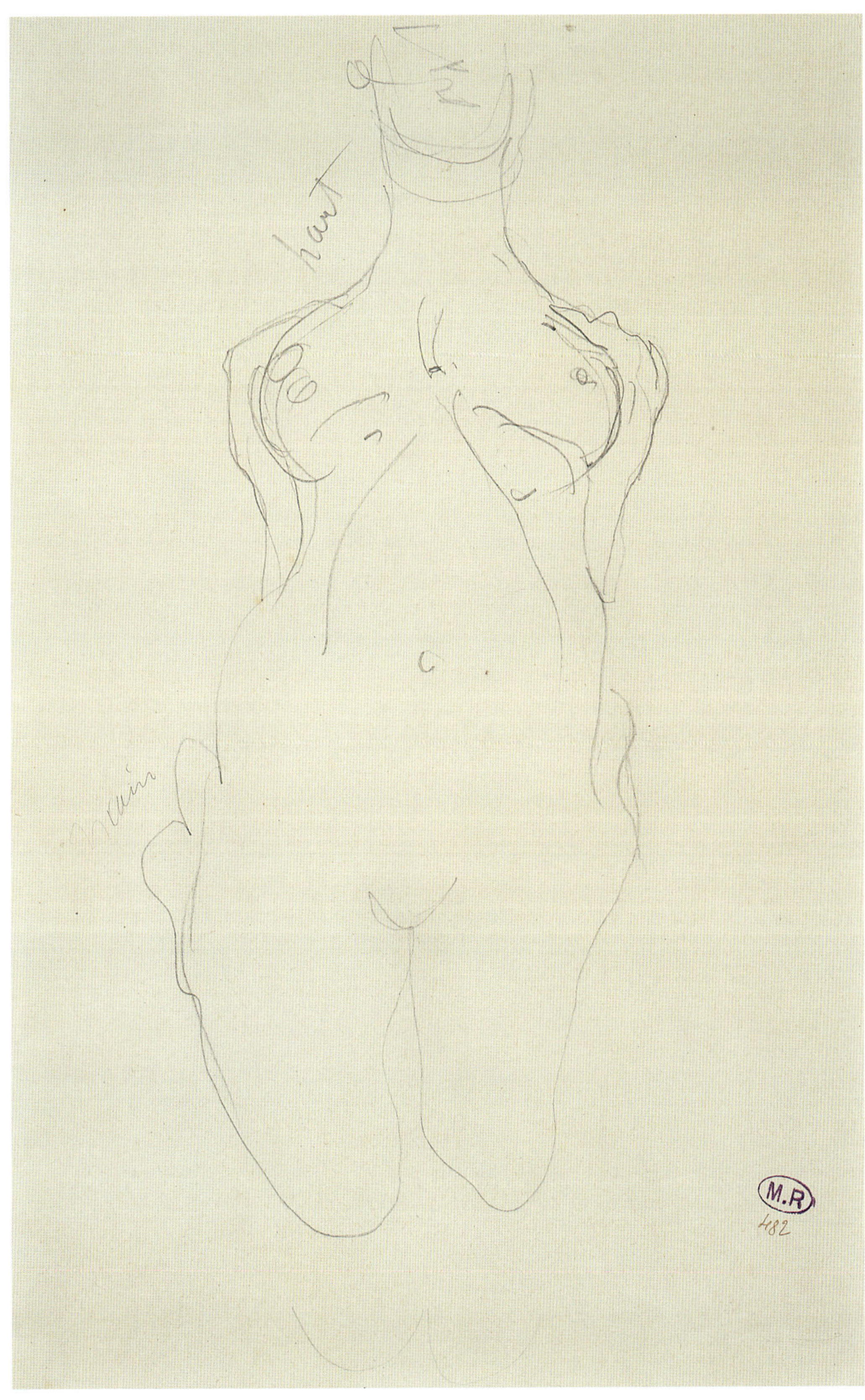

Kneeling Female Nude c.1900 (cat. 84)

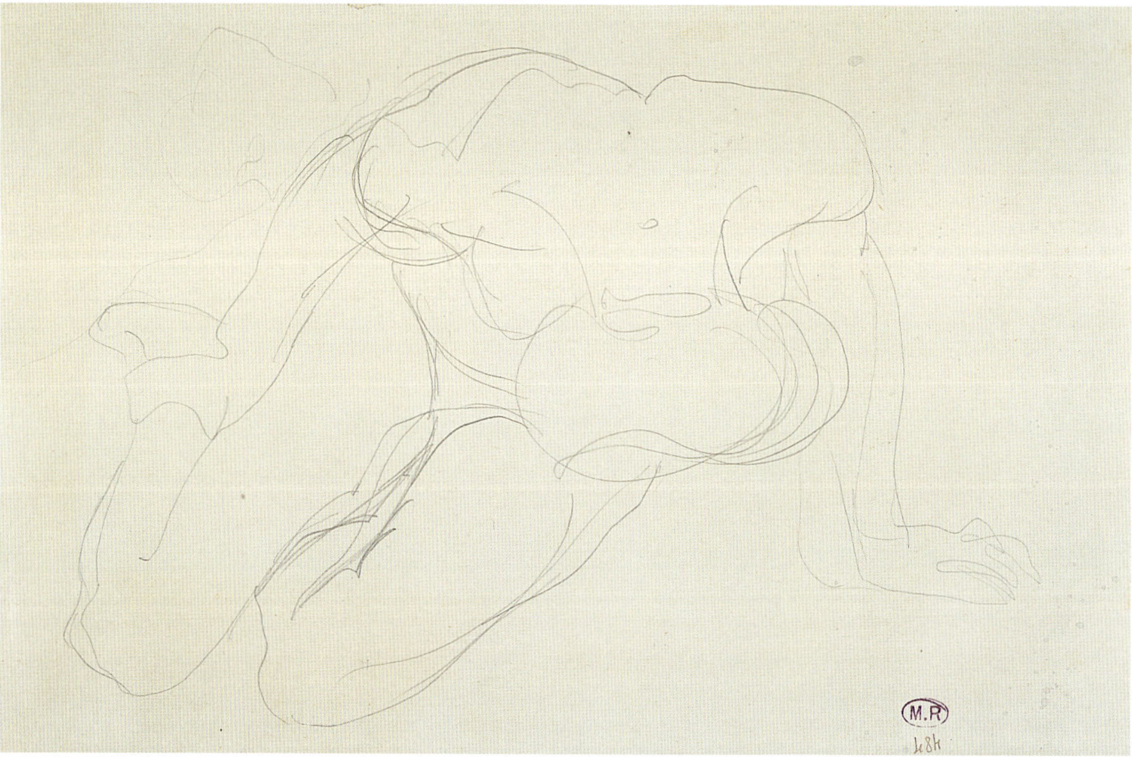

Seated Female Nude c.1900 (cat. 85)

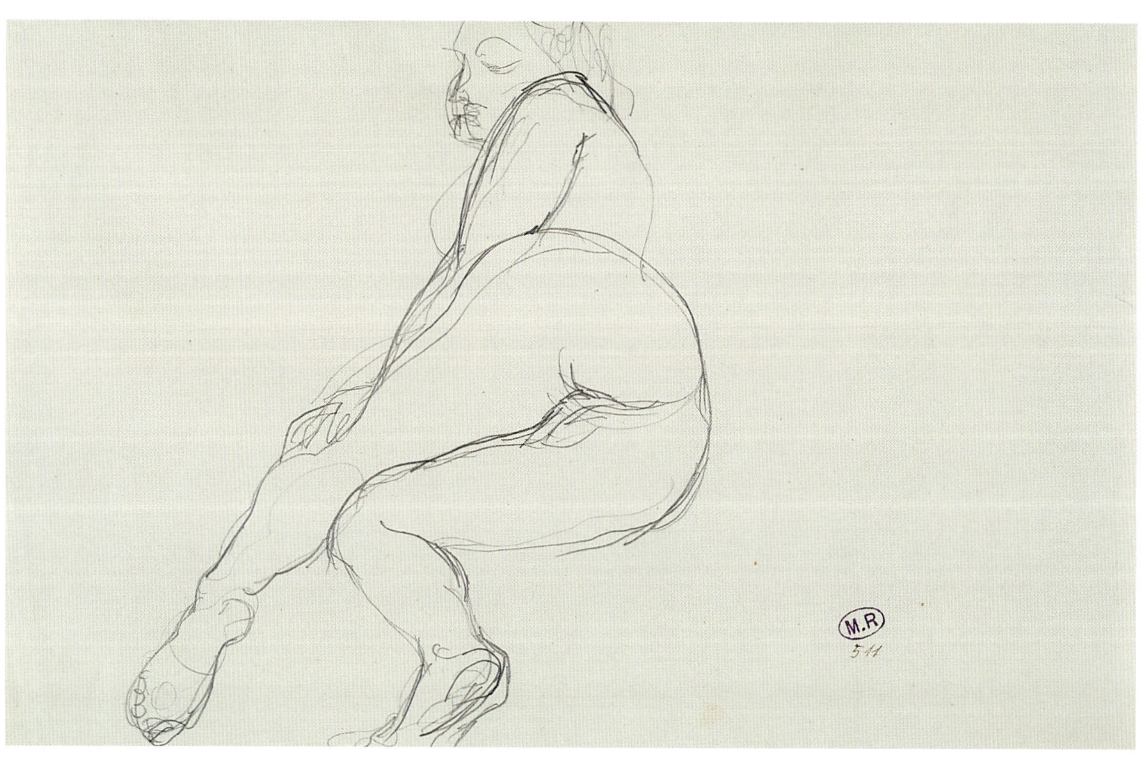

Reclining Female Nude c.1900 (cat. 88)

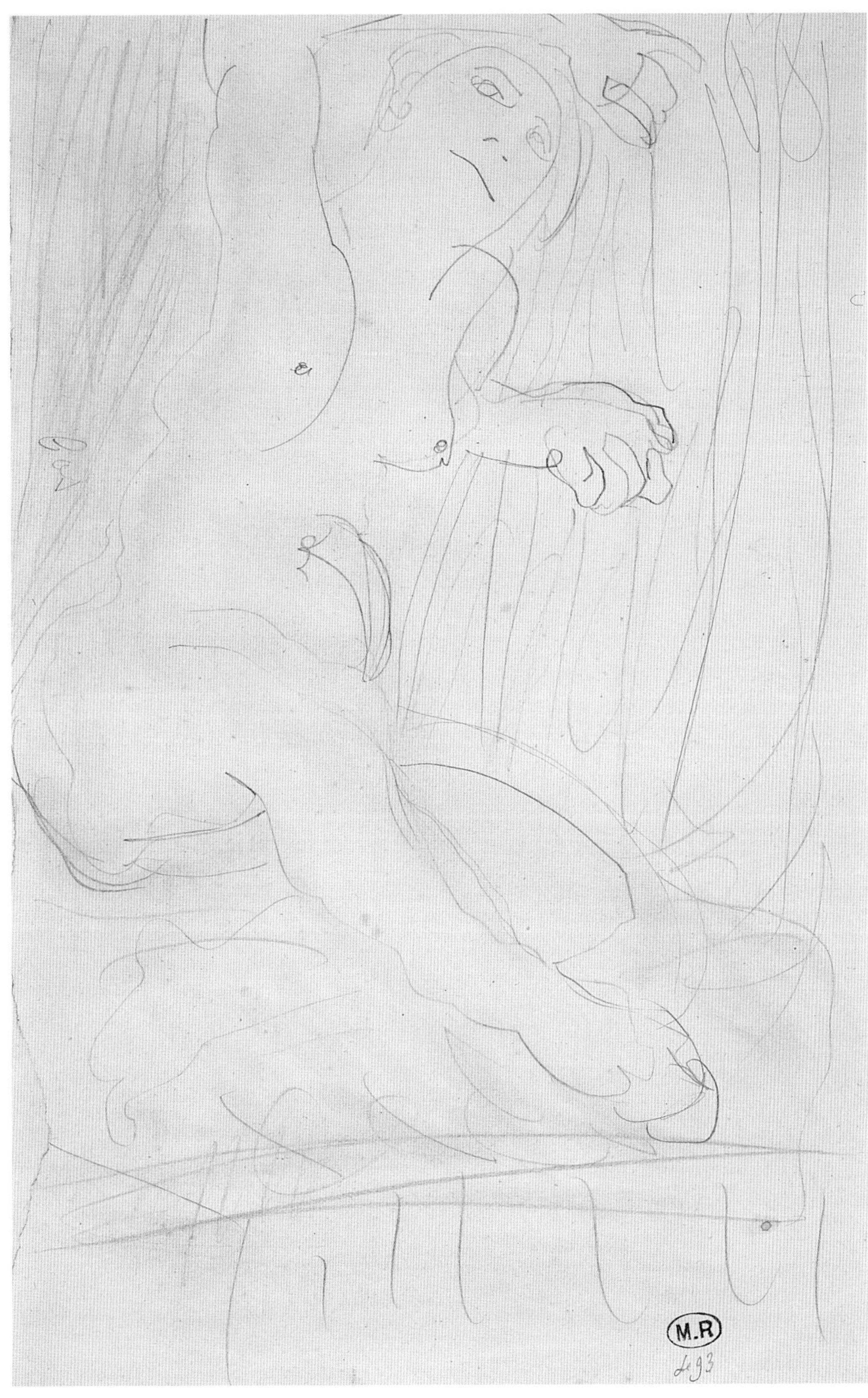

Seated Female Nude c.1900 (cat. 86)

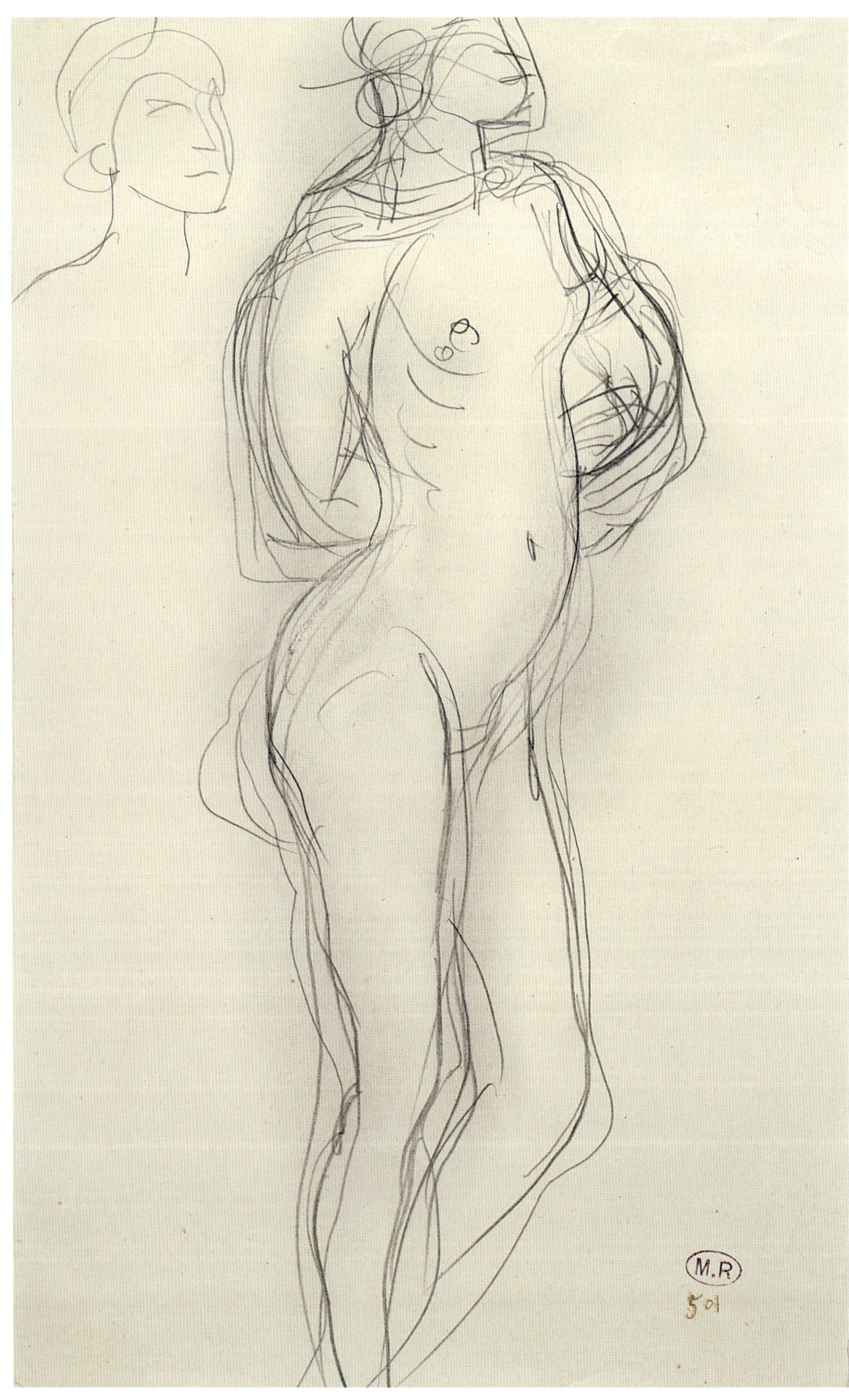

Female Nude c.1900 (cat. 87)

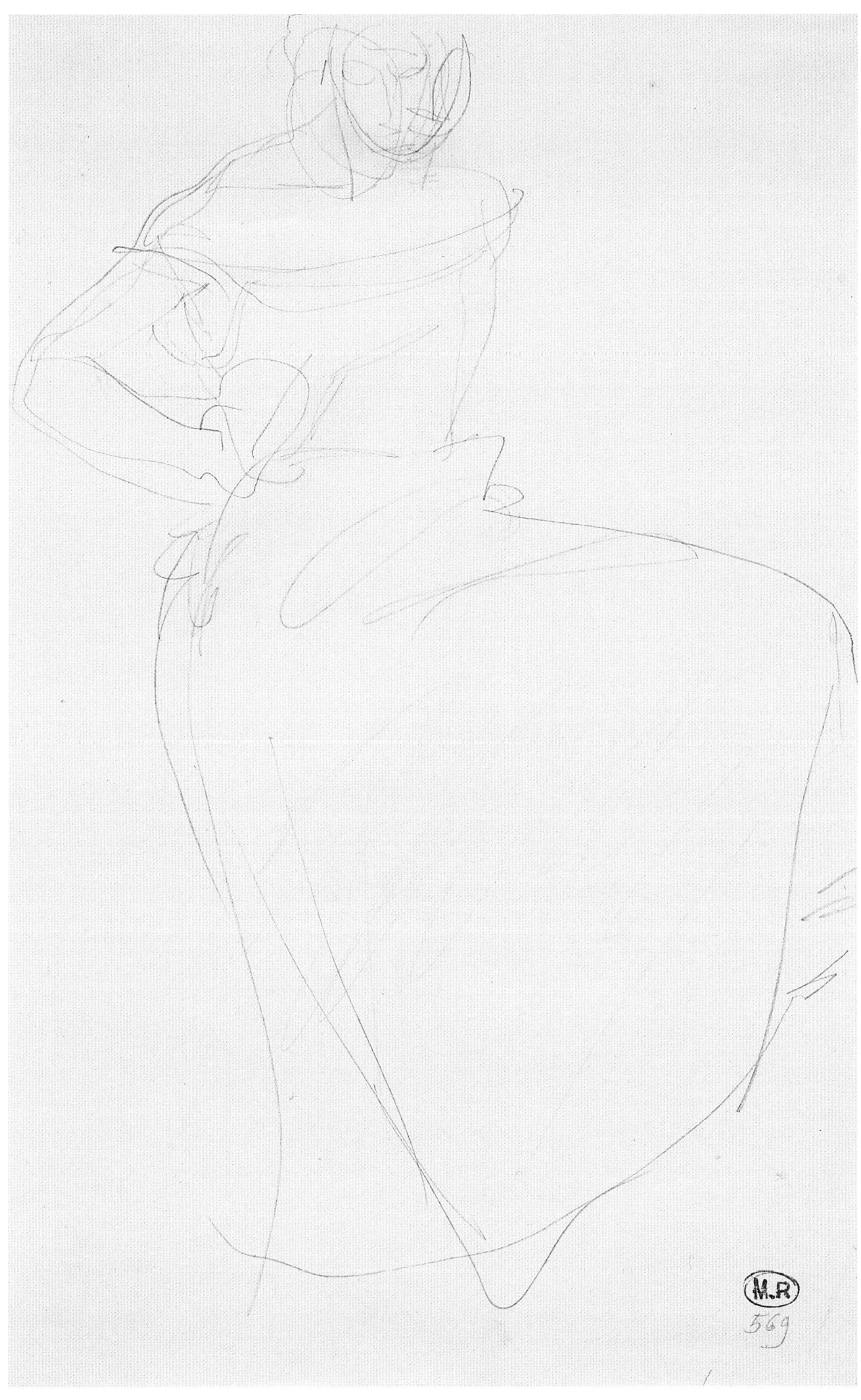

Draped, Seated Female Nude c.1900 (cat. 89)

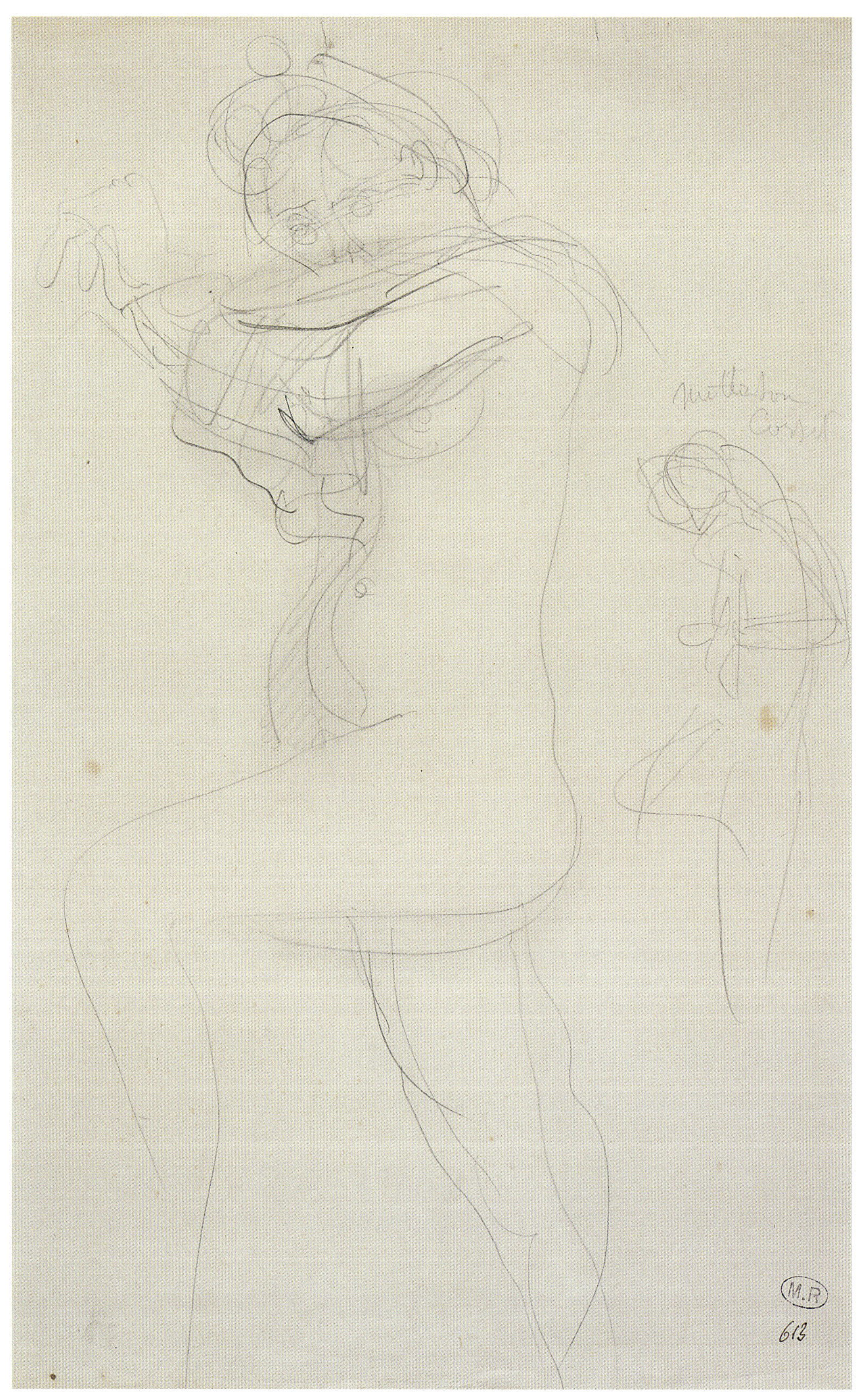

Female Nude *c.*1900 (cat. 90)

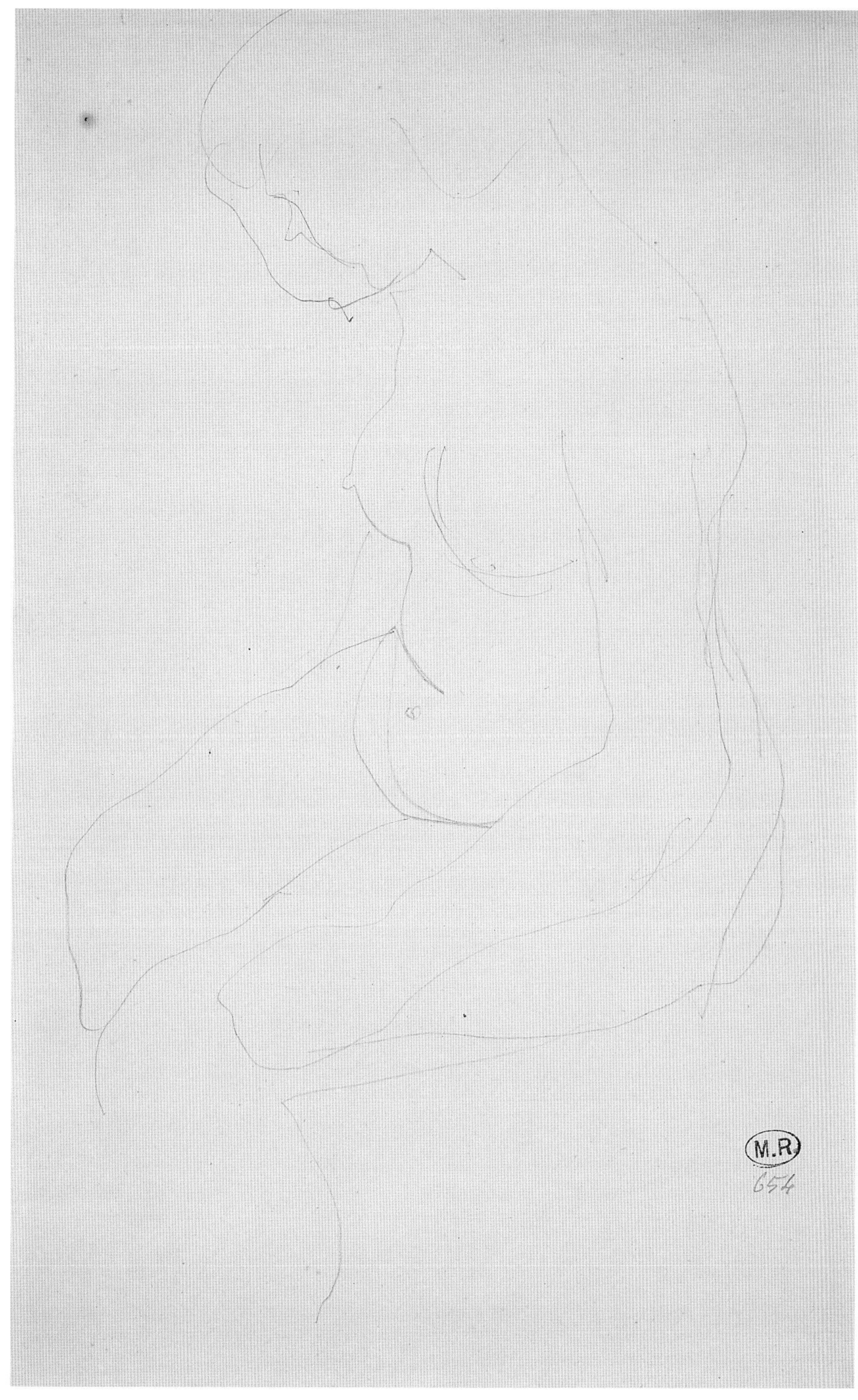

Seated Female Nude *c.*1900 (cat. 91)

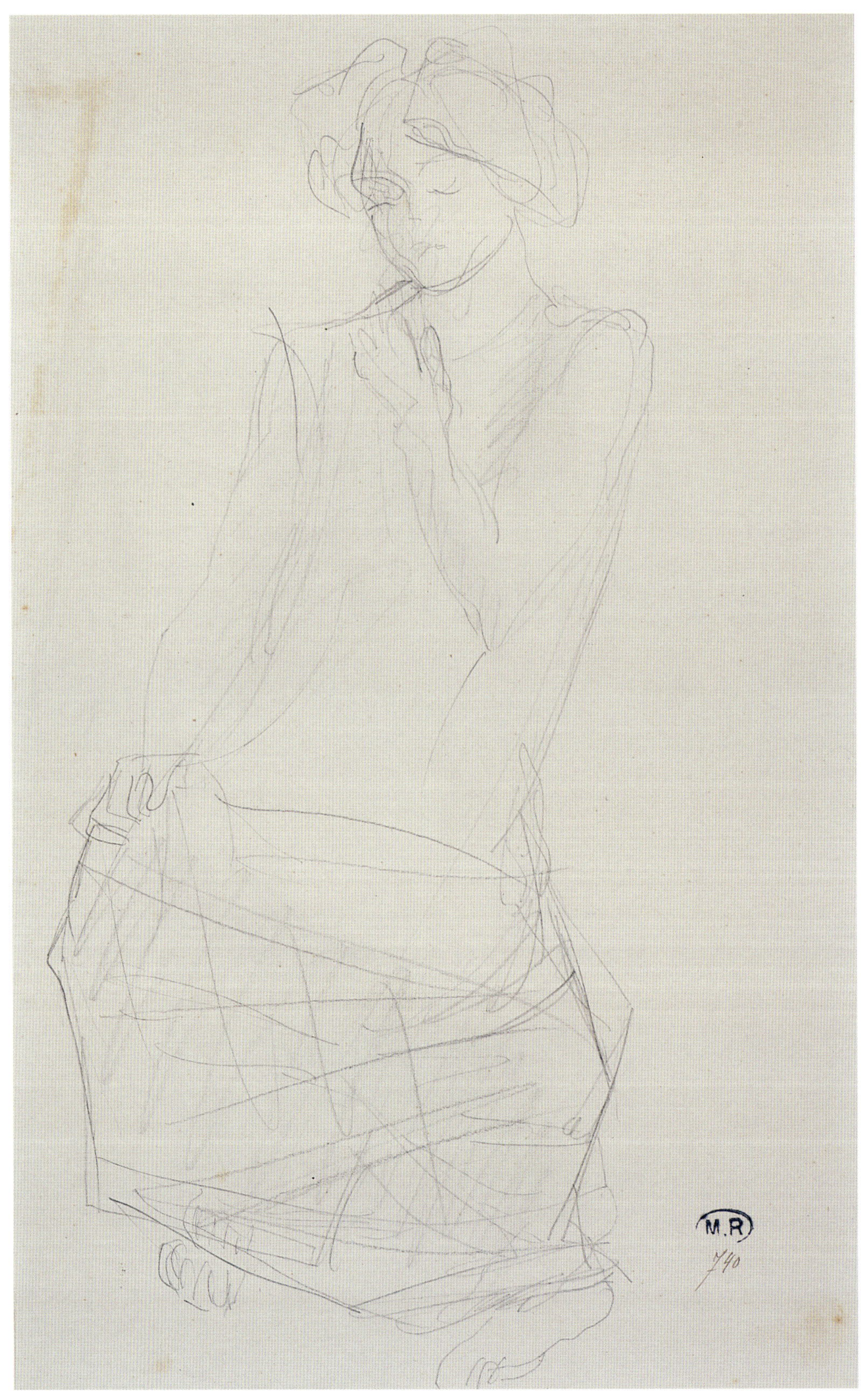

Draped, Seated Female Nude c.1900 (cat. 92)

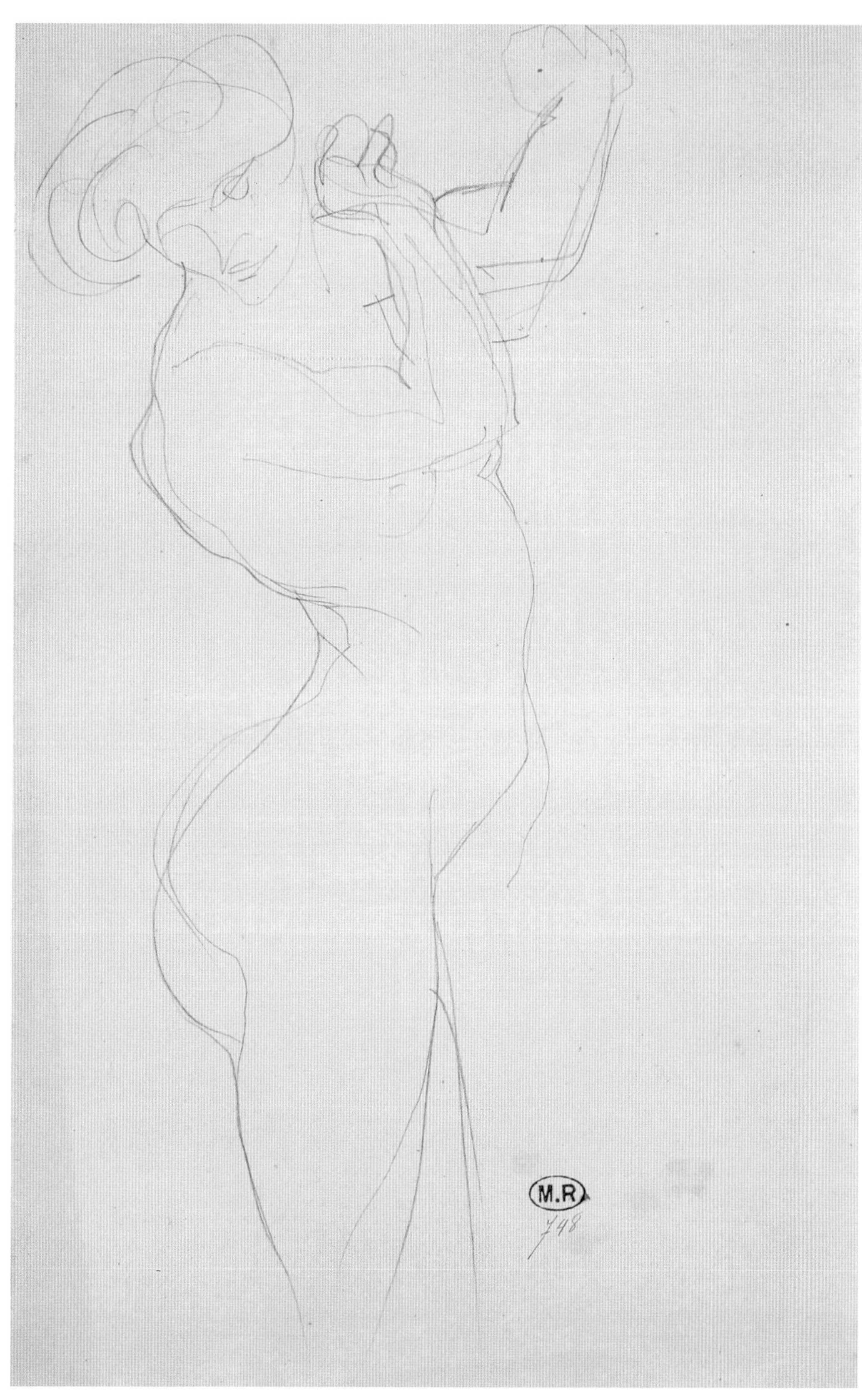

Standing Female Nude c.1900 (cat. 93)

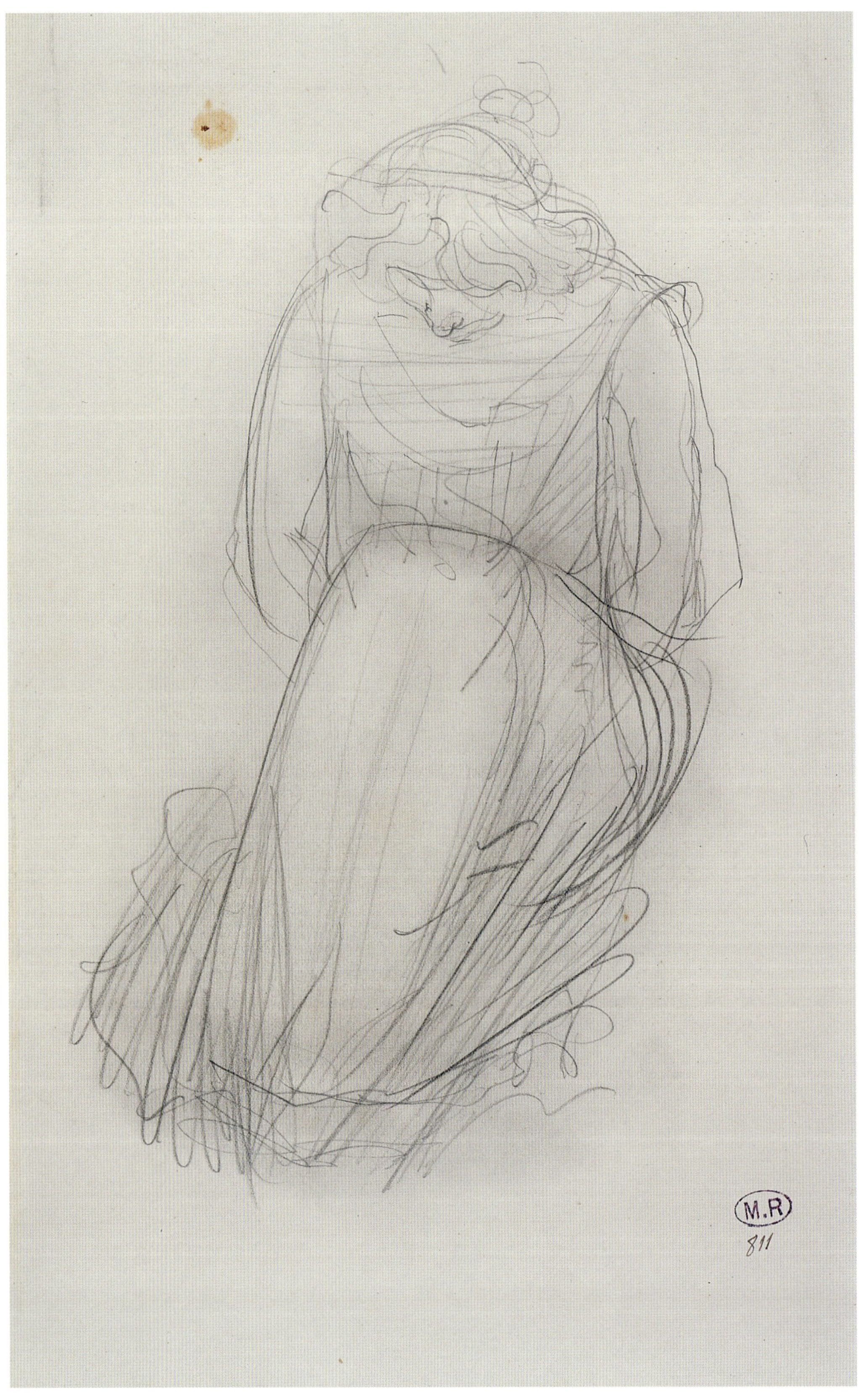

Draped, Seated Female Nude c.1900 (cat. 94)

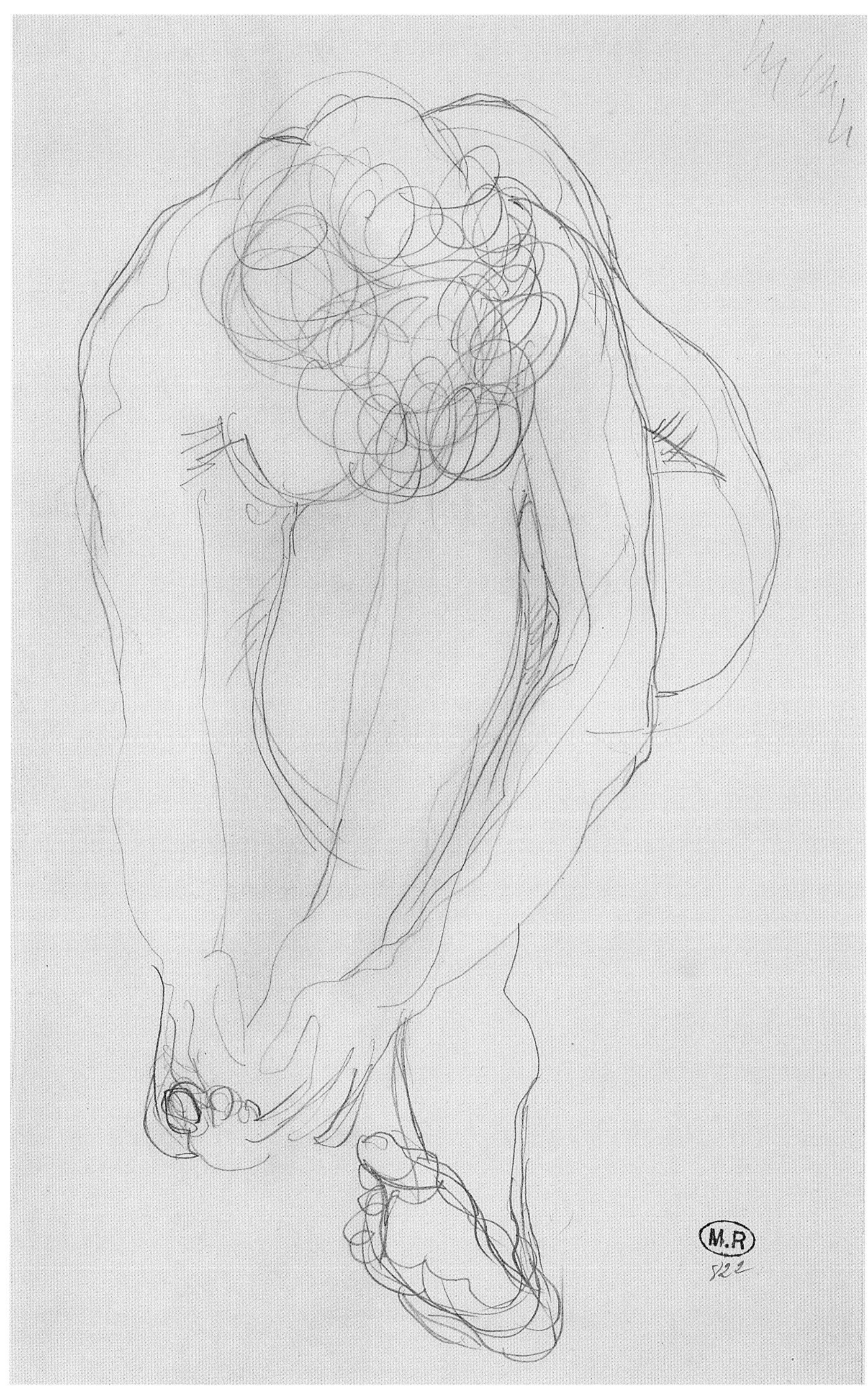

Seated Female Nude c.1900 (cat. 95)

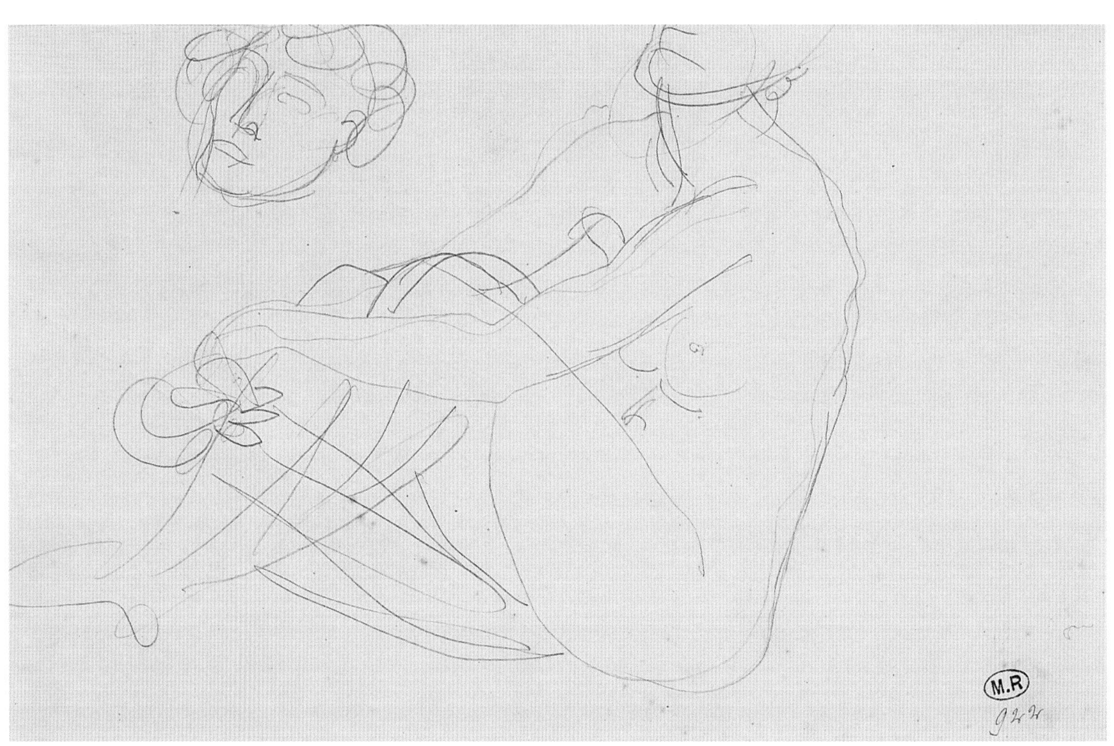

Seated Female Nude c.1900 (cat. 96)

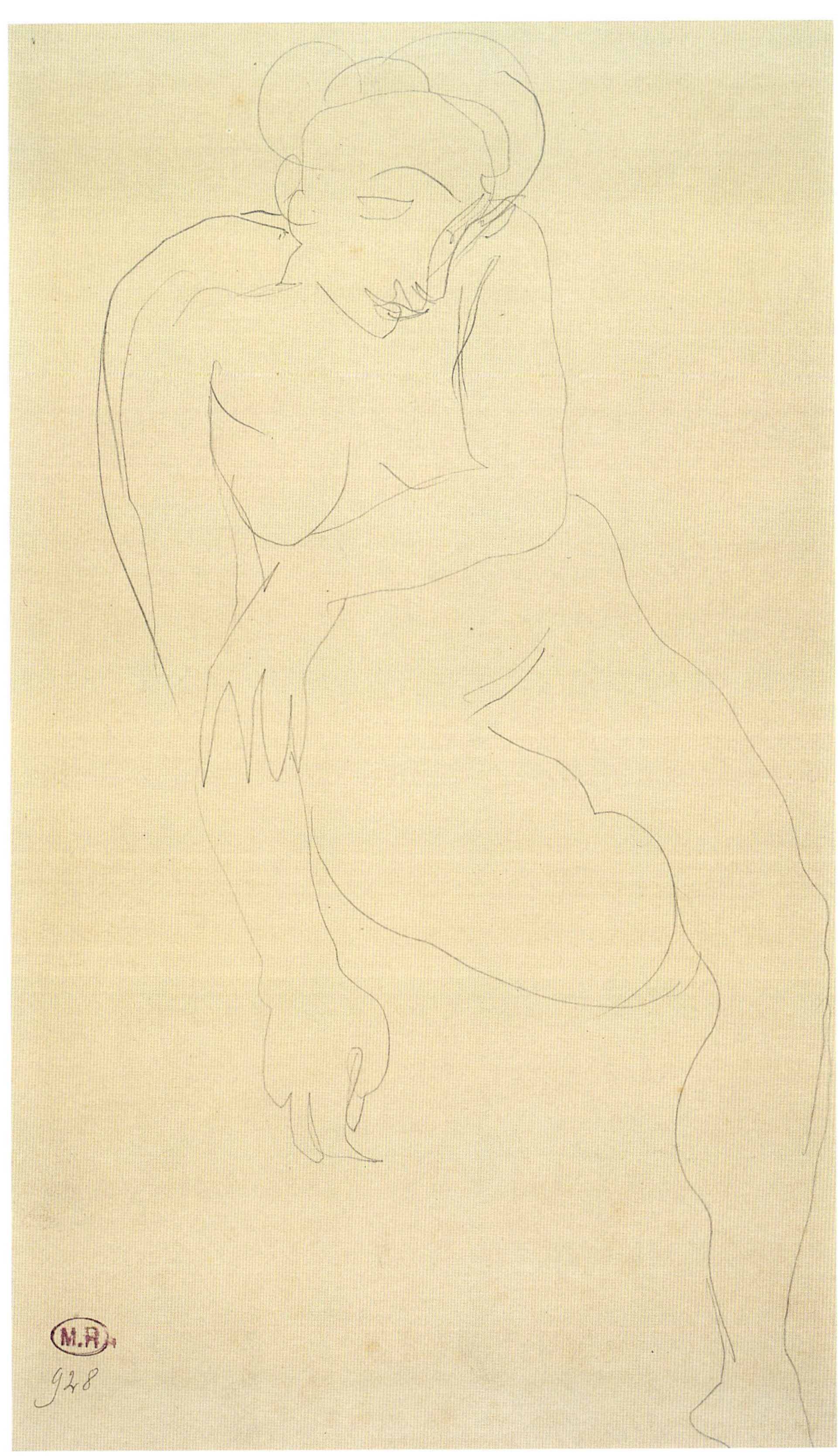

Seated Female Nude c.1900 (cat. 97)

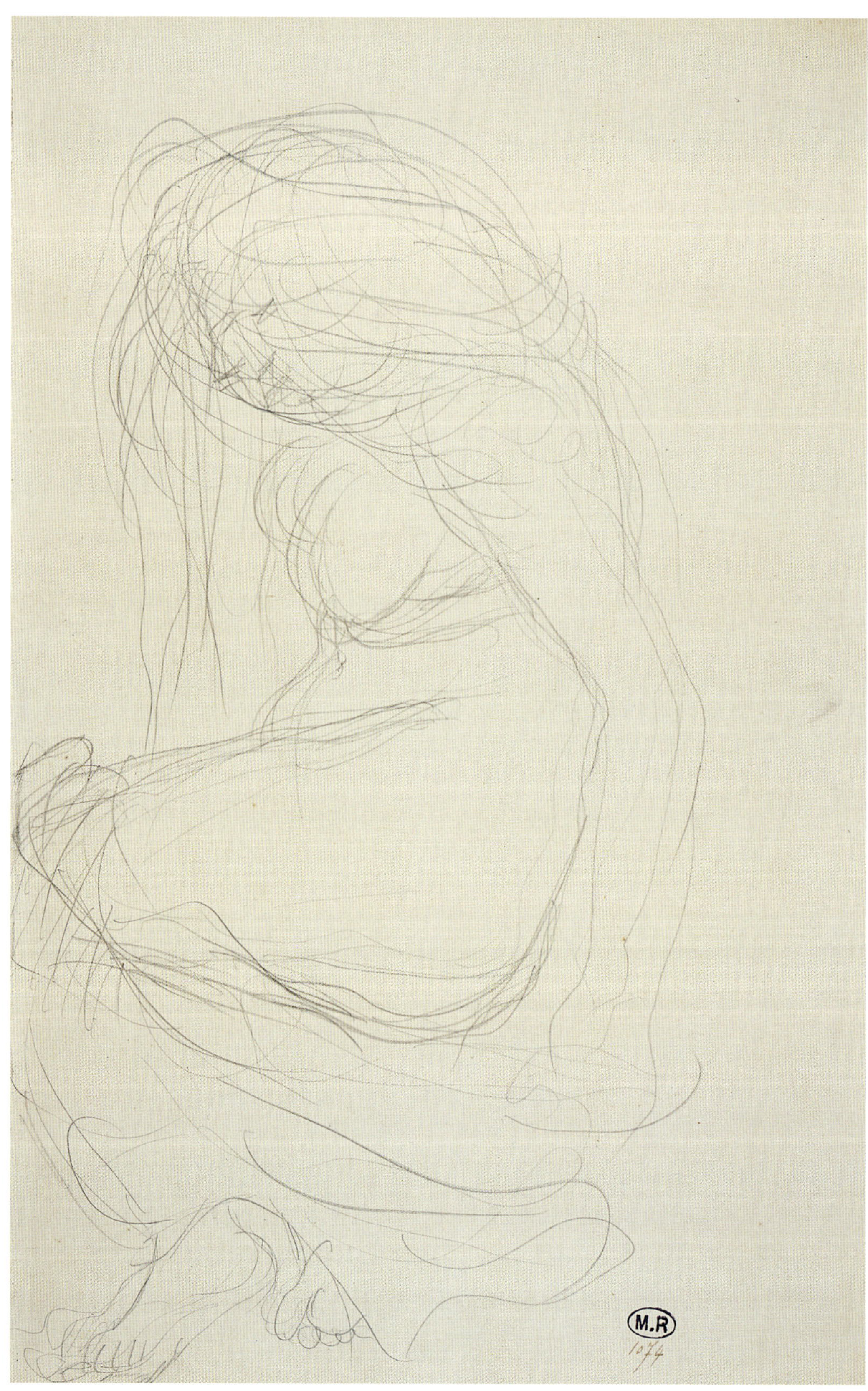

Seated Female Nude c.1900 (cat. 98)

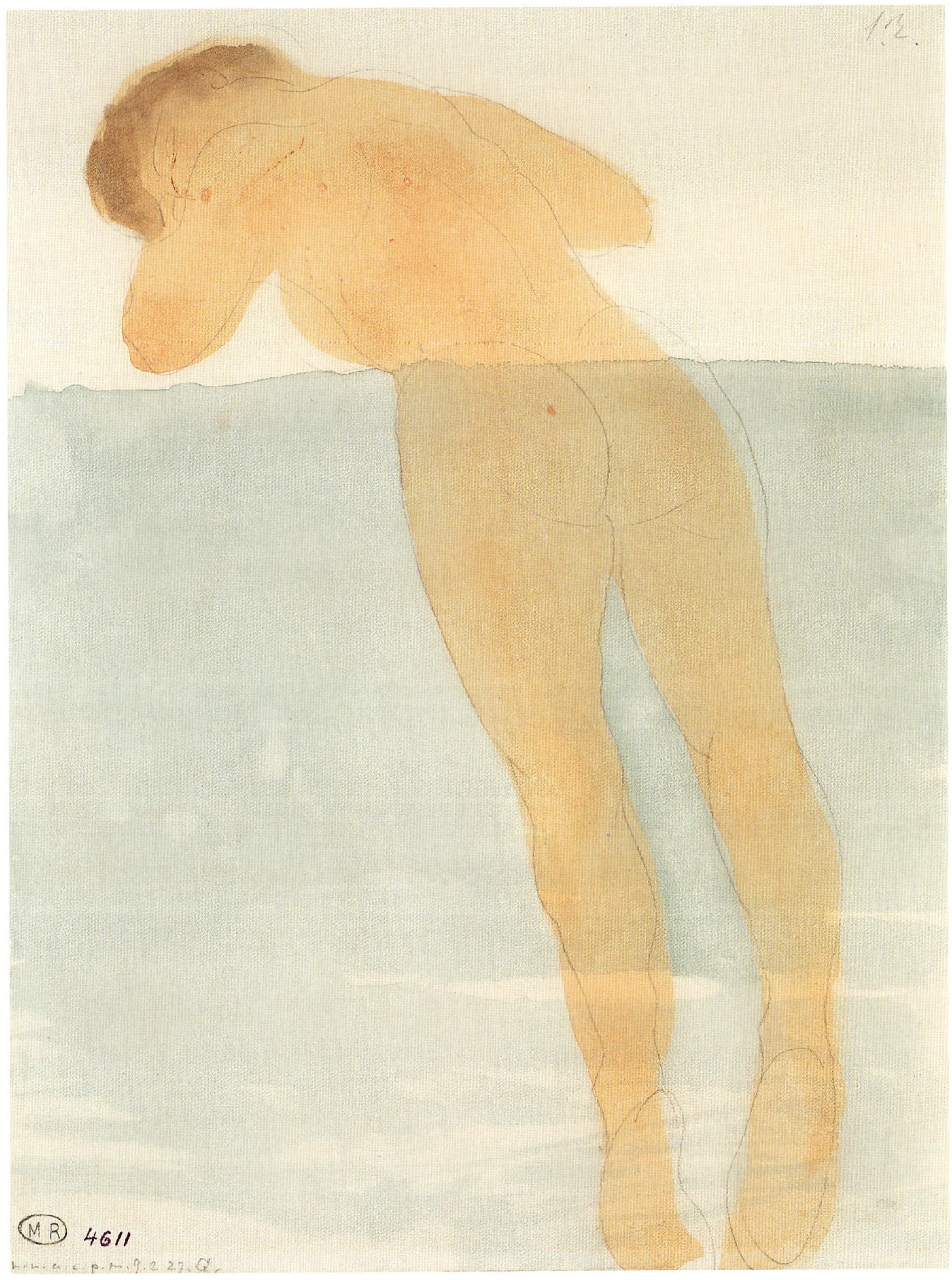

Reclining Female Nude c.1900 (cat. 83)

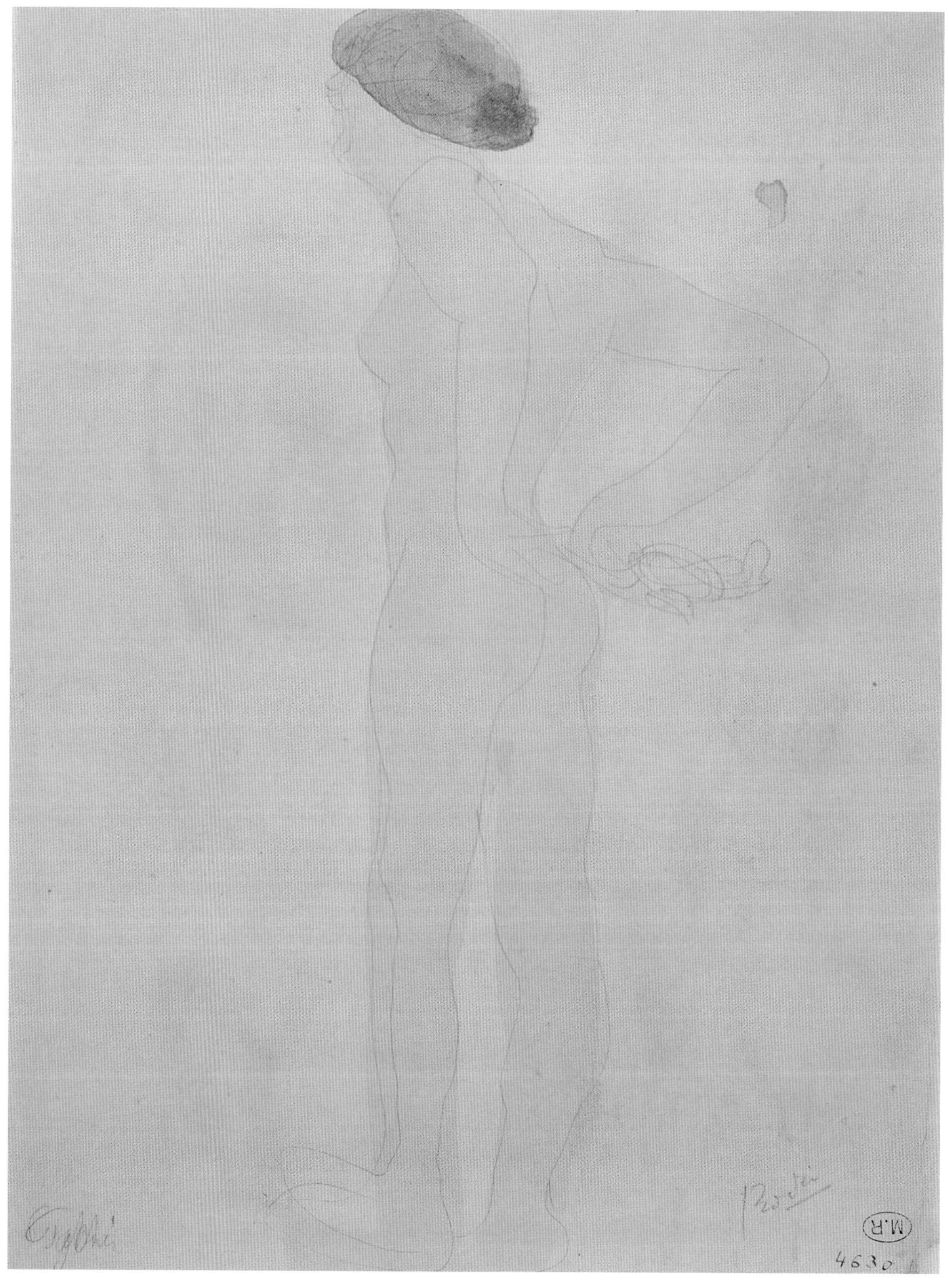

Psyche c.1900 (cat. 99)

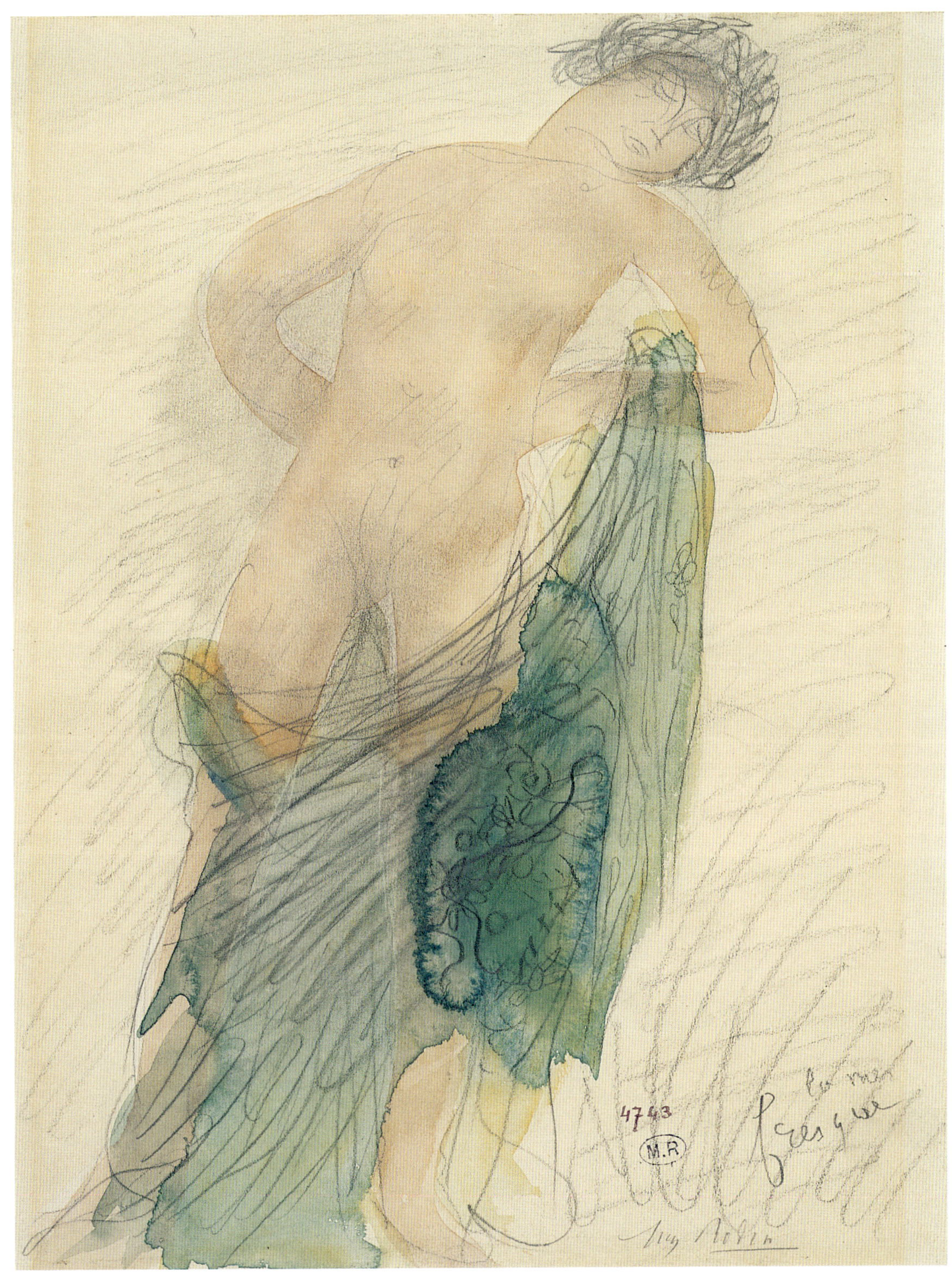

The Sea c.1900 (cat. 101)

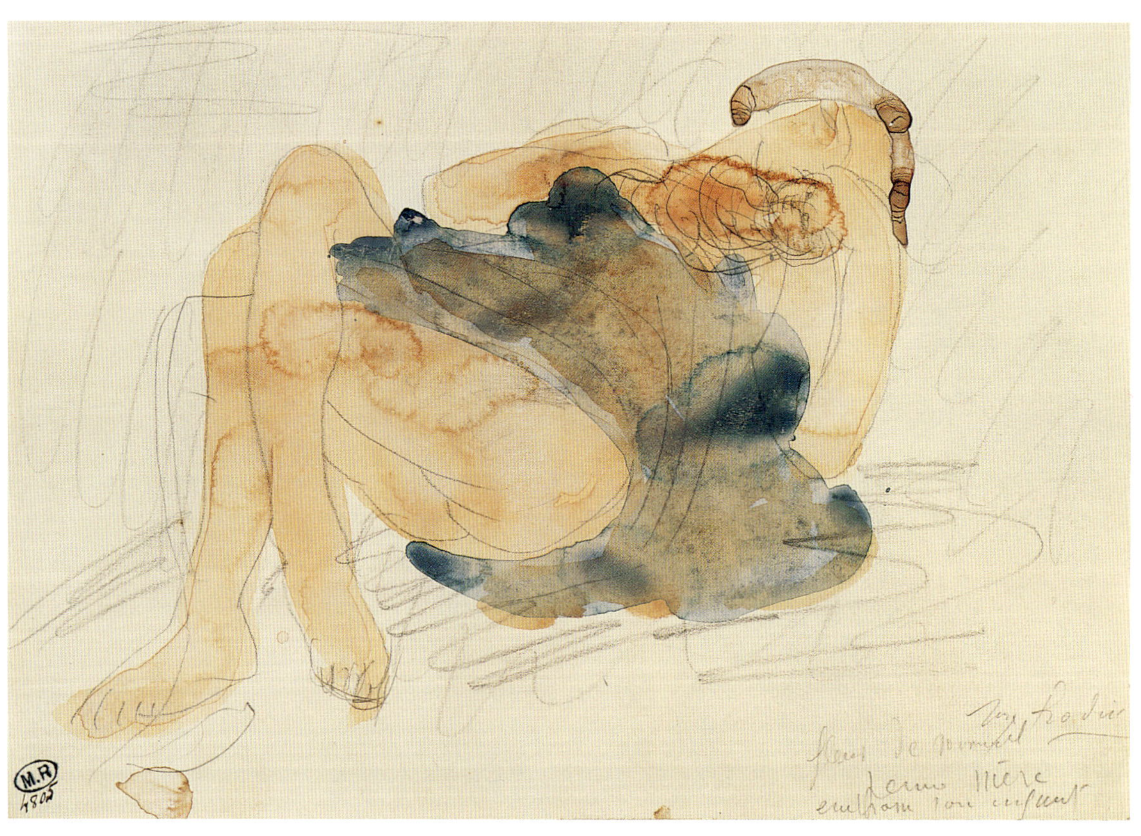

Night Flower (Young Mother and Child) c.1900 (cat. 102)

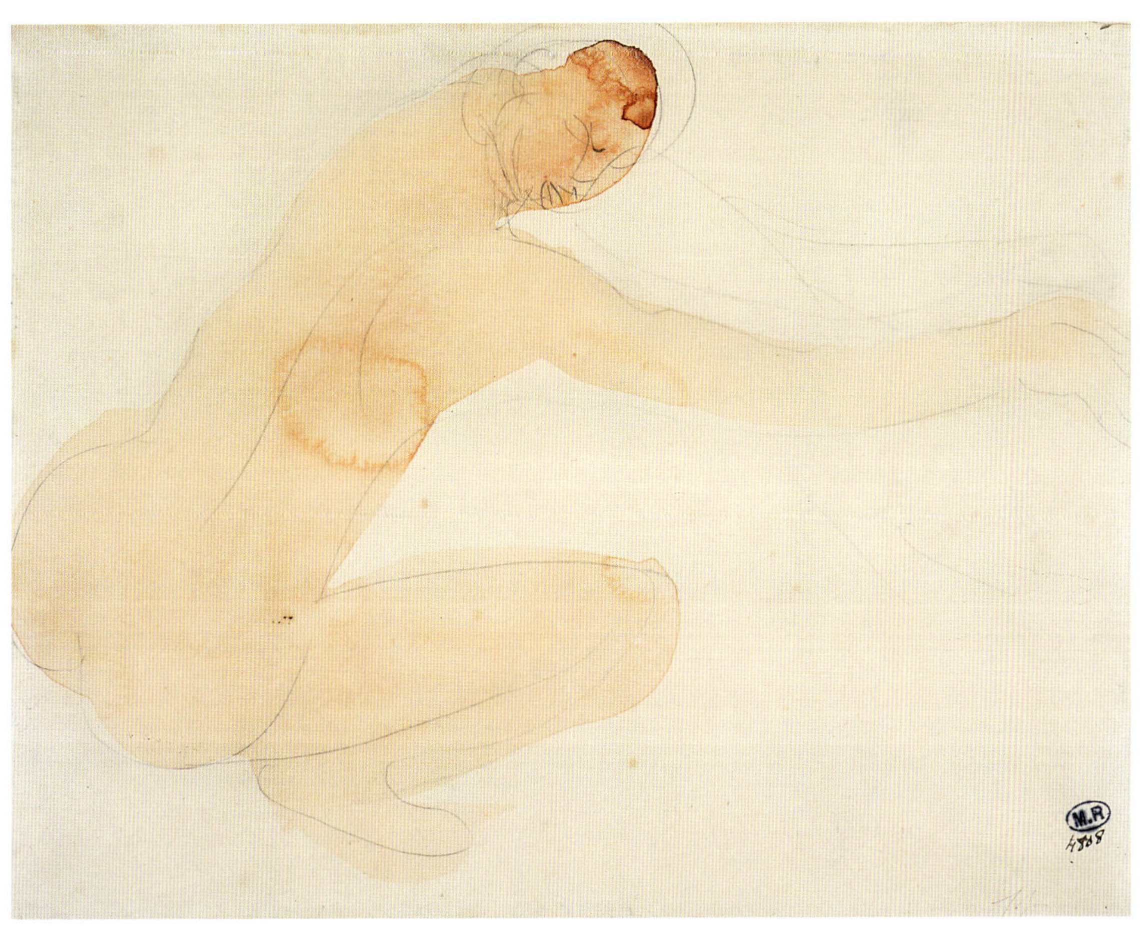

Crouching Female Nude c.1900 (cat. 103)

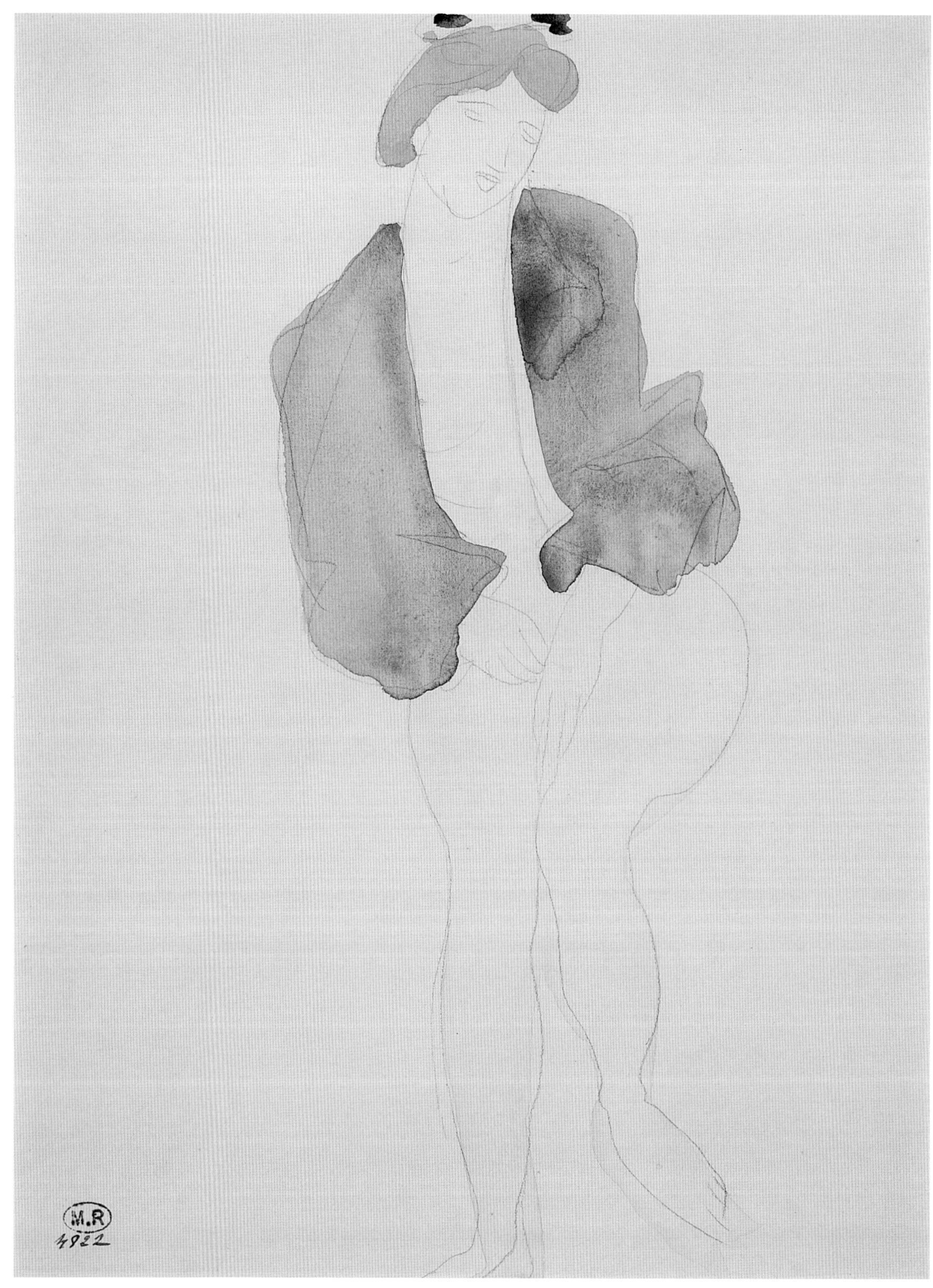

Draped, Seated Female Nude c.1900 (cat. 104)

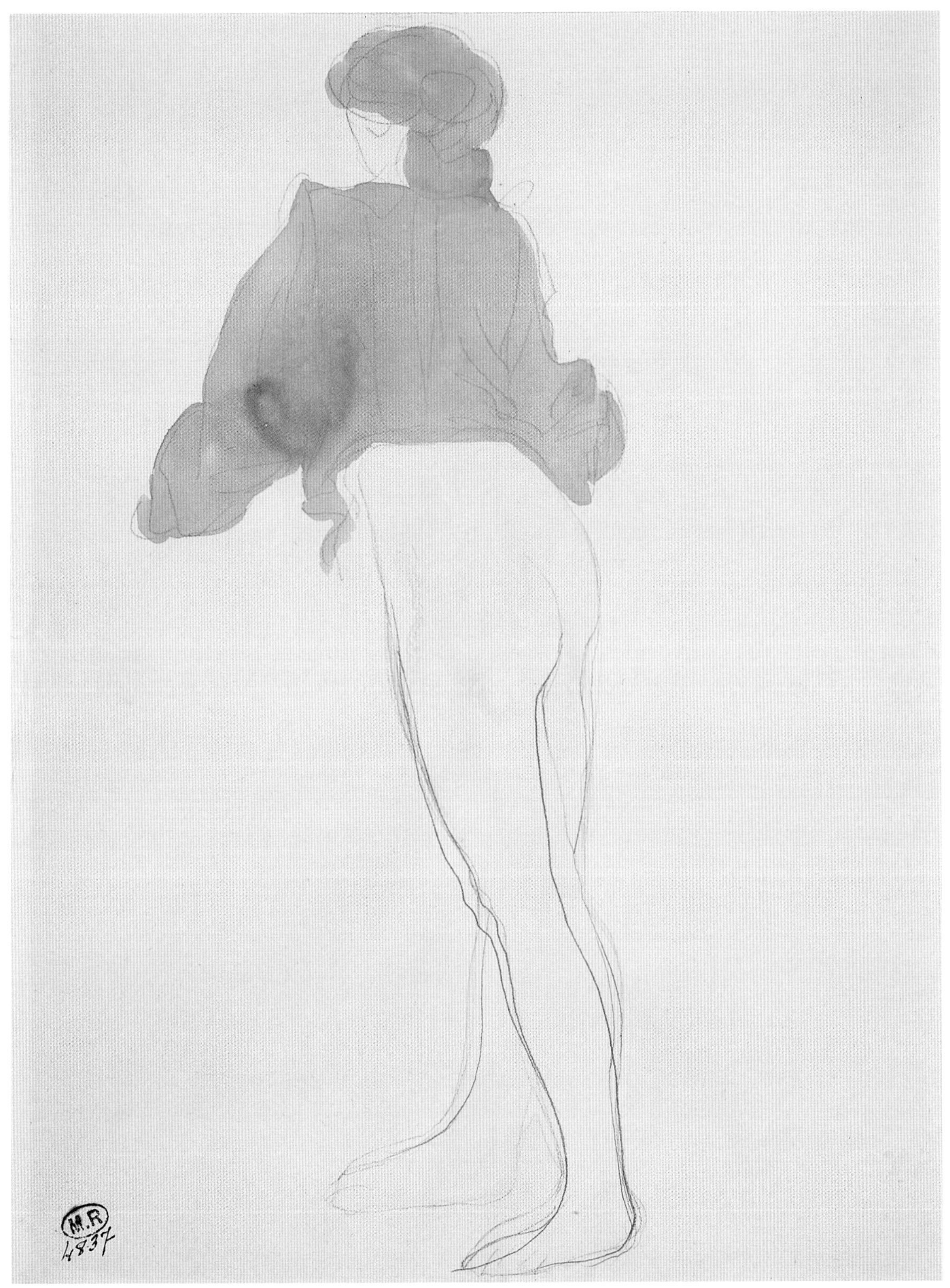

Draped Female Nude *c*.1900 (cat. 105)

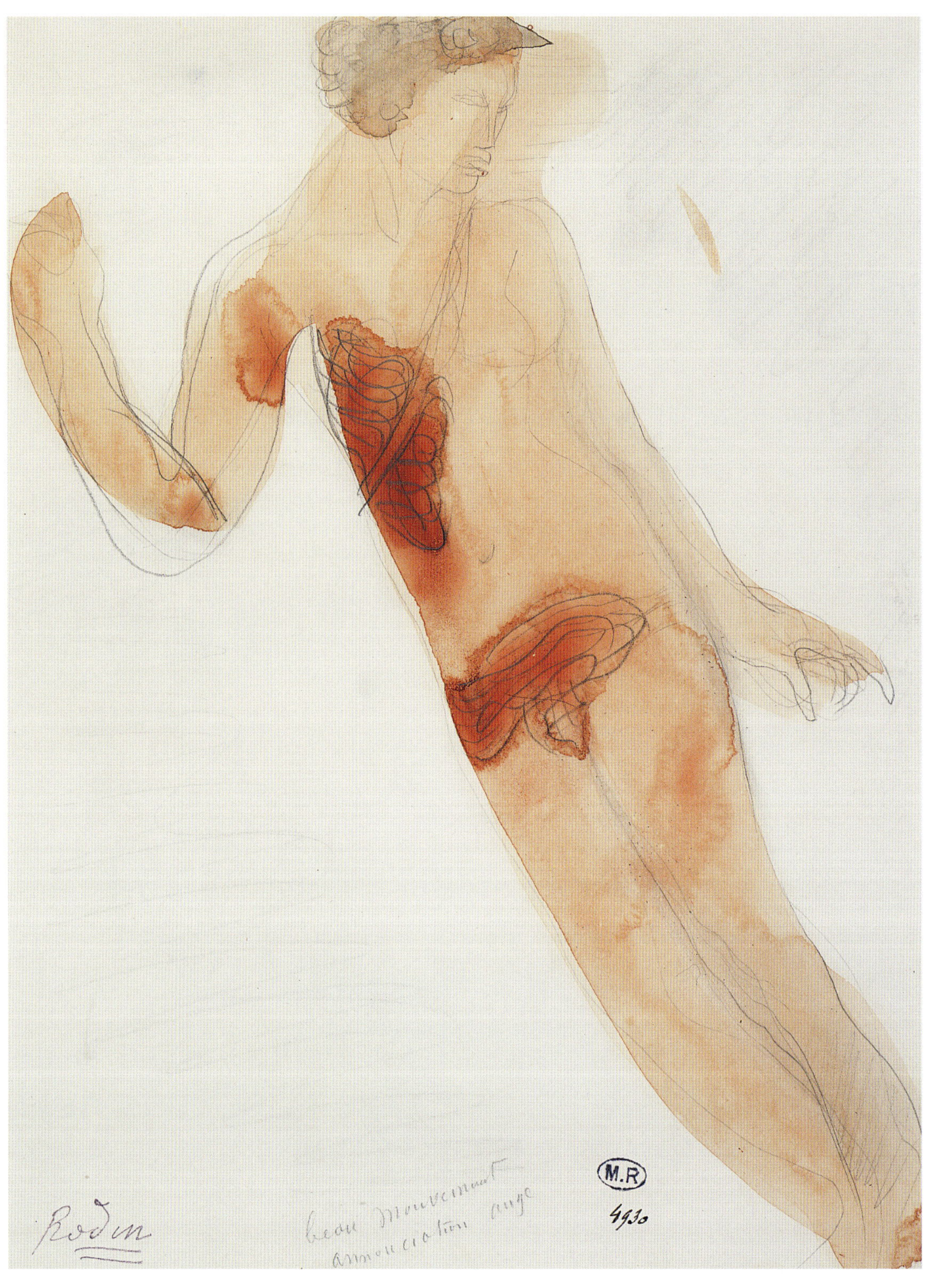

Annunciation c.1900 (cat. 106)

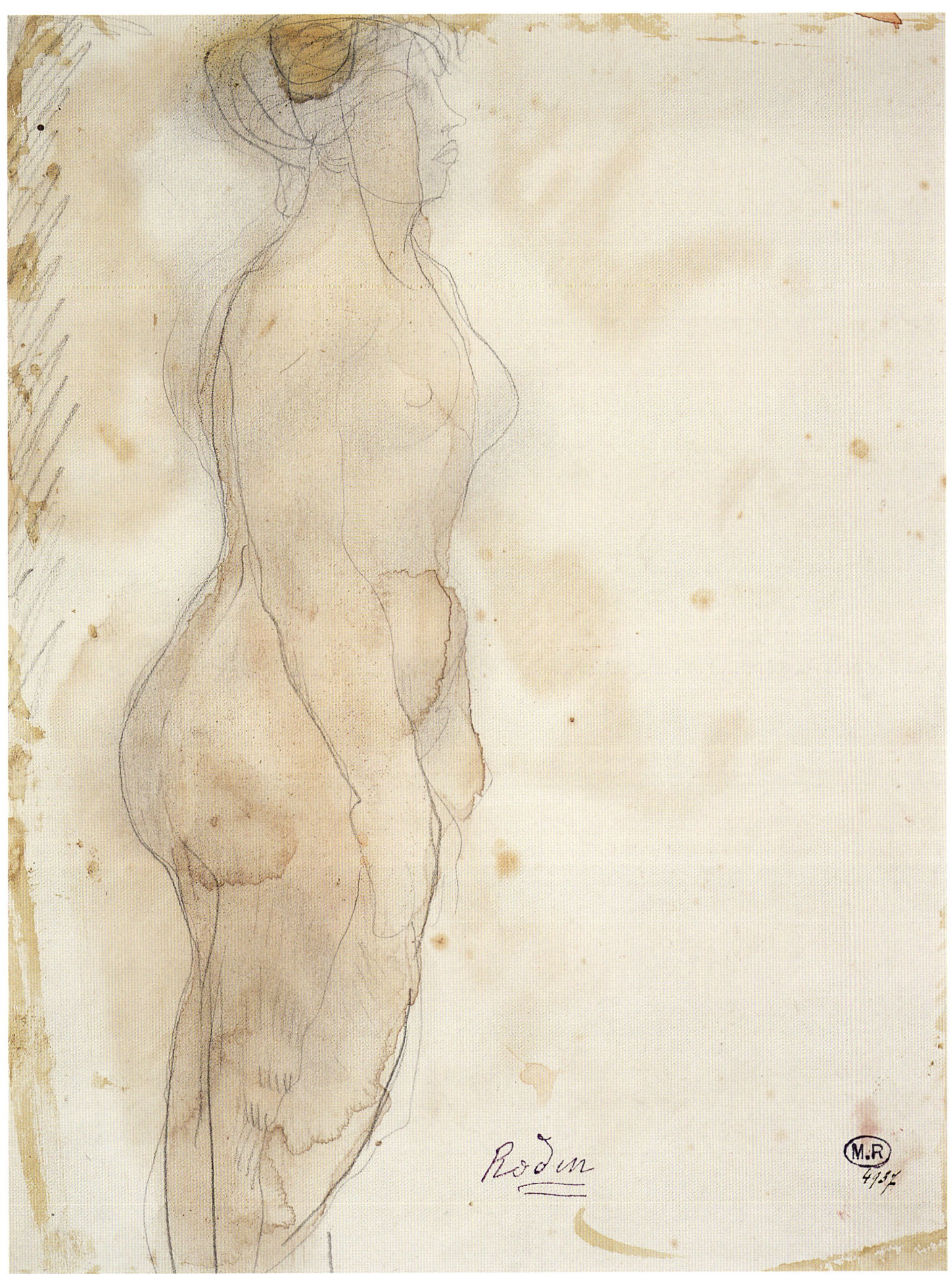

Standing Female Nude c.1900 (cat. 107)

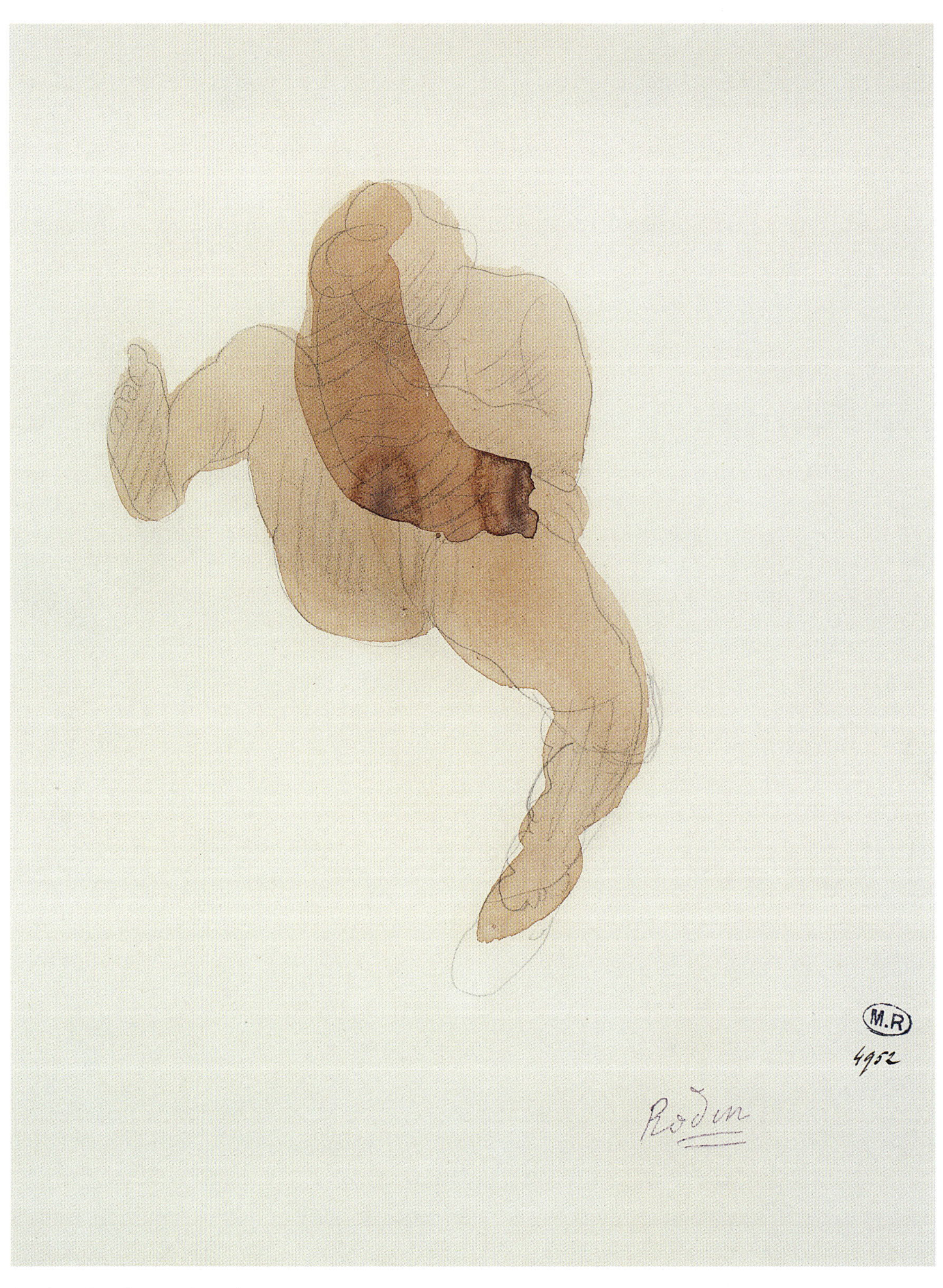

Seated Female Nude c.1900 (cat. 108)

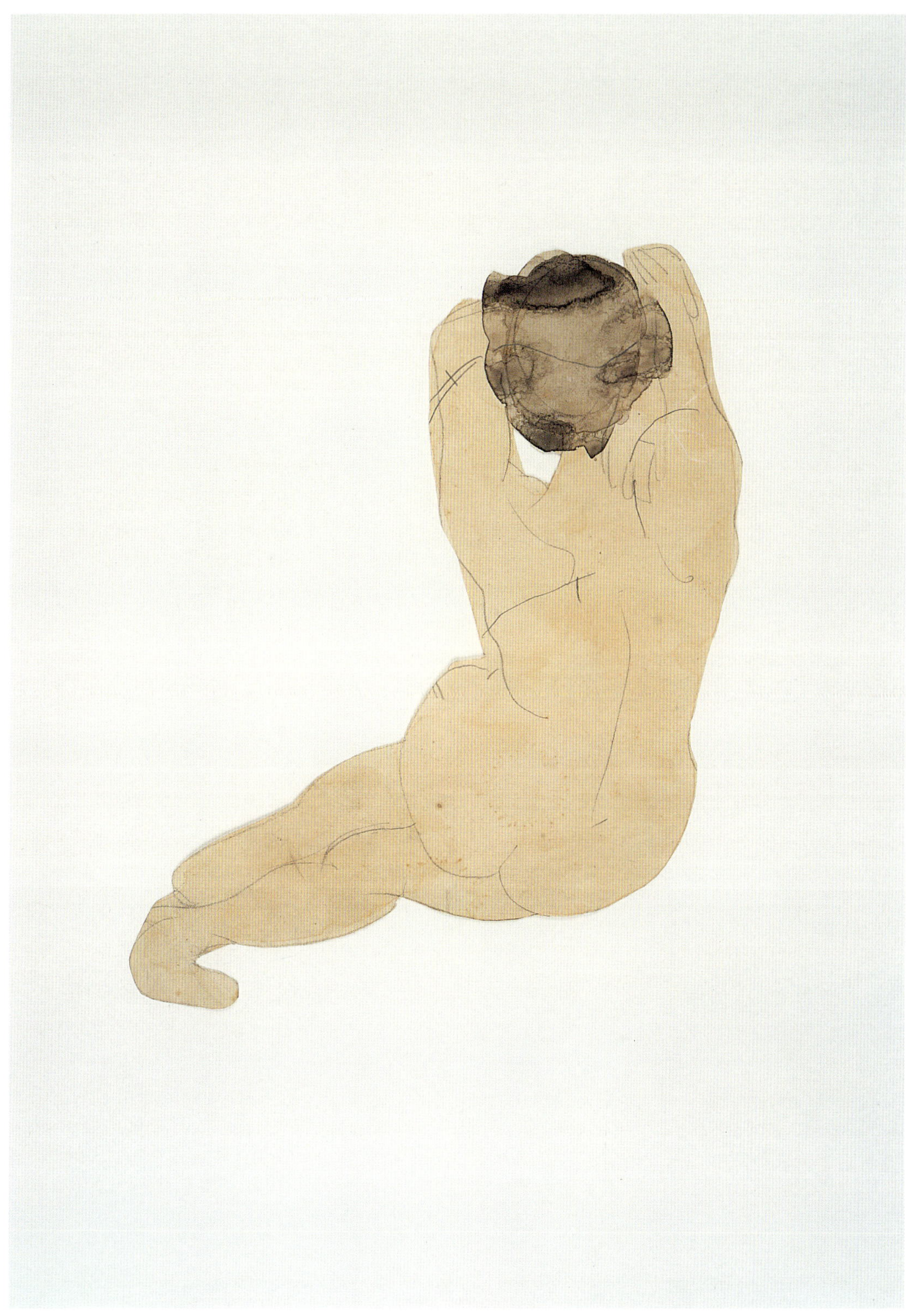

Seated Female Nude *c.*1900 (cat. 109)

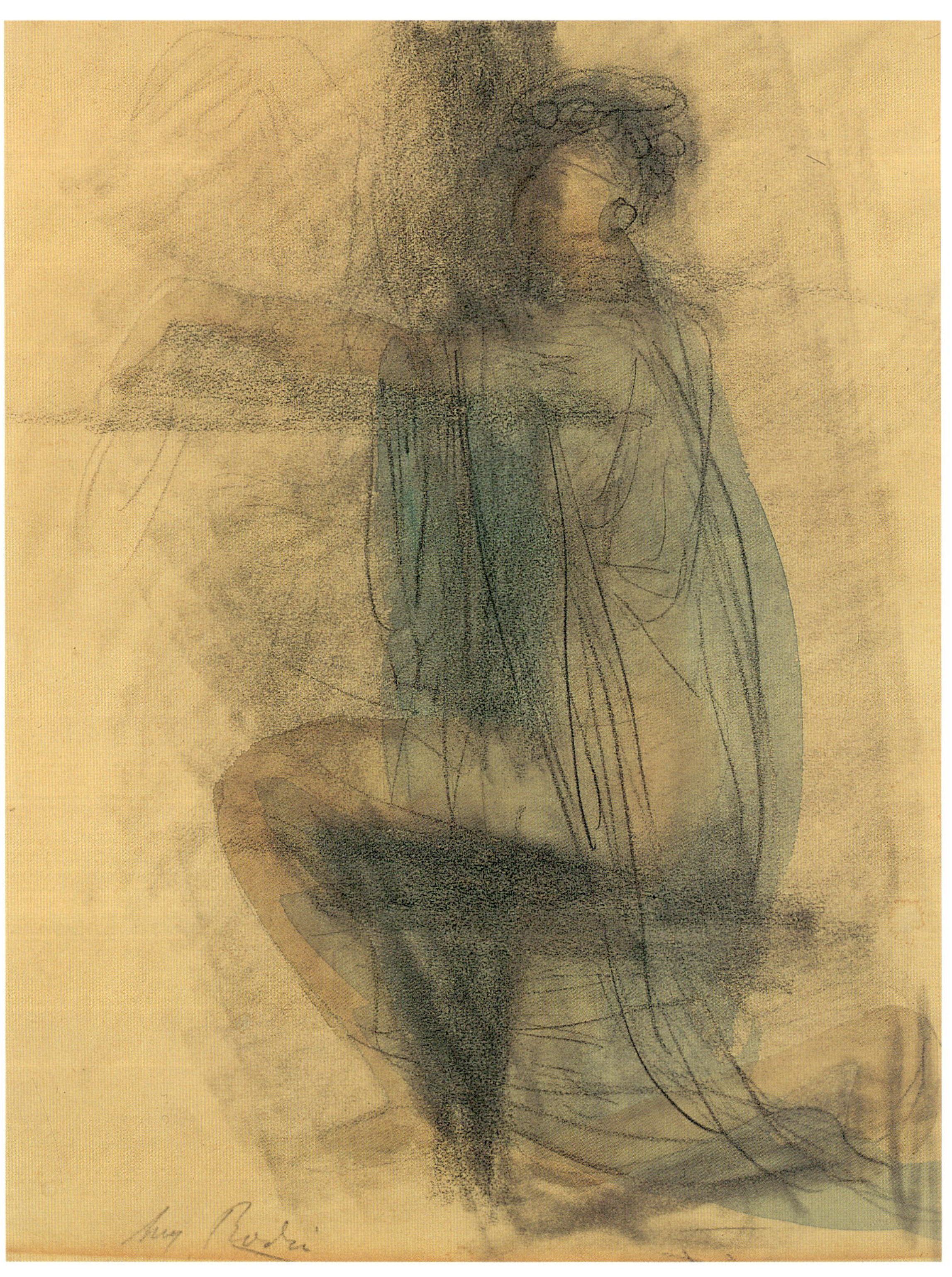

Female Dancer 1906 (cat. 113)

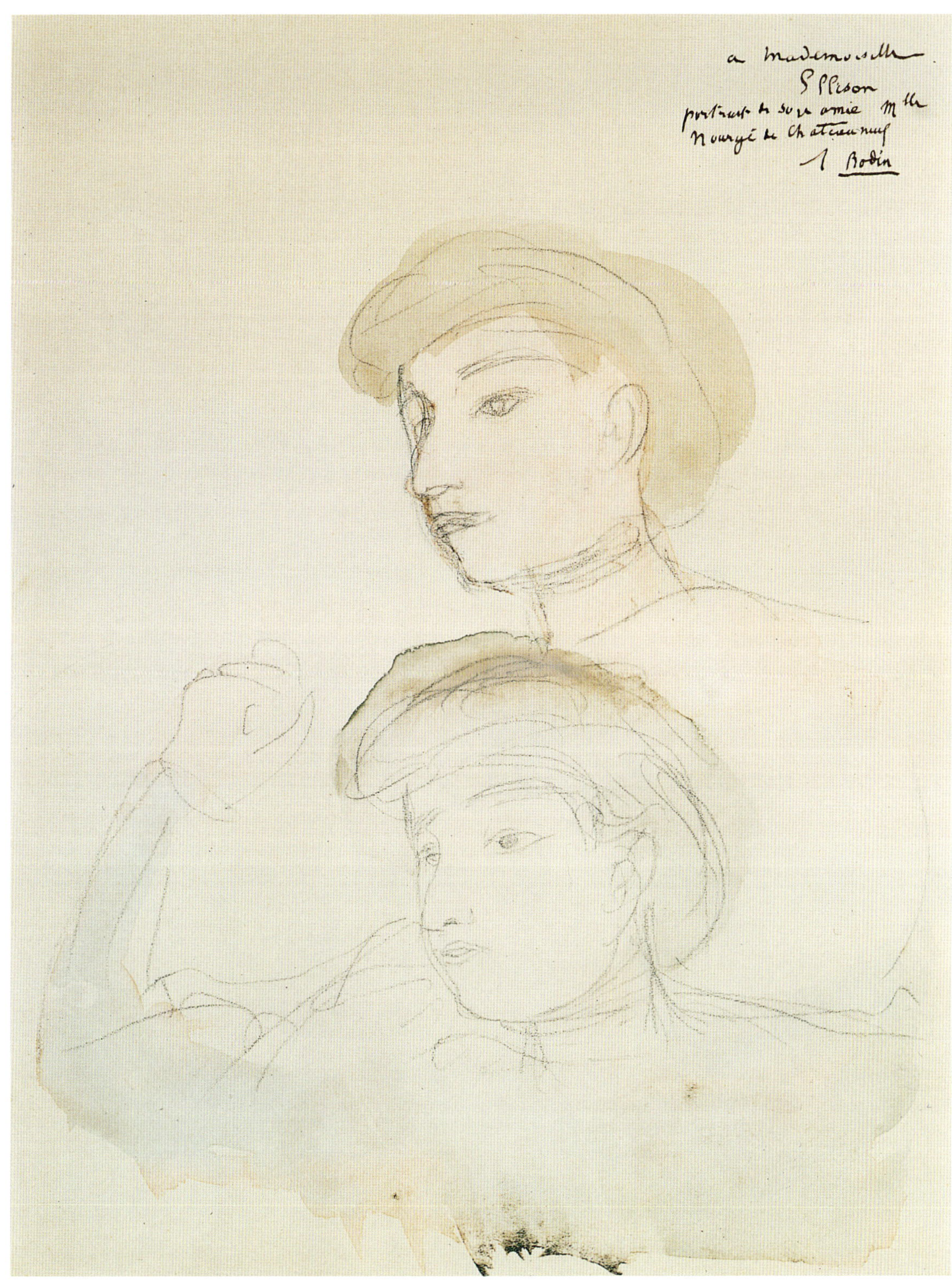

Portrait of a Woman (Portrait of the Countess Nouvre Rohozinska) 1906 (cat. 114)

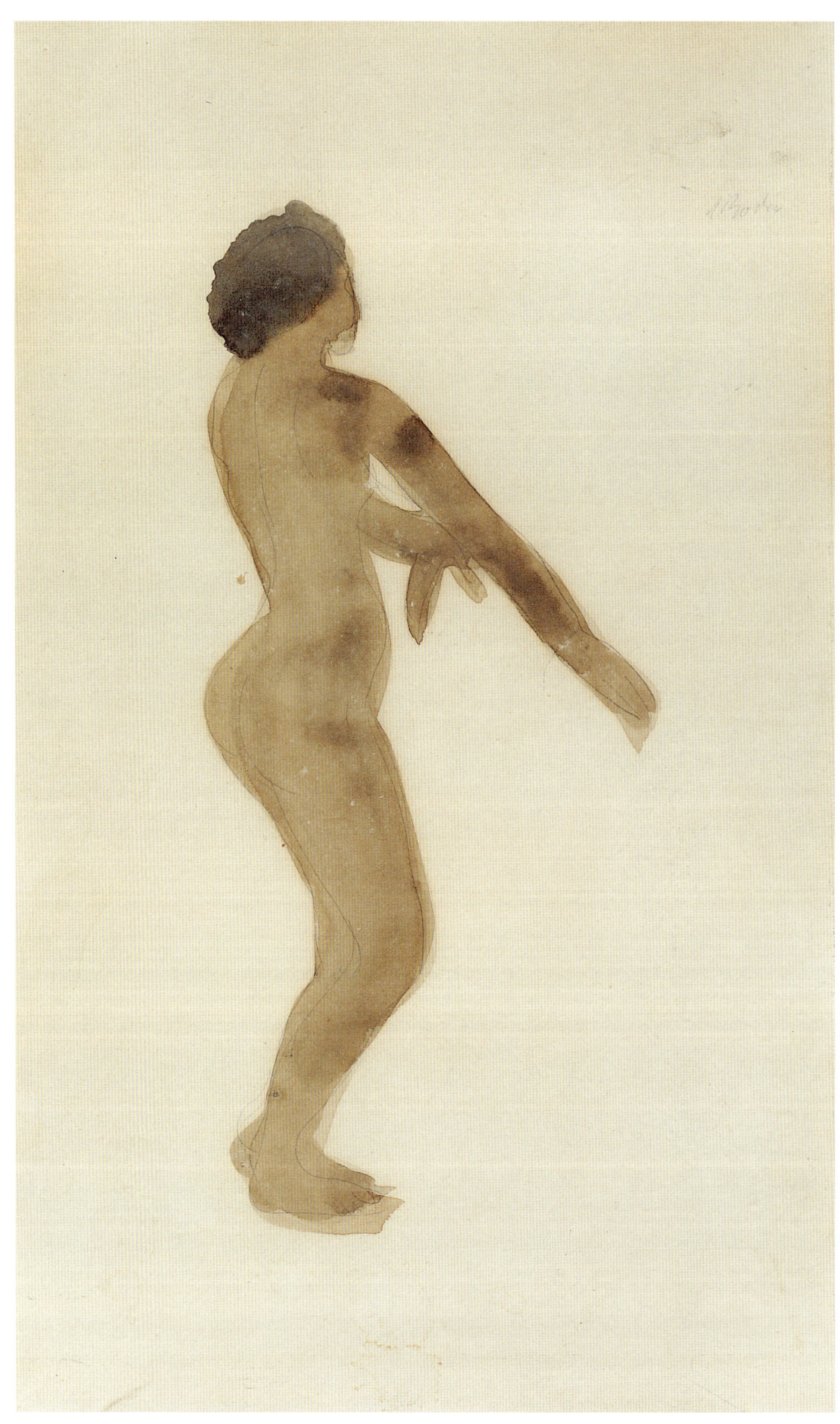

Nude (no date) (cat. 115)

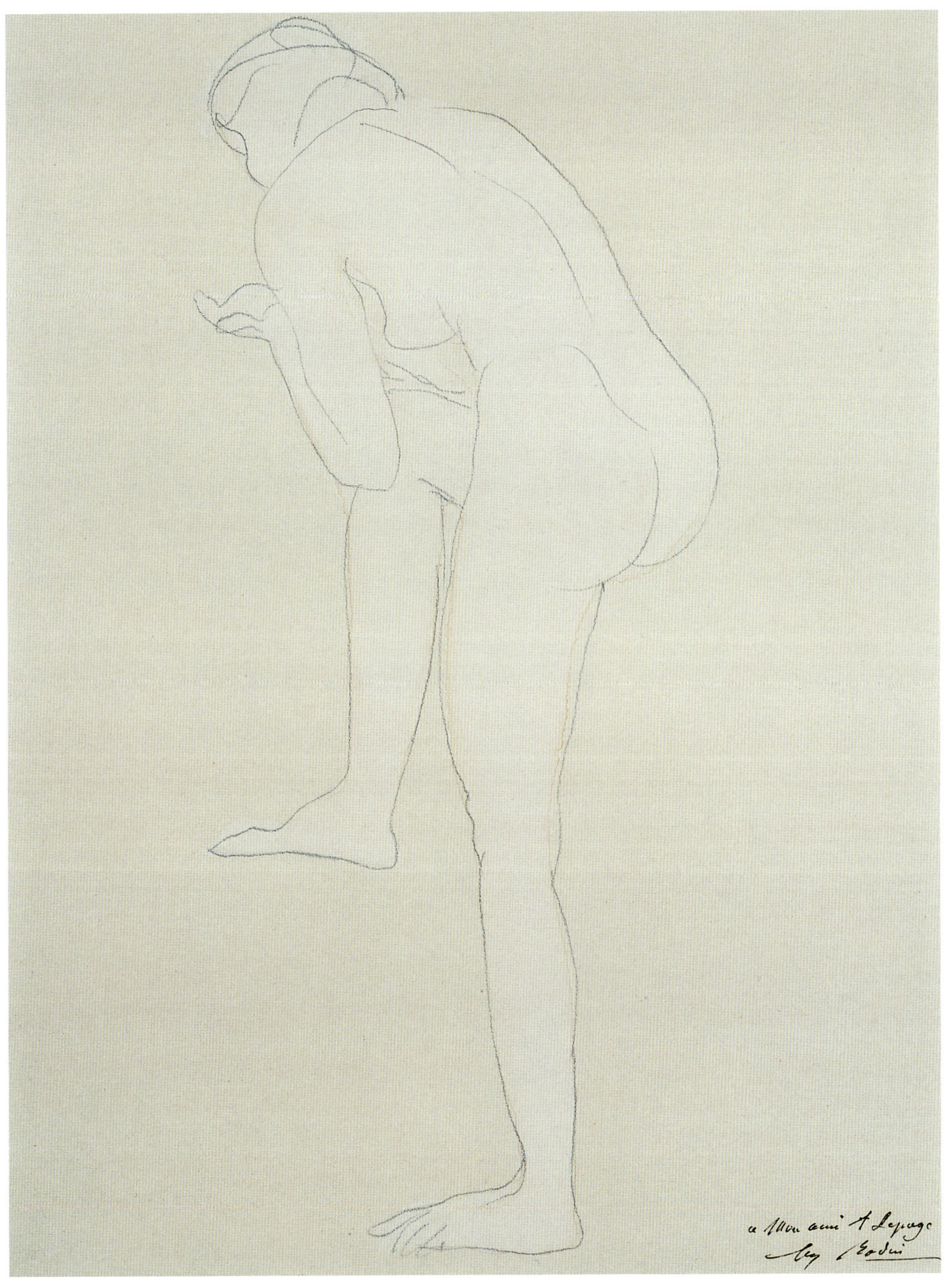

Standing Nude c.1900 (cat. 111)

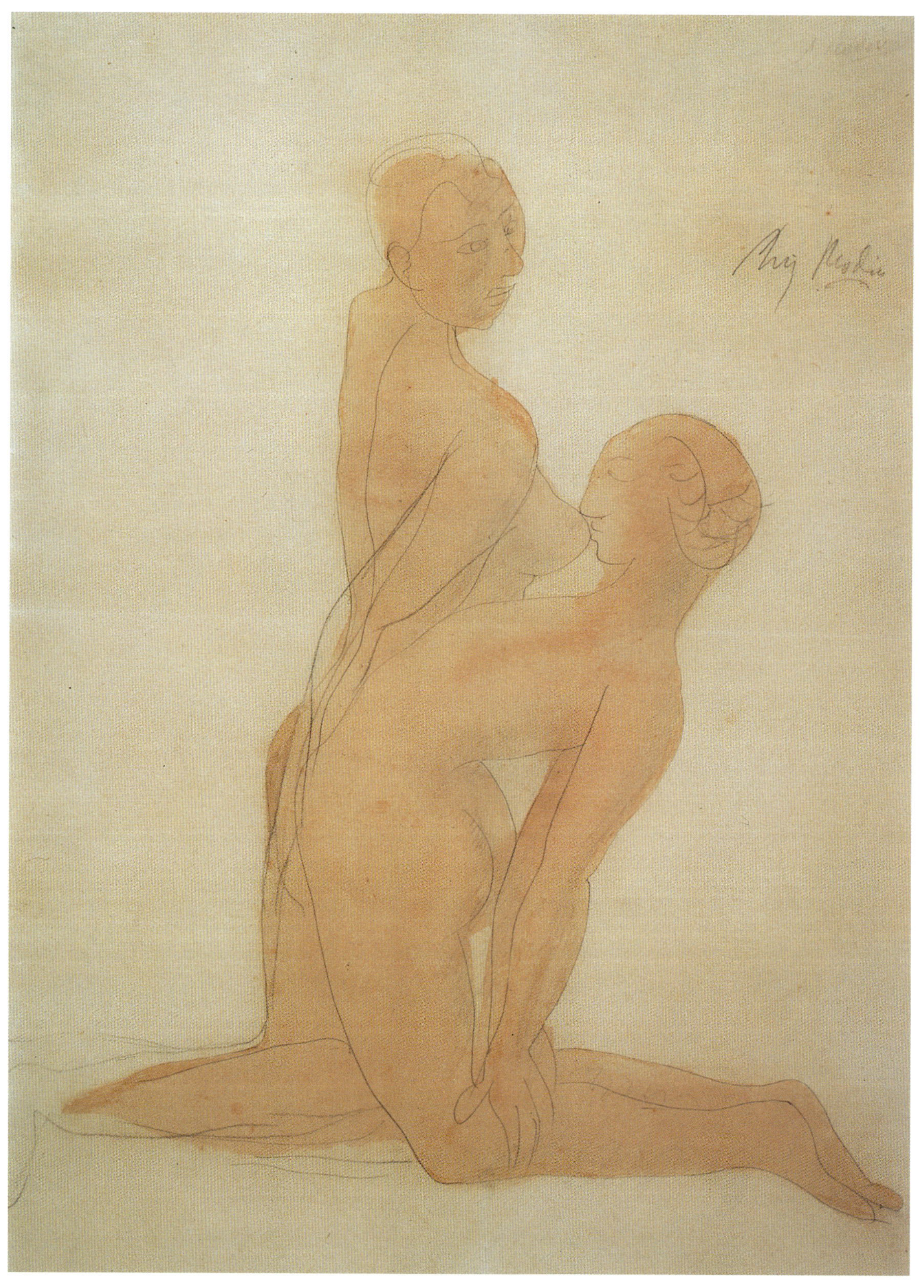

Two Kneeling Nudes c.1900 (cat. 110)

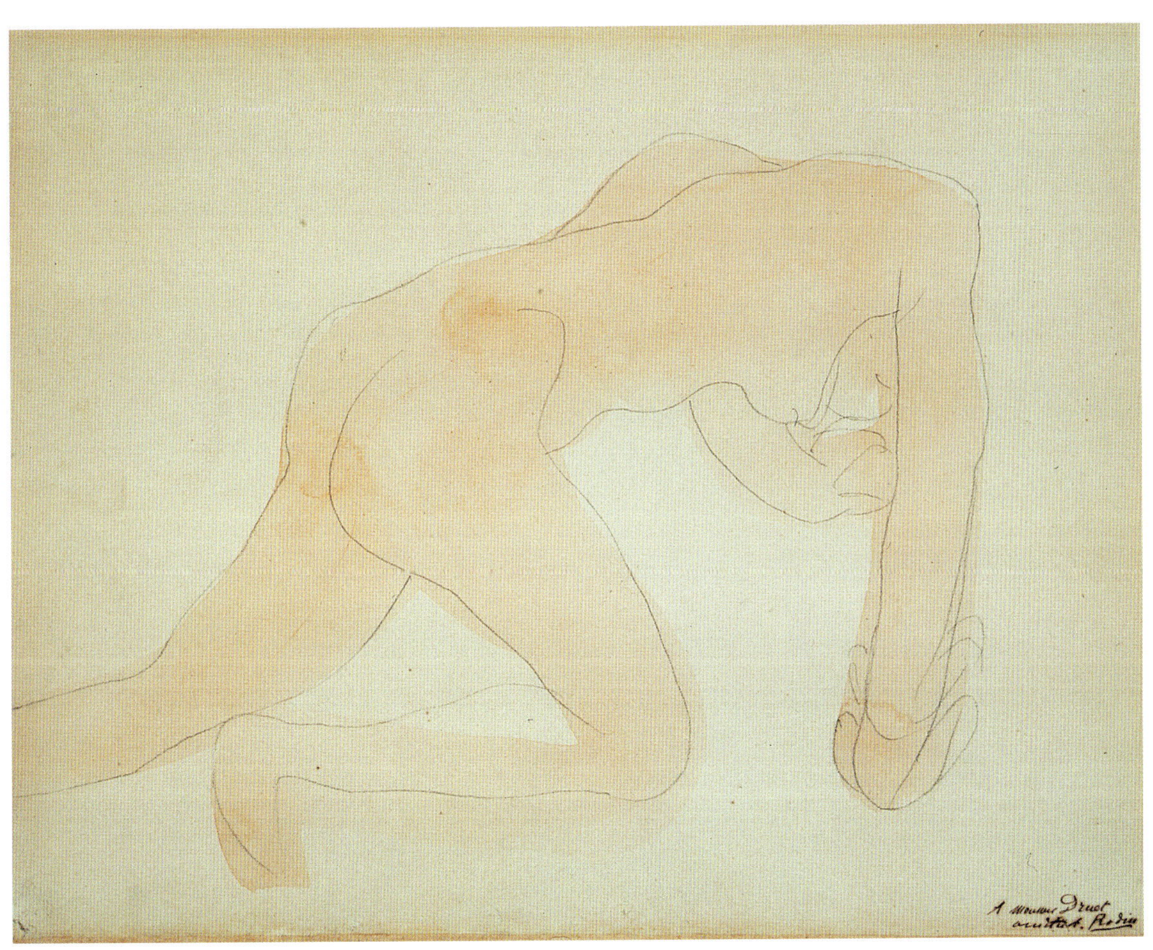

Kneeling Female Nude after 1900 (cat. 112)

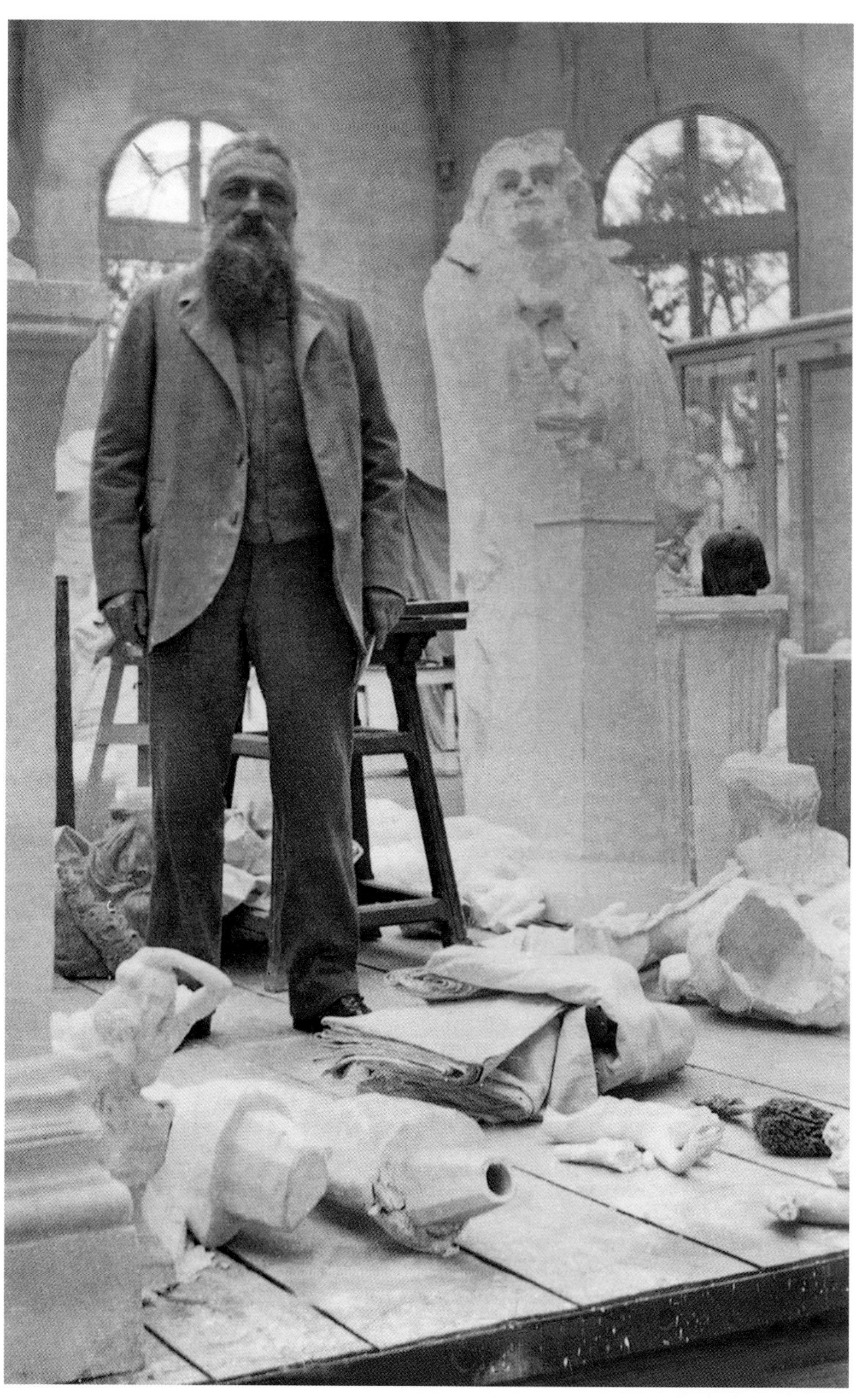

Eugène DRUET *Rodin in his Studio Surrounded by his Plaster Works* 1902 Gelatin silver photograph 25.3 x 25.0 cm
Musée Rodin

THE SCULPTOR WRITES: RODIN IN CORRESPONDENCE WITH MELBOURNE[1]

Jaynie Anderson and Paul Paffen

Eight letters from Auguste Rodin (1840–1917), preserved in the Bernard Hall Archive at the National Gallery of Australia Research Library, reveal the circumstances in which the National Gallery of Victoria acquired sculpture directly from Rodin's studio.[2] Bernard Hall (1859–1935), the Director of the National Gallery of Victoria,[3] visited Europe in 1905 as the first purchaser overseas for the Felton Bequest,[4] with authority to spend £3,600 acquiring works for the Gallery. Before leaving Australia, Hall indicated that sculpture would be amongst his acquisitions, claiming that he knew two good friends of Rodin through whom he could get an introduction to the famous French sculptor: '[W]e might be lucky enough to get something of his. Casts, directly from him, I think, could certainly be obtained.'[5] Two other sculptors were specifically named to the Trustees, John Macallan Swan (1847–1910) and Alfred Gilbert (1854–1934);[6] and Hall would also search for replacements for the two lions that stood outside the front entrance of the Gallery, for which purpose he would visit *animalier* sculptors in Paris.

Soon after arriving in London on 6 February 1905, Hall visited the Whistler Memorial Exhibition organised by the International Society of Sculptors, Painters and Gravers, of which Rodin was President, succeeding James Abbott McNeil Whistler (1834–1903). Hall was present at the Society's gala banquet to mark the opening of the exhibition, held at the fashionable Café Royal and attended by Rodin.

While, at the very least, Hall would have seen Rodin at the dinner, the two men did definitely meet in April 1905. Hall first arrived to buy works in Paris on 13 April and called Rodin on 16 April to make arrangements for a meeting the following day. His diary for 17 April indicates that at 3.00 pm he met the Australian expatriate artist, Rupert Bunny (1864–1947),[7] in whose company he called on Rodin, presumably at his studio at the Dépôt des Marbres at 5.30 pm.[8] Plans were made for the three men to meet again at Rodin's studio at Meudon, in Val Fleury, on the outskirts of Paris, at 1.00 pm on Tuesday 18 April.

That same afternoon, at Rodin's suggestion, Hall visited the Palais du Luxembourg, the great Parisian museum for the work of living artists, where he saw Rodin's original bust of Jean-Paul Laurens (1838–1921).[9] Hall wrote to Rodin the next day, ordering a reproduction in bronze of the Laurens bust and confirming his acceptance of Rodin's price of 2,500 francs (£100).

Hall's decision to acquire the bust may have been partly influenced by the fact that Laurens had taught several Melbourne artists at the Académie Julian in Paris. Bunny was one of them. In 1886 he commenced studies under Laurens and, despite traversing a very different artistic path, he commented later: 'his *élève* (pupil) I have always remained'.[10] Bunny's admiration for Laurens may have carried some weight in deciding the purchase, but Hall's ultimate motive for acquiring the bust lies more reasonably with his 'profound respect' for the French sculptor and his creations.[11]

In his letter to Rodin, Hall instructed that the bust must arrive in London before the end of May in good time for his return passage to Australia.[12] Rodin's response, dated 21 April 1905, revealed details of the other transactions that were made or proposed at Meudon, and reassured Hall regarding delivery and that these would be signature works.

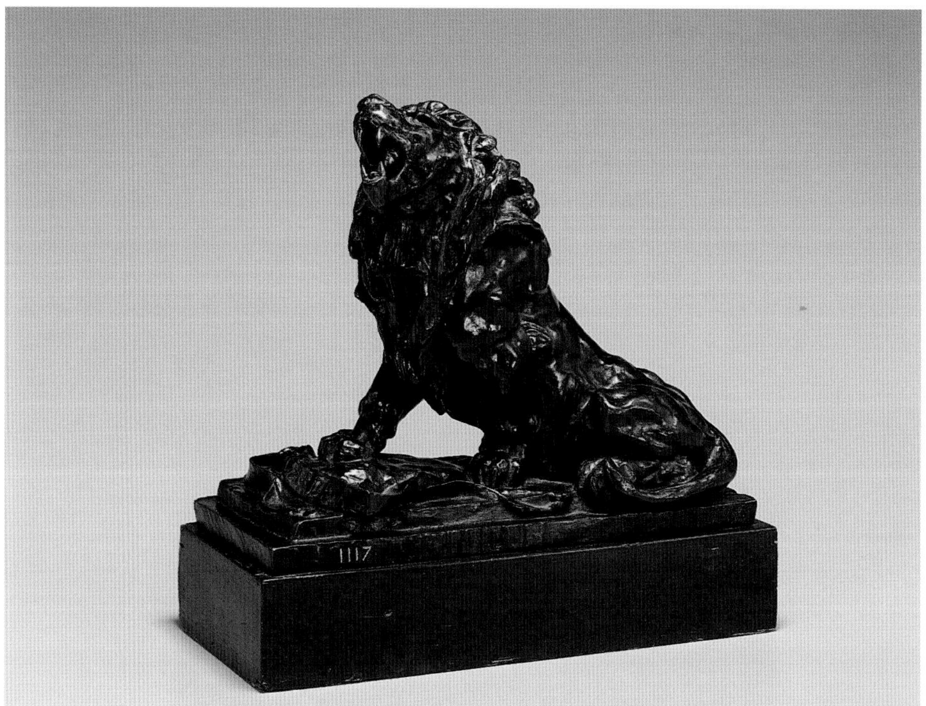

The Crying Lion 1881 (cat. 116)

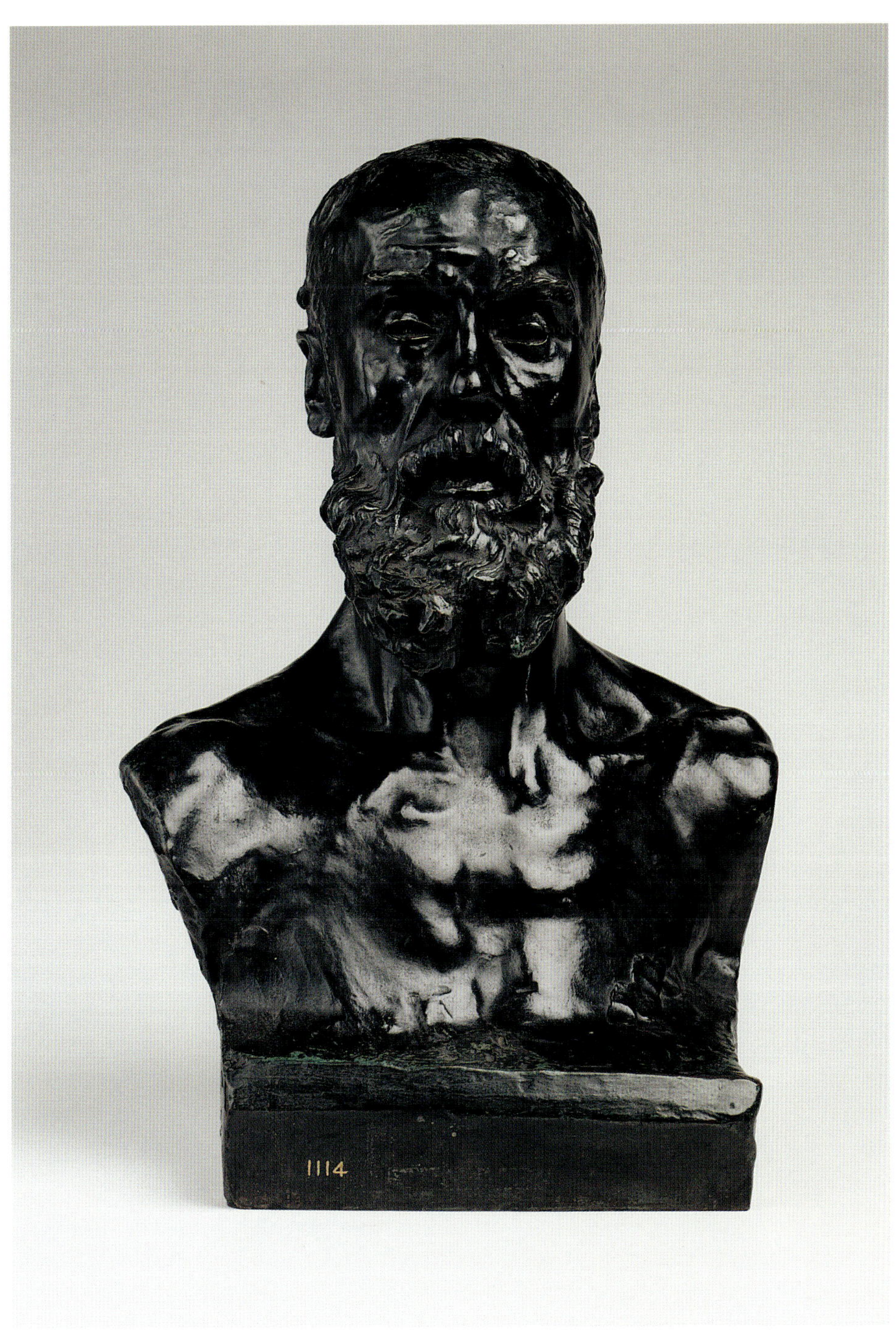

Jean-Paul Laurens 1881–82 (cat. 117)

Monsieur,
En réponse à votre lettre du 19 a. je viens vous dire que je pourrai vous donner le bronze de Jean Paul Laurens absolument pareil à celui qui existe au Luxembourg et à la date que vous mentionnez c'est à dire, à la fin du mai. En même temps je vous enverrai une copie du petit lion si le prix de 1800 frs. vous convient. La tête de Minerve part cette semaine pour l'adresse de Londres que vous m'avez indiquée et je vaillerai à ce qu'aucune pièce ne soit expédiée avant que j'y aie gravé mon nom ainsi que vous me le demandez.
Veuillez, Monsieur, agréer l'expression de mes sentiments très distingués.
Aug. Rodin.
N.B. Vous pouvez compter que le petit lion sera le même que celui que vous avez vu.[13]

Sir,
In response to your letter of 19 April, I can inform you that I will be able to give you a bronze of Jean-Paul Laurens which is absolutely the same as the one in the Luxembourg and by the date you mention, that is, the end of May. At the same time I will send you a copy of the little lion if the price of 1800 francs suits you. The head of Minerva leaves this week for the address in London you gave me and I assure you that none of the pieces will be sent without my first engraving my name as you have requested.
Yours sincerely,
Aug. Rodin.
N.B. Rest assured that the lion will be the same as the one you have seen.

At Meudon, on a table near the door, stood a small bronze lion, *Le Lion qui pleure* (*The Crying Lion*, sometimes known as *The Wounded Lion*) – one of Rodin's rare animal pieces and a recollection of his apprenticeship with Antoine-Louis Barye (1796–1875). Hall asked if he could obtain a copy of it and what its price would be. While the idea of purchasing the small lion was pondered by Hall overnight, he did decide on one work immediately – an exquisite marble head, *Minerve sans casque*, known as *Minerva Without a Helmet*, for 6,000 francs (£239).[14]

The model for Minerva was Mariana Mattiocco della Torre, considered by Rodin to be the most beautiful woman in Paris. Mariana married the Australian Impressionist painter John Peter Russell (1858–1930) on 8 February 1888 and, over many years, the two sustained a friendship with Rodin. From his home on Belle-Île off the coast of Brittany, Russell wrote to Vincent van Gogh on 22 July 1888, remarking that before he left Paris he had lunched with Rodin 'who has finished a fine head of my wife'.[15] Rodin modelled Mariana's portrait in wax in 1888 and later, in about 1896, he used her as a model for his sculptural subjects of classical goddesses.[16] Rodin's frequent use of Mariana as a model generated a great deal of speculation concerning their relationship, and Mariana was often discussed in letters between Rodin and Russell. A silver bust of Mariana, commissioned by Russell in 1889, is also a topic that they discussed in their letters. Rodin was extremely fond of this work and included it in his exhibition at the Pavillon de l'Alma in 1900. Although it was Russell's wish that the silver bust of his wife should go to the Art Gallery of New South Wales, his daughter Jeanne bequeathed the work to the Musée Rodin in Paris, who in turn gave it to the Musée des Jacobins de Morlaix.

The replica of *Minerva Without a Helmet* arrived promptly in London. The London agents for the Felton Bequest, St Barbe Sladen and Wing, acknowledged that they had taken delivery of the marble head on 26 April 1905 and, under Hall's instructions, sent Rodin a draft for 6,000 francs.

On the day the London agents sent the payment for the *Minerva Without a Helmet,* Hall also wrote to Rodin, in reply to the sculptor's letter of 21 April 1905. He was delighted that Rodin could deliver the two pieces of sculpture by the end of May (referring to the bust of Laurens and the small bronze lion). But as he had wanted to purchase the lion for 1,000 francs, and Rodin's price as stated in his letter was 1,800 francs, Hall decided that, for the moment, he would leave aside its acquisition. This letter crossed one that was written to Hall on Rodin's behalf, apparently believing that the price of 1,800 francs had been accepted. When he discovered that this was not the case, Rodin reduced the price to 1,500 francs.[17] In reply, Hall graciously declined Rodin's offer,[18] and Rodin came down no further in price. Two years later the National Gallery of Victoria bought the same object for 2,500 francs – the price that Hall had paid in 1905 for the bust of Laurens.

On 14 May 1905, during his second sojourn in Paris, Hall contacted Rodin saying that he wished to inspect the bust of Laurens before it was sent to London and he visited Rodin the following afternoon.[19] The arrival in London of the bust, however, prompted further correspondence. On 23 May, Hall wrote to Rodin explaining that when the bust had been unpacked the previous day it was found to have suffered some damage, either in packing or in transit. The 'nose, beard and left eyebrow appear to have been rubbed down to the yellow metal' – the patina had been 'rubbed away completely' in those places. In order to have this rectified before the bust was transported to Australia, Hall asked for instructions for it to be returned to Paris, if necessary, to undergo repairs by Rodin. He ended his letter by saying that he had sent Rodin an illustrated catalogue of the Melbourne collection which he hoped would interest the sculptor.[20]

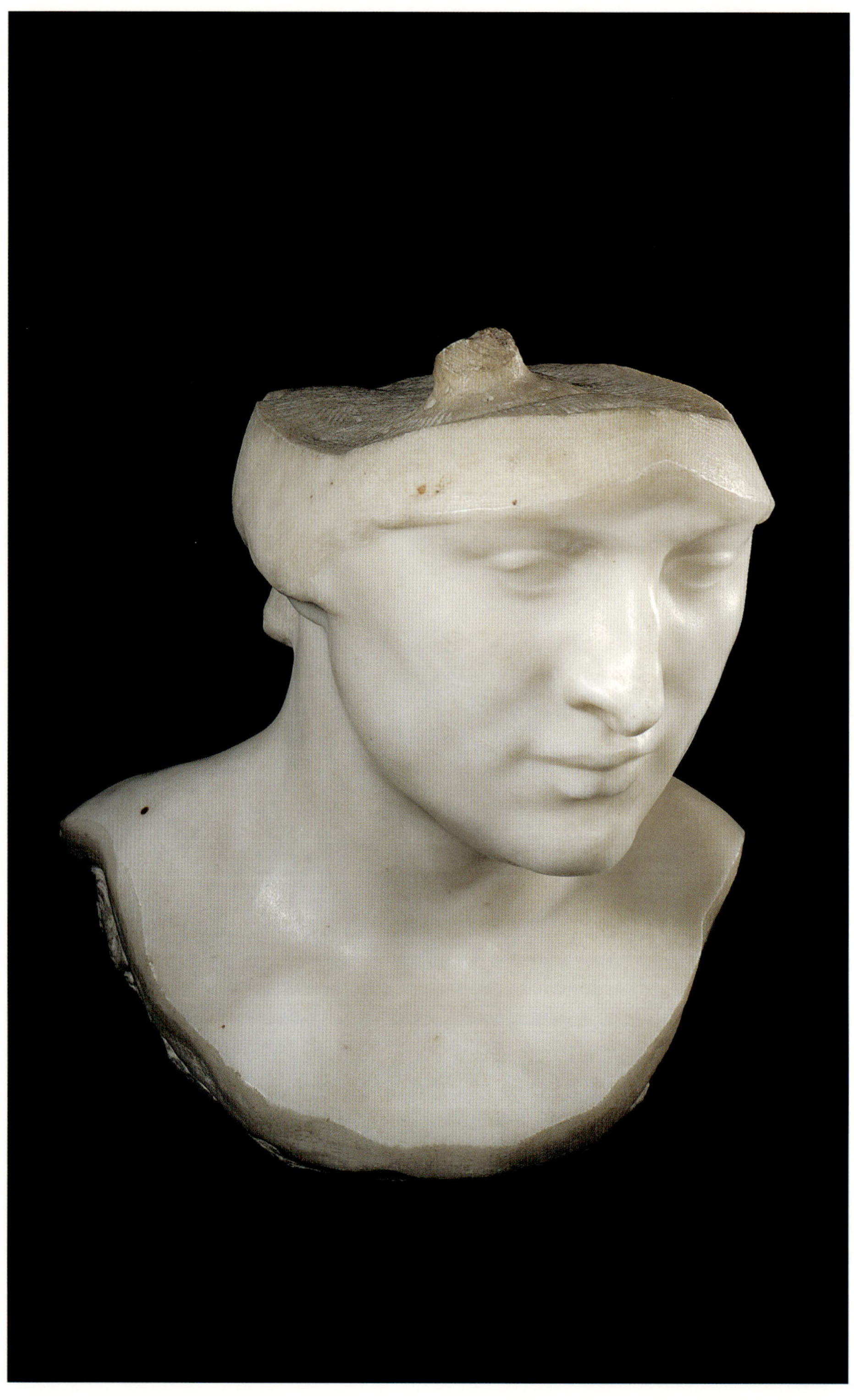

Minerva Without a Helmet c.1896 Marble 20.8 x 28.0 x 24.0 cm Felton Bequest 1905 National Gallery of Victoria, Melbourne

On 1 June 1905, Hall wrote to Rodin that the bust was being sent to have the damage put right as soon as possible, for everything needed to be packed the next week for the voyage to Australia. The previous day, the London agents had written to Rodin, saying that at Hall's request they had had the bronze repacked and sent back to Paris for repairs.[21] The repaired bust did not reach London in time to make the journey to Melbourne with Hall's other purchases, and charges incurred for its further travelling to and from Paris fell upon Rodin. Deciding whose responsibility it was to pay for the unexpected freight charges became a complicated matter untangled by St Barbe, Sladen, and Wing, Rodin and the continental firm of shipping agents Rosenberg, Loewe and Company.[22]

Some two years after his first visit to Rodin in Paris, Hall wrote to him on 7 March 1907, referring to the small bronze lion that he had seen in the Meudon studio, to inquire whether the sculptor had ever used it as a sketch for a larger piece.[23] Hall had in mind a space for such a piece, and in the next mail he sent Rodin a photograph of the front of the building housing the Public Library, Museums and National Gallery of Victoria in Swanston Street, Melbourne.[24] The intention was to show Rodin the site – where two 'decrepit zinc lions [that] are falling to pieces' had stood for a number of decades on either side of the top

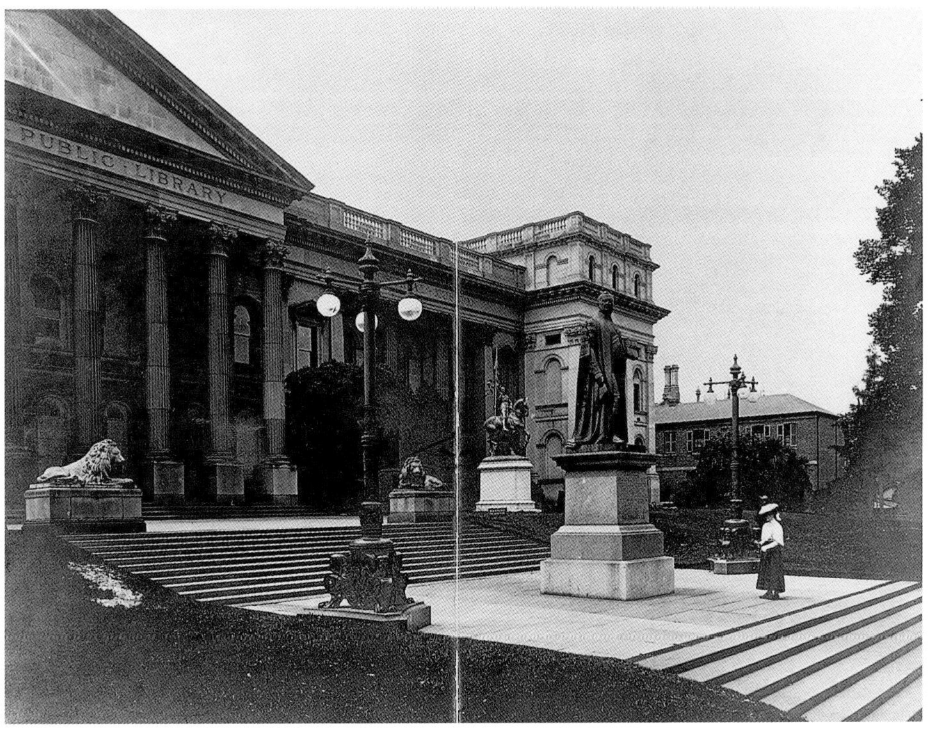

Facade of the National Gallery of Victoria, Melbourne c.1907 Gelatin silver photograph 16.0 x 21.2 cm Musée Rodin

step leading to the portico of the main entrance of the building. The lions, which were acquired in 1876 for £68 5s on the advice of the first President of the Trustees, Sir Redmond Barry, had not weathered well. Hall considered that the space they occupied was 'an excellent one' for two animal groups. In order to put his proposal to the Trustees, Hall asked Rodin to send him a photograph or sketch of the small bronze lion, with an estimate for its life-size reproduction – such a piece, he believed, would 'nobly' fill one of two pedestals.[25]

Rodin responded eagerly to Hall's proposition for the lion sculpture, and stated that, if he were given the commission, the one grand roaring lion should occupy the position in the middle of the architecture – that it should be well made and be slightly larger than life-size; the estimate would be between 20,000 and 25,000 francs. Should Hall choose a pair of lions, one for each side, their aspect could follow the example of the pair by Barye at one of the entrances to the Louvre, being the same lion reversed.[26]

But Hall had a different idea. On 11 June 1907, he wrote to explain clearly to Rodin that he did not wish to repeat the lion in reverse as the Louvre had done, but 'to have two distinct works … to get as a companion to your Lion, a Lioness and Cubs' – a work that Hall saw in 1905 in J.M. Swan's studio in London. Rodin was asked to understand that an unavoidable delay would occur before any final decision was made, for the proposal still had to be put to the Trustees and Hall was waiting to hear definitely from Swan. Plans therefore were not for Rodin's animal statuary to stand either in tandem outside the Gallery or in one grand place, but for the great French sculptor's work to be placed in dialogue with the work of his contemporary English counterpart.[27] This did not deter Rodin, who remained keenly interested in the project.

> Sir
> J'ai répondu à Messrs St. Barbe, Haden and Wing à London, au sujet de votre offre d'achat du petit Lion en bronze que vous aviez remarquée dans mon atelier en 1905.
> J'ai informé vos correspondants que cette pièce est à disposition pour deux mille cinq cents francs.
> Mais je me souviens de votre projet d'agrandissement de ce bronze pour décorer la façade du Musée de Melbourne, que vous m'aviez exposé dans votre lettre de 7 mars 1907.
> Ce projet m'intéresse fort, et j'aurais été tres heureux de savour si vous comptez lui donner suite.
> Je vous remercie vivement, et vous prie d'agréer, Sir, l'expression de mes sentiments très dintingués.
> A. Rodin[28]

Sir,
I have replied to Messrs St Barbe, Haden and Wing in London, concerning your offer to purchase the little bronze lion that you saw in my studio in 1905. I told your agents that this piece is available for 2500 francs. But I remember your project for enlarging this bronze for decorating the façade of the Museum in Melbourne, that you proposed in your letter of 7 March 1907. This project interests me greatly and I would be happy to know if you are thinking of following this through.
Thank you very much
Yours sincerely,
A. Rodin

By May 1908, with no clear action decided by the Trustees, Hall felt the matter had dragged on for too long, and to the Trustees he noted:

> Neither of these sculptors are young men, & I know of no others who would be equal to them in this kind of work. Besides it is important that we do not forfeit the notion that we are in earnest. This is a very real asset, in putting us in sympathy with the genuine artist, as opposed to the scheming of the merely popular & commercial ones.[29]

Three months later, perceptive to the balancing act that had to be performed during the passage of time when no decision was made, Hall again wrote to the Trustees:

> I can assure the Trustees that the treatment we accord to these artists will make all the difference in the way they approach their task & the heart they put into the Commission entrusted to them, or the good understanding we have with them as to the terms of purchase on its satisfactory completion.
>
> At present we are simply irritating them, as it would be almost impossible to make clear to them the necessity for this delay. In any case, it will take months to arrange the details to select the designs, to have them well "paired" & to agree about terms of purchase all of which, I submit, can be attended to from this end.[30]

In October 1908, the Trustees contacted Rodin regarding the small bronze lion that Hall had seen in the Meudon studio, and which featured in the photograph that Rodin had sent to Melbourne. They offered £100 (2,500 francs) for it. Should Rodin accept this offer, which he did, the Trustees asked that he send the piece to St Barbe Sladen and Wing. The Felton Bequest Committee had no London adviser at this time, so the Trustees approached J.M. Swan to assess its condition.[31] The transaction was successfully completed in early January 1909.[32] Rodin's bronze lion, measuring 28 cms in height, dated 1881, then made its way to Melbourne.[33]

The purchase of the small lion by the Trustees of the National Gallery of Victoria was the pay-off for not proceeding to acquire a large work by Rodin for the front of the Gallery. It was actually Hall who suggested the acquisition, and he wrote to Rodin unofficially a week after the Trustees had sent their offer, hoping that the lion he had seen in the studio at Meudon was still available, for he had admired its patina. He also offered his apologies to Rodin for his silence on the proposed life-sized lion sculpture. In short, he explained that nothing had been settled until recently when 'to insure our getting a pair, perfectly matched in both balance & treatment – we have decided to ask Mr. Swan to give us designs for both groups'. The reason given for this decision was the difficulty in supervising work undertaken in different studios across the Channel, let alone from Melbourne.[34]

The plan that had been communicated to Rodin in Hall's letter of October 1908 was in fact suggested to the Trustees by Hall twelve months earlier, when he gave his opinion 'that the best course would be to give the commission <u>for the pair</u> to Mr. Swan & to purchase the little lion from M. Rodin at his price of £100 (It was a beautiful bit of bronze).[35] Another reason for Hall choosing this course was that Swan's work was more likely to have the direct, personal supervision of the artist, whereas Rodin's was not. The Trustees called for photographs of both groups, which Hall gave to them. He noted that the works appeared to be finely conceived, 'but I foresee an objection to their being "paired". The base (in bronze) required for the 2 cubs in Mr. Swan's "Deluge" being so <u>much deeper</u> than that of the lion will give it a more bulky appearance & tend to destroy the <u>balance</u> or adjustment, which is a most desirable feature to obtain'. There was an alternative plan, namely to ask Rodin to collaborate with Swan 'on the basis of the "Deluge", but there may be an awkwardness in etiquette about doing this, as also, because M. Rodin has given up modelling animals, whereas Mr. Swan has a mass of material to draw upon'.[36]

Rodin was disappointed that a life-sized version of *The Crying Lion* was not realised for Melbourne. However, he did make a larger version of the sculpture, with the assistance of Victor Peter (1840–1918), which was sold in 1915 to the American collector, Samuel Colt, and is now in the Bristol Museum, Rhode Island, Connecticut. His impression of the Melbourne Gallery may well have been tarnished over this long, drawn-out incident and its unsatisfactory conclusion.

While overseas in 1910, the Australian artist, Ambrose Patterson (1877–1966), contacted the Trustees, offering them three remarkable works by Rodin – the bronze *Les Bourgeois de Calais* (*The Burghers of Calais*) for £2,000, a bronze of *Saint Jean-Baptiste* (*Saint John the Baptist Preaching*) for £720, and *Le Baiser* (*The Kiss*) in marble for £800.[37] These were all declined by the Trustees, but they decided to contact Rodin to ask what statuary he could supply, and at what price. An official letter to Rodin, written on behalf of the Trustees by the Chief Librarian and Secretary, dated 12 July 1910, declared that:

> The Trustees of the National Gallery of Victoria would be glad to learn whether you have any finished examples of your own sculpture which would be suitable for Gallery purposes. If you have any such works and are willing to dispose of them, I am directed to ask you whether you would be so good as to forward full particulars for the information of the National Gallery Committee. The Committee specially desires to have photographs of any work that may be available, and any description or notes (either in French or English) giving details of the work would be much appreciated.[38]

Rodin appears to have ignored the letter and the Trustees failed to pursue the matter. Following Swan's death on 14 February 1910, the Trustees took no further action regarding that sculptor's models of the animal groups for the entrance of the institution.[39] While the work of neither Rodin nor Swan came to stand in front of the Swanston Street building, other works by Rodin were acquired during Hall's term as Director of the National Gallery of Victoria, but these were purchased in 1921, after the famous French sculptor's death.[40]

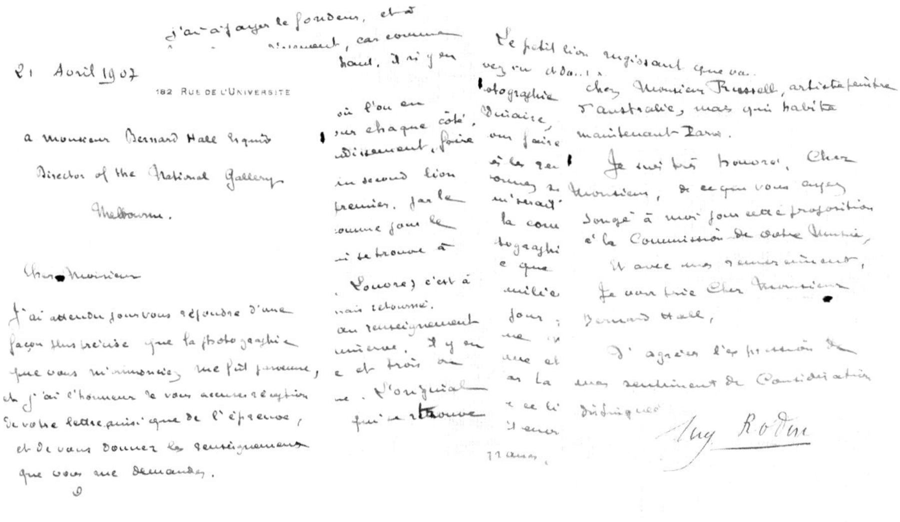

21 Avril 1907

182 Rue de l'Université

a Monsieur Bernard Hall Esquire

Director of the National Gallery

Melbourne.

Cher Monsieur

J'ai attendu pour vous répondre d'une façon plus précise que la photographie que vous m'annonciez me fût parvenue, et j'ai l'honneur de vous accuser réception de votre lettre ainsi que de l'épreuve, et de vous donner les renseignements que vous me demandez.

[illegible]

Le petit lion rugissant que vous avez vu … chez Monsieur Russell, artiste peintre d'Australie, mais qui habite maintenant Paris.

Je suis très honoré, Cher Monsieur, de ce que vous ayez songé à moi pour cette proposition à la Commission de votre Musée,

Et avec mes remerciements,

Je vous prie Cher Monsieur Bernard Hall,

d'agréer l'expression de mes sentiments de considération distingués

Aug Rodin

Letter from Auguste Rodin to Bernard Hall, 21 April 1907 Bernard Hall Archive National Gallery of Australia Research Library 2:7

1 The research underlying this essay was undertaken with the support of an Australian Research Council grant (2000) to Professor Jaynie Anderson (University of Melbourne), 'Australia's patrimony exemplified by the history of the multicultural collections at the National Gallery of Victoria (1850–2000)'. It is part of a large study on the politics of acquisition at the National Gallery of Victoria, to be published in 2002. The project is a collaborative one between the recipient of the grant and her Senior Research Assistant, Dr Paul Paffen, School of Fine Arts, Classical Studies and Archaeology, University of Melbourne.

2 Bernard Hall (BH) Archive. National Gallery of Australia Research Library, items 1:71-2, 74, 77, 79; 2:7; 232-3, 341.

3 Lindsay Bernard Hall (1859–1935) was Director of the National Gallery of Victoria and the Gallery Schools for forty-three years, 1892–1935.

4 Melbourne merchant Alfred Felton (1831–1904) left a generous bequest to the National Gallery of Victoria (NGV), which raised its purchasing power to international level. On 30 December 1904, the Hon. Edward Langton, President of the Gallery Trustees, requested Hall 'to proceed to Europe as soon as possible'. BH Archive, NGARL, 3:267.

5 Bernard Hall, Suggestions for expenditure of the Felton Bequest Monies in collecting works of art [1904], BH Archive, NGARL, 3:416.

6 When Hall returned to Australia, in addition to the works by Rodin which are discussed in this essay, he had purchased sculpture by Rodin's master, Antoine-Louis Barye (1796–1875), and works by Alfred Gilbert.

7 Papers of Bernard Hall, State Library of Victoria, MS 10549.

8 Cartes de visite de Monsieur Bernard Hall, Monsieur C.R.W. Bunny, April 1905, Archives of the Musée Rodin, Paris.

9 BH letter to Rodin, 19 April 1905, Archives of the Musée Rodin, Paris.

10 *Magazine of Art*, vol. 18, 1895, p. 392. Other artists who received their early training in Melbourne before going abroad and who were taught by Laurens in Paris at the Académie Julian included Grace Joel (1865–1924), Aby Altson (1864–after 1937), David Davies (1864–1939) and James Peter Quinn (1871–1951).

11 Bunny is said to have recalled in later life that Hall's decisions to purchase famous pieces in Paris were 'sometimes prompted and advised by Bunny himself', Colette Reddin, *Rupert Bunny Himself: His final years in Melbourne*, Armadale, Victoria: The author, 1987, p. 253.

12 BH letter to Rodin, 19 April 1905, Archives of the Musée Rodin, Paris.

13 Rodin letter to BH, 21 April 1905, BH Archive, NGARL, 1:74.
Translation by catalogue editor.

14 Before acquiring a work, Hall was usually meticulous about obtaining all relevant details. But curiously, regarding the *Minerva Without a Helmet*, this process took almost two years. He wrote to Rodin in March 1907 asking 'for catalogue purposes' for the location of the original statue and date of its production, and the number of replicas that were made of it. BH letter to Rodin, 7 March 1907, Archives of the Musée Rodin, Paris. The information was given by Rodin in a letter of April 1907, in which he said that the original bronze was owned by John Russell. BH Archive, NGARL, 2:7.

15 John Russell letter to Vincent van Gogh, 22 July [1888], Letter no. 501b, in *The Complete Letters of Vincent van Gogh*, vol. 2, London: Thames and Hudson, 1958, p. 595.

16 Clare Vincent, 'Rodin at the Metropolitan Museum of Art: A history of the collection', *The Metropolitan Museum of Art Bulletin*, Spring 1981, p. 37.

17 Letter initialled FL [for Auguste Rodin] to BH, 29 April 1905, BH Archive, NGARL, 2:233.

18 BH letter to Rodin, 12 May 1905, Archives of the Musée Rodin, Paris.

19 Card from BH to Rodin, 14 May 1905, Archives of the Musée Rodin, Paris.

20 BH letter to Rodin, 23 May 1905, Archives of the Musée Rodin, Paris.

21 St Barbe Sladen and Wing letter to Rodin, Meudon, Val Fleury, Paris, 31 May 1905, Archives of the Musée Rodin, Paris.

22 St Barbe Sladen and Wing letter to Rodin, Meudon, Val Fleury, Paris, 4 July 1905, Archives of the Musée Rodin, Paris.

23 Archives of the Musée Rodin, Paris.

24 Until 1968 the Public Library, Museums and National Gallery of Victoria were housed in a single building on Swanston Street, Melbourne, now the home of the State Library of Victoria. The photograph is today in the archives of the Musée Rodin, Paris.

25 BH letter to Rodin, 7 March 1907, Archives of the Musée Rodin, Paris.

26 Rodin letter to BH, 27 April 1907, BH Archive, NGARL, 1:79.

27 BH letter to Rodin, 11 June 1907, Archives of the Musée Rodin, Paris.

28 Rodin letter to BH, 20 November 1908, BH Archive, NGARL, 2:341. Transcript by Lucina Ward, Assistant Curator, NGA (see also L. Ward, 'Inside Rodin's Studio: A sculptor, a director and some letters', *artonview,* Summer 2001/2002, issue 28. Translation by catalogue editor.)

29 BH to Trustees, Memorandum on Mr Swan's letter, 28 May 1908, BH Archive, NGARL, 3:200 (draft version).

30 BH to the Chairman of the National Gallery Committee, 26 August 1908, BH Archive, NGARL, 3:201 (draft version).

31 A.M. Bazin, Acting Chief Librarian and Secretary, Public Library, Museums and National Gallery of Victoria, letter to Rodin, 14 October 1908, Archives of the Musée Rodin, Paris. Rodin was also informed of this procedure by St Barbe Sladen and Wing, letter to Rodin, 17 November 1908, Archives of the Musée Rodin, Paris.

32 St Barbe Sladen and Wing, letters to Rodin, 6 January 1909 and 8 January 1909, Archives of the Musée Rodin, Paris.

33 Other versions of Rodin's bronze *The Crying Lion* are at Walters Art Gallery, Baltimore, Museo Nacional de Arte Decorativo, Buenos Aires, the California Palace of the Legion of Honor, San Francisco and the Iris and B. Gerald Cantor Foundation, Los Angeles (cat. 4).

34 BH letter to Rodin, 21 October 1908, Archives of the Musée Rodin, Paris.

35 Hall notes that he wrote to the Trustees with this opinion in a letter dated 30 October 1907. See BH letter to the Chairman of the National Gallery Committee, 26 August 1908, BH Archive, NGARL, 3:201 (draft version).

36 BH to the Chairman of the National Gallery Committee, 26 August 1908, BH Archives, NGA.

37 Minutes of the Trustees, National Gallery of Victoria (MTNGV), 26 May, 1910, State Library of Victoria.

38 E.L.Armstrong, Chief Librarian and Secretary, Public Library, Museums and National Gallery of Victoria, letter to Rodin, 182 rue de l'Université, Paris, 12 July 1910, Archives of the Musée Rodin, Paris.

39 MTNGV, 26 May 1910, State Library of Victoria.

40 In 1921 the Felton Bequest purchased finished versions in bronze of the *Kissing Babes* and *The Thinker*. These were acquired for £350 and £950 respectively.

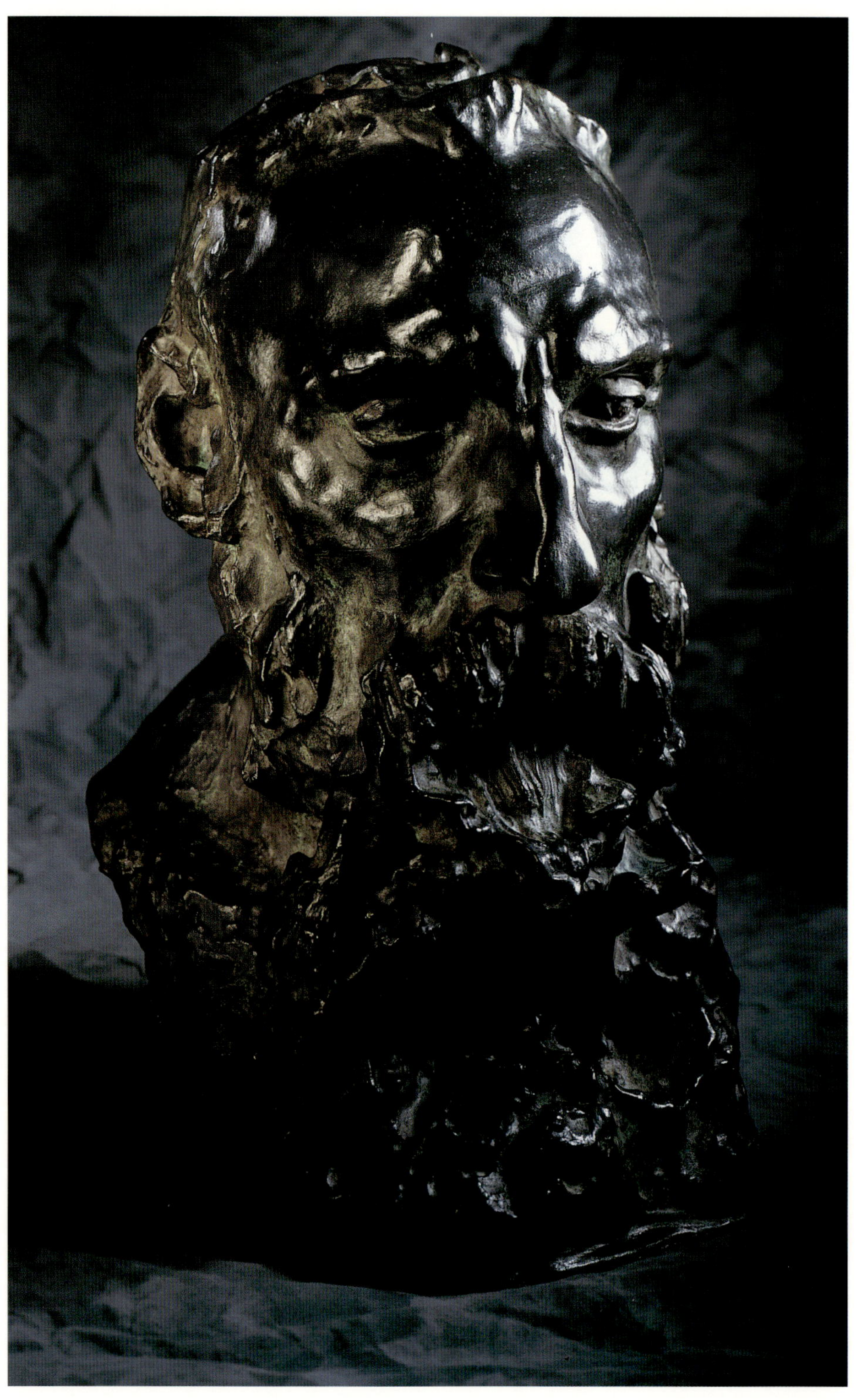

Camille CLAUDEL *Bust of Rodin* 1888–92 (cat. 75)

CHRONOLOGY

1840
François-Auguste-René Rodin was born in the working-class Mouffetard district in Paris on 12 November 1840. His father, Jean-Baptiste Rodin (1803–1883), was a clerk in the police force and his mother, Marie Cheffer (*c.*1806–1871), was a native of Lorraine who had come to Paris in the 1830s. His elder sister, Anna-Marie, known as Maria (1837–1862), had a powerful influence over her brother; she entered a convent in 1861.

1847–54
Rodin attended primary school run by the Christian Brothers, the Ecole des Frères de la Doctrine Chrétienne, and then went to a private boarding school in Beauvais, run by his uncle Hippolyte Rodin.

1854–57
Rodin enrolled at the Ecole Impériale Spéciale de Dessin et de Mathématiques (Special Imperial School of Drawing and Mathematics), known as the 'Petite Ecole'. The curriculum stressed the copying of approved styles and learning techniques applicable to the decorative arts. Although the stated purpose of the school was training for a decorative arts career, many of the students regarded the Petite Ecole as a stepping stone to the Ecole des Beaux-Arts (Fine Arts Academy).

One of Rodin's professors was Horace Lecoq de Boisbaudran (1802–1897) who trained his students to draw from memory and from the moving model, and encouraged them to develop a personal style. At the end of 1855, Rodin won a second prize for drawing and the following year he won first prize.

1857–59
The Ecole Supérieure des Beaux-Arts was a prerequisite for success for an artist in nineteenth-century France. The school provided an entrée to the ateliers (see note 26, p. 73) of the most prestigious professors, who could then endorse work for the Salon (see note 5, p. 13). Rodin failed three times to gain admission to the school; he was successful in the drawing competitions, but his sculpture was refused.

1858–62
Rodin helped to support his family by working as a craftsman or ornamenter, working for a succession of jewellers, masons and craftsmen supplying the large market for decorative objects and embellishments to buildings. Rodin also struggled tenaciously at his own work, continuing his own study with great self-discipline. He was involved in a cooperative atelier, then rented his own space, and attended evening life-drawing sessions.

1862–63
Devastated by the death of his sister Marie, Rodin entered the order of Pères du Très-Saint-Sacrement (Monastery of the Most Holy Sacrament) as a novice. The head of the order, Pierre-Julien Eymard, encouraged Rodin to devote

himself instead to art. Rodin modelled a bust of Eymard (see page 19).

Returning to the secular world, Rodin also worked on decorative sculpture for the Théâtre des Gobelins. He also began work on bust using a hired – but not professional – model: Bibi, a local workman, had a broken nose, and Rodin's plaster was later known as *The Man with the Broken Nose*.

1864

Rodin attended the classes of the *animalier* sculptor Antoine-Louis Barye (1796–1875) at the Musée d'Histoire Naturelle (Museum of Natural History). Rodin also drew live animals in the menagerie of the Jardin de Plantes (Botanical Gardens), at the zoo and at the horse markets. He also studied the anatomy of humans at the Ecole de Médecine (Medical School) and on the streets. Rodin met a young seamstress, Rose Beuret (1844–1917), who became his mistress, studio assistant and life-long companion.

As his reputation as a modeller grew, Rodin's status changed and he was employed by the successful sculptor Albert-Ernest Carrier-Belleuse (1824–1887). One of the most prolific and versatile nineteenth-century sculptors, Carrier-Belleuse ran a huge atelier and hired assistants as modellers, mould makers and marble carvers. Rodin worked intermittently with Carrier-Belleuse until 1882, learning entrepreneurial and delegation skills.

1865

The Mask of the Man with the Broken Nose was refused by the Salon. *The Mask* was a fragment of *The Man with the Broken Nose* – Rodin had been unable to keep his studio warm during a particularly cold winter and his clay model froze and broke, the back of the head falling off.

1866–69

Carrier-Belleuse was commissioned to provide ornamentation for the Hôtel de la Païva, a private town-house on the Champs-Elysées. Rodin and Jules Dalou (1838–1902) also worked on the decoration of this the elaborate residence. Rodin worked for a range of other sculptors and artisans during this period.

Auguste Beuret (1866–1934), Rodin's only son whom he never acknowledged, was born to Rose Beuret.

1870–71

When the Franco-Prussian War began, Rodin was conscripted as a corporal into the 158th Regiment of the Garde Nationale (National Guard) in Paris, then invalided out because of his short-sightedness. In the in the wake of the war, the decorative trades collapsed and Rodin joined Carrier-Belleuse in Brussels.

When Parisians opposed the national government – claiming it was too conservative, too royalist, and too ready to accept a humiliating peace with Prussia – and elected a municipal council known as the Commune, the resulting upheavals meant that employment in Paris was difficult. Rodin was forced to support himself in Belgium from 1871 until 1877. Rose Beuret joined Rodin at Ixelles, near Brussels, at the end of 1871.

1872–74

After Rodin and Carrier-Belleuse quarrelled – Rodin was ambitious and wanted to make and sell sculpture under his own name – their collaboration ended. Another of Carrier-Belleuse's sculptors, Antoine Van Rasbourgh (1831–1902), won the commission for allegorical groups to decorate the Paris stock exchange, the Bourse du Commerce. He and Rodin went into partnership undertaking artistic and industrial sculpture, and later worked in Antwerp on a monument to the burgomaster François Loos, a large fountain with Michelangelo-like seated figures of *Industry, Commerce, Navigation* and *Art* (1874–1876).

Rodin exhibited portrait busts of his Belgian friends and small-scale works that possess an eighteenth-century charm. He developed *The Man with the Broken Nose* into a bust, exhibiting it in plaster in the Brussels Salon of 1872. He also returned briefly to Paris with a marble version of bust, shown under the title *Portrait de M.B.–* in the Salon of 1875. Rodin also painted landscapes during his time in Belgium.

1875–76

Using a Belgian soldier as his model, Rodin began working on a standing nude figure that was later known as *The Age of Bronze*. In the winter of 1875–1876 Rodin travelled to Italy (Turin, Genoa, Rome, Naples, Siena and Florence), hoping to discover the 'secrets' of Michelangelo (1475–1564); he returned to Brussels equally impressed with Donatello (*c.*1386–1466), Raphael (1483–1520) and the art of Antiquity. The trip was crucial to his development.

1877–78

Back in Belgium, Rodin resumed work on the standing nude male figure. The sculpture was exhibited at the Cercle Artistique de Brussels (Brussels Art Society), then at the Salon in Paris, and became Rodin's first *succès de scandale.* Rodin was accused of casting *The Age of Bronze* from life, of making a cast direct from the human body. Although this charge was later repudiated, this episode caused Rodin much anguish.

Rodin returned to Paris and made an extensive tour of French cathedrals during the autumn and winter of 1877. He also began work on a larger than life figure, *Saint John the Baptist Preaching*, and *Adam* and *Eve*, figures that were eventually incorporated into *The Gates of Hell.*

1879

Rodin submitted the head of *Saint John the Baptist Preaching* to the Salon of 1879. He also entered *The Call to Arms* in the competition for a monument commemorating the defence of Paris during the Franco-Prussian War in 1870 – but his work was not shortlisted. Rodin accepted a commission for the statue's enlargement in 1916 and it was inaugurated in 1920 as *The Defence of Verdun.*

Rodin worked on several decorative projects in Marseilles, Nice and Strasbourg, and was employed at the Sèvres porcelain factory, under director Carrier-Belleuse.

1880

A group of eight leading artists petitioned the government for Rodin to be officially considered for State commissions. An order was made for a cast in bronze of *The Age of Bronze*. Rodin was also invited to design a monumental portal for the proposed Musée des Arts Décoratifs (Museum of Decorative Arts). Although the museum was never completed, the project occupied Rodin for many years and became known as *The Gates of Hell.*

State patronage entitled Rodin to a shared studio at the Dépôt des Marbres

(Storehouse for Marble Sculptures), 182 rue de l'Université, Paris – he occupied additional spaces until his death – and financed a constant supply of models and technicians. He worked on *The Thinker*, *The Three Shades* and *Fallen Caryatid with Stone*.

1881
Rodin worked intensively on *The Gates of Hell*. He also made busts of fellow artists Alphonse Legros (1837–1911), Jean-Paul Laurens (1838–1921), and Carrier-Belleuse. *Saint John the Baptist Preaching* and *Adam* were exhibited at the Salon and the French State commissioned a bronze casting of *Saint John the Baptist Preaching*.

1882
Rodin visited London and exhibited work at the 1882 Royal Academy summer exhibition. He also made his first drypoints with Legros.

1883
Rodin met Camille Claudel (1864–1943) while supervising a sculpture class. She was his collaborator, mistress and model for ten years.

Victor Hugo (1802–1885) agreed that Rodin could make his bust, on the condition that he did not pose. Rodin made hundreds of preparatory drawings of the French hero in his home. His first exhibition of drawings was held at the Cercle des Arts Libéraux (Liberal Arts Society), Paris.

1884
The municipal council of Calais commissioned a monument to Eustache de Saint-Pierre, the first of the Burghers who, in 1347, had offered their lives to the English in return for an end to the siege on Calais. Rodin submitted a maquette depicting all six Burghers – moving, bending, turning and bound to one another.

Rodin had his first exhibition at the Galérie Georges Petit, Paris. His busts of Victor Hugo and Jules Dalou were exhibited in the Salon, and the reviews were very positive.

1885
Rodin was awarded the commission for the Calais monument known as *The Burghers of Calais*. He made further maquettes and then worked individually on each of the six figures, modelling them first nude and then draped, in progressively larger stages.

Renting a larger studio at 117 rue de Vaugirard, to accommodate the Burgher figures, Rodin also continued to work on *The Gates of Hell* in his spaces at the Dépôt des Marbres. He announced that the gates would be ready for casting in six months. When the plans for building the museum were cancelled, Rodin was freed from a deadline. The work remained standing in his studio, and the artist revised intermittently the figure groups and architectural mouldings throughout the late 1880s and the 1890s.

Rodin also worked on a monument to his friend the painter Jules Bastien-Lepage (1848–1884). The town of Damvillers commissioned the monument, which was awarded to Rodin in the following year, and dedicated in 1889.

1886
Rodin prepared a maquette for a monument to General Patrick Lynch, his only equestrian figure. He also modelled many representations of Claudel.
The first group of figures from *The Gates*

of Hell were enlarged and exhibited as independent works at the Galérie Georges Petit. Rodin also enlarged the figures for *The Burghers of Calais*.

He also worked on a series of illustrations for Charles Baudelaire's notorious volume of poetry, *Les Fleurs du Mal* (*The Flowers of Evil*) (1857).

1887
Three of the Burghers were exhibited at the Galérie Georges Petit. Although Rodin continued to work on the General Lynch project, the monument did not progress beyond the maquette stage.

1888
The French State commissioned an enlargement in marble of *The Kiss* for the 1889 Exposition Universelle (Universal Exhibition). *The Thinker* was first exhibited in Copenhagen, under the title *The Poet*.

Rodin and Claudel spent much of their time at 113 boulevard d'Italie, where he rented a studio for her.

1889
Rodin received commissions for the *Monument to Claude Lorrain*, to be erected in Nancy, and for a *Monument to Victor Hugo* for the Panthéon. The Lorrain maquettes were shown at Durand-Ruel and the monument was inaugurated in 1892. Rodin also worked on a number of studies for the Hugo project.

A joint exhibition with Claude Monet (1840–1926) at the Galérie Georges Petit displayed thirty-six of Rodin's works and confirmed his reputation. The complete group of *The Burghers of Calais* was shown for the first time. Gustave Geoffroy (1855–1926) wrote the introduction to the catalogue. Rodin was also a founding member of the Sociéte Nationale des Beaux-Arts (National Fine Arts Society), and vice-president of the sculpture section.

1890
Rodin's project for the *Monument to Victor Hugo* was rejected. The commissioners objected to lack of formality of his naked Hugo, seated on a rock and surrounded by female muses.

The painter Pierre Puvis de Chavannes (1824–1898) posed for Rodin. Rodin accepted commissions for a bust of the artist in 1890 and for a monument to Puvis for the Panthéon in 1911.

Rodin rented the Folie Neufbourg in the Clos Payen, 68 boulevard d'Italie, across the road from Claudel's studio. The lovers journeyed to Touraine and Anjou.

1891–92
The Luxembourg Gardens were provided as an alternative site for Rodin's *Monument to Victor Hugo*. Although the work was never completed, various versions of this monument exist in plaster. The plaster with *Tragic Muse*, but without *Meditation*, was exhibited at the 1897 Salon. The marble figure of the poet alone was exhibited at the 1902 Salon as *Victor Hugo*. The figure, mounted on a plinth of large angular blocks, was unveiled in the gardens of the Palais Royal in 1909.

The Société des Gens de Lettres (Society of Authors) commissioned a monument to the great writer Honoré de Balzac (1799–1850). The project consumed Rodin during this period – he read widely and made studies of the writer's head from living models and portraits.

Rodin was made Officer of the Légion d'Honneur.

1893
Rodin rented the Villa des Brillants, a modest building in the suburb of Meudon, south of Paris. In 1895 he purchased the Villa (now the Musée Rodin, Meudon). Emile Antoine Bourdelle (1861–1929) was employed as an assistant.

Rodin succeeded Dalou as the vice-president of the Sociéte Nationale des Beaux-Arts and president of its sculpture section. The Sociéte provided exhibition possibilities for contemporary artists and from 1890, when its first Salon was held, existed as an alternative to the official Salon.

The subscription to pay for *The Burghers of Calais*, dormant since 1886, was renewed. Rodin visited Calais to study the siting of the monument in 1894 – it was erected on a pedestal and inaugurated in 1895.

Rodin's decade-long relationship with Claudel ended. He continued to extend support to her as an artist, but she resented his interference. She had a breakdown in 1905 and was institutionalised in 1913.

1894
Rodin continued to struggle with the *Monument to Balzac*. He modelled *Study of the Nude Balzac* and *Balzac in a Dominican Robe*.

Accompanied by the politician Georges Clemenceau (1841–1929), and the art critics and writers Octave Mirbeau (1848–1917) and Geoffroy, Rodin visited Monet at Giverny and met Paul Cézanne (1839–1906). Rodin also developed a friendship with the sculptor Medardo Rosso (1858–1928) and they exchanged works.

1895
Hostile reviews adversely affected Rodin's health and he suffered depression during this period.

1896
Rodin modelled a new athletic Balzac. The exhibition *Rodin–Puvis de Chavannes–Carrière* was held at Musée Rath, Geneva.

1897
The maquette for the Balzac monument was finished and enlarged.
Les Dessins d'Auguste Rodin, with 142 photogravure drawings and a foreword by Mirbeau, was published by Maison Goupil (known as the Goupil Album).

1898
The Société des Artistes Français and the Société Nationale de Beaux-Arts exhibited together for the first time – the Salon of 1898 contained more than seven thousand works. Rodin exhibited the *Monument to Balzac* and a marble version of *The Kiss*. The Sociéte des Gens de Lettres turned down the statue of *Balzac* and a violent press campaign ensued. Although he received several offers, Rodin refused to relinquish the work and it was not cast during his lifetime.

Rodin worked on the *Monument to Labour*. The initial conception of this project had brought together all of the important contemporary sculptors of the day, and was supposed to do for the 1900 Exposition Universelle (Universal Exhibition) what the Eiffel Tower had done in 1889. It did not come to fruition.

1899
Rodin installed his first solo exhibition in Brussels – comprising some sixty works, most of which were plaster and fifteen of which were large-scale, plus drawings and

photographs. Judith Cladel (1873–1958) lectured, and then toured with the show to Rotterdam, Amsterdam and The Hague. Rodin joined the exhibition in Amsterdam, and particularly admired Rembrandt's paintings in the Rijksmuseum.

Rodin again turned his attention to *The Gates of Hell*, planning a full-sized plaster cast of it for the 1900 Exposition Universelle.

1900
Rodin raised the funds to build a pavilion on the place de l'Alma, Paris, for a huge retrospective of his work. Organised by Rodin himself, and timed to coincide with the Exposition Universelle, the exhibition included 168 sculptures, and drawings and photographs.

Eugène Druet (1867–1916), an amateur photographer and café owner, managed the exhibition. Profits came from the exhibition tickets, sales of works and casts and photographs by Druet of Rodin's sculpture. Prefaces to the catalogue were contributed by Eugene Carrière (1849–1906), Laurens, Monet and Albert Besnard (1849–1934), and the works were introduced by Arsène Alexandre (1859–1937).

The exhibition confirmed Rodin's fame as the greatest living sculptor. He became a celebrity and was much in demand – royalty, politicians, society and young writers and artists visited him at Meudon, including King Edward VII (1908), and Mrs Roosevelt (1910). Orders flowed from museums and many patrons, especially English and Americans, solicited portraits from Rodin.

Rodin was appointed Chevalier de l'Ordre de Léopold de Belgique (Knight of the Order of Leopold of Belgium).

1901
Rodin purchased land adjacent to the Villa des Brillants and the Pavillon de l'Alma was rebuilt at Meudon. In 1906 he also bought fragments of a seventeenth-century château, hoping to have it reconstructed on the property to house his collection of Antique sculpture. Although this project proved too costly, the façade was reconstructed and later incorporated into Rodin's tomb.

After 1901, Rodin concentrated on portrait busts and small informal sculptures. He devoted much of his time to drawing and the supervision of his many assistants in the execution of marble versions of his sculptures, many of which were commissioned during this period.

1902
The photographer Edward Steichen (1879–1973) visited Rodin at Meudon to photograph the artist and his work. He again came to Meudon in 1908 to photograph *Balzac* by moonlight. Rodin travelled to London, Prague and Vienna.

Rodin met the poet Rainer Maria Rilke (1875–1926) who became his secretary between 1905 and 1906. He illustrated Mirbeau's *Le Jardin des Supplices (The Torture Garden)*; the lithographs of his drawings were executed by Auguste Clot (1858–1936), and published by Ambroise Vollard (1867–1939).

1903
Rilke's *Auguste Rodin* and Cladel's *Auguste Rodin: Pris sur la vie* (*Auguste Rodin: His life*) were published. Rodin was elected President of the International

Society of Painters, Sculptures and Gravers in London, successor to James McNeill Whistler (1834–1903). The large-format plaster of *The Thinker* was exhibited at the International Society in London, then at the Salon in Paris. An exhibition, organised by dancer and choreographer Loïe Fuller (1862–1928), was shown at the National Arts Club, New York. Rodin was appointed Commander of the Légion d'Honneur.

1904
Painter Gwen John (1876–1939) posed for his *Monument to Whistler* but the statue was never cast full-size. Rodin met and became infatuated with Claire Coudert de Choiseul, known as the duchesse de Choiseul who dominated his life between 1909 and 1912.

1905
Rodin was appointed a member of the Conseil Supérieur des Beaux Arts (Senior Council of the Fine Arts) and awarded an honorary degree by the University of Jena. Later he was awarded honorary doctorates by the University of Glasgow (1906) and the University of Oxford (1907).

1906
The Thinker was installed in front of the Panthéon. Rodin completed many busts, including one of George Bernard Shaw (1856–1950), who came to Meudon to pose.

In the summer, King Sisowath and the Royal Ballet of Cambodia came to France. Rodin carried out a large number of watercolours of the dancers, following them from Paris to the Exposition Coloniale (Colonial Exhibition) in Marseilles. This marked the beginning of Rodin's fascination with dancing and dancers as models. The same year he also sketched at dancing school run by Isadora Duncan (1878–1927), and met the Japanese actress Ohta Hisa (1868–1945), better known as Hanako, who would pose for him in 1908, and of whom he would also make drawings. In 1912 Rodin also modelled Vaslav Nijinsky (1890–1950), soon after having seen the first performance of Debussy's ballet *L'Après-midi d'un faune.*

Rodin was appointed a full member of the Academy of Fine Arts of Berlin.

1907
A major exhibition of more than three hundred drawings was shown at the Galérie Bernheim Jeune, Paris. Further exhibitions devoted to his drawings were held at the Manes Society, Prague (1909), and at the Lyons Library (1912).

1908
Rodin began living at the Hôtel Biron (now the Musée Rodin, Paris). The State purchased the Hôtel Biron, making the Beaux-Arts responsible for its administration, in 1911.

1909
A major exhibition held at the Galérie Devambez, Paris included 135 drawings and four photographs by Jacques-Ernest Bulloz (1858–1942) of the statue of Balzac.

During this period Rodin also executed a number of portraits of statesmen and wealthy patrons, some friends and admirers, and others with whom his relationship was more distant, such as he composer Gustav Mahler (1860–1911). Clemenceau sat for Rodin eighteen times in 1911.

1910
An exhibition of drawings, *The Thinker* and Steichen's photographs was held at Photo Secession Gallery (Gallery 291), New York.

Rodin was made a Grand Officer of the Légion d'Honneur.

1911
Rodin's reminiscences and ideas about art were published by Paul Gsell (1870–1947): *L'Art: Entretiens réunis par Paul Gsell* (translated as *Conversations with Paul Gsell*).

The National Art Collections Fund, London, purchased a cast of *The Burghers of Calais* for the gardens at Westminster, (now Victoria Tower Gardens, near the Houses of Parliament) and a large cast of *The Walking Man* was presented to the French Government for its embassy at the Palazzo Farnese, Rome. The work was removed in 1912 and sent to Lyons. The idea for the creation of a Rodin museum at the Hôtel Biron gained momentum and occupied Rodin for the rest of his life.

1912
The Rodin room opened at the Metropolitan Museum, New York. Exhibitions of his work were held in Venice, Rome and Chicago.

1913
Rodin's collection of Antiquities was exhibited at the Faculté de Médecine (Faculty of Medicine), Paris.

1914–15
Les Cathédrales de France, containing reproductions of his studies of architectural detail and his meditations on the Gothic age, was published by Armand Colin. Clot completed the facsimiles of the drawings and Charles Morice (1861–1919) wrote the preface. This volume was the culmination of Rodin's lifelong habit of making pilgrimages to French cathedrals.

Accompanied by Cladel, Rodin and Beurat escaped to London at the commencement of the war. Rodin presented eighteen sculptures to the Victoria and Albert Museum, London. They also travelled to Rome, where Rodin made a bust of Pope Benedict XV, and to Florence.

1916
Rodin suffered a severe stroke. After lengthy negotiations, the French government designated the Hôtel Biron as the future Musée Rodin (it opened to the public in 1919). The State received three successive donations of work owned by the artist, including an enormous number of plasters and drawings, the artist's library and a huge archive of photographs, correspondence and news clippings.

1917
Rodin and Rose Beuret were married on 29 January, two weeks before her death. Rodin died at Meudon on the 17 November.

Chronology compiled by Lucina Ward

CHECKLIST OF WORKS IN THE EXHIBITION

IRIS AND B. GERALD CANTOR FOUNDATION, LOS ANGELES

The following works are in the collection of the Iris and B. Gerald Cantor Foundation, Los Angeles unless otherwise specified

SCULPTURE

Monuments, Portraits & Symbolic Figures (1860–1909)

1 *Bust of Jean-Baptiste Rodin*
1860, cast 1980
Bronze, 41.0 x 28.6 x 24.1 cm
2/12, Godard Foundry, Paris
Issued by Musée Rodin, Paris
CC 1139

2 *Mask of the Man with the Broken Nose*
1863–64, probably cast 1970s
Bronze, 31.8 x 18.4 x 15.2 cm
3/12, Coubertin Foundry, Paris
Issued by Musée Rodin, Paris
CC 1605

3 *The Call to Arms*
1879, date of cast unknown
Bronze, 113.0 x 57.2 x 38.1 cm
Edition unknown, Alexis Rudier Foundry, Paris
CC 1546

4 *The Crying Lion*
1881, date of cast unknown
Bronze, 20.0 x 33.7 x 15.2 cm
Edition unknown
Issued by Musée Rodin, Paris
CC 14700

5 *Idyll of Ixelles*
1885, cast 1981
Bronze, 53.3 x 37.1 x 37.1 cm
4/8, Coubertin Foundry, Paris
Issued by Musée Rodin, Paris
CC 1682

6 *Maquette for General Lynch*
1886, cast 1981
Bronze, 45.1 x 34.9 x 20.0 cm
5/edition unknown, Godard Foundry, Paris
Issued by Musée Rodin, Paris
CC 1567

7 *Study for the Monument to Claude Lorrain*
1889, cast 1992
Bronze, 50.5 x 20.3 x 20.3 cm
5/8, Godard Foundry, Paris
Issued by Musée Rodin, Paris
CC 1570

8 *Tragic Head*
1890–96, cast 1963
Bronze, 16.5 x 12.7 x 12.1 cm
6/12, Georges Rudier Foundry, Paris
Issued by Musée Rodin, Paris
CC 1472

9 *The Benedictions*
1894, cast 1955
Bronze, 90.2 x 61.0 x 48.3 cm
Edition unknown, Georges Rudier Foundry, Paris
Issued by Musée Rodin, Paris
CC 1386

10 *Romeo and Juliet*
1902, cast before 1917
Bronze, 68.6 x 50.8 x 33.0 cm
Edition unknown, Alexis Rudier Foundry, Paris
CC 1414

11 *Study for the Monument to Whistler*
1905–06, cast 1983
Bronze, 62.9 x 33.0 x 34.3 cm
3/8, Godard Foundry, Paris
Issued by Musée Rodin, Paris
CC 1569

12 *Whistler's Muse*
1907, cast 1991
Bronze, 223.5 x 90.2 x 108.9 cm
IV/IV Coubertin Foundry, Paris
Issued by Musée Rodin, Paris
CC 1627

13 *Mask of Hanako (type D)*
1908, cast 1979
Bronze, 20.0 x 17.8 x 15.2 cm
8/12, Godard Foundry, Paris
Issued by Musée Rodin, Paris
CC 4140

14 *Gustav Mahler*
1909, cast at a later date
Bronze, 33.0 x 34.3 x 30.5 cm
Edition unknown, Alexis Rudier Foundry, Paris
Issued by Musée Rodin, Paris
Collection: Iris and B. Gerald Cantor
Promised Gift to the Iris and B. Gerald Cantor Foundation
CC 1444

Figures & Partial Figures (1876–1910)

15 *The Age of Bronze (reduction)*
1876, reduction *c.*1903–04, date of cast unknown
Bronze, 66.0 x 21.6 x 17.8 cm
Edition unknown, Alexis Rudier Foundry, Paris
CC 1484

16 *Monumental Head of Saint John the Baptist*
*c.*1879, cast 1988
Bronze, 54.6 x 52.7 x 38.6 cm
III/IV, Godard Foundry, Paris
Issued by Musée Rodin, Paris
CC 1451

17 *Saint John the Baptist Preaching*
*c.*1880, cast 1962
Bronze, 50.2 x 27.9 x 23.2 cm
Edition unknown, Georges Rudier Foundry, Paris.
Issued by Musée Rodin, Paris
CC 1560

18 *Meditation (with arms)*
Originally conceived for *The Gates of Hell*, *c.*1885–87; enlarged *c.*1896, separated from the definitive *Monument to Victor Hugo* as an independent sculpture after 1900, cast 1980
Bronze, 154.9 x 63.5 x 63.5 cm
9/edition unknown, Coubertin Foundry, Paris
Issued by Musée Rodin, Paris
CC 1618

19 *The Walking Man*
*c.*1889, date of cast unknown
Bronze, 83.8 x 51.4 x 50.8 cm
Edition unknown
CC 1060

20 *The Flying Figure*
*c.*1890–91, date of cast unknown
Bronze, 52.1 x 74.9 x 30.5 cm
12/12, Georges Rudier Foundry, Paris
Issued by Musée Rodin, Paris
CC 1302

21 *Tragic Muse*
1894–96, cast 1986
Bronze, 33.0 x 64.8 x 38.7 cm
3/8, Godard Foundry, Paris
Issued by Musée Rodin, Paris
CC 1446

22 *Illusions Received by the Earth (The Fallen Angel)*
1895, cast 1983
Bronze, 39.4 x 68.6 x 39.4 cm
1/8, Coubertin Foundry, Paris
Issued by Musée Rodin, Paris
Collection: Iris and B. Gerald Cantor
Promised Gift to the Iris and B. Gerald Cantor Foundation
CC 1341

23 *Half-length Figure of a Woman (The Martyr)*
before 1900, cast 1966
Bronze, 78.7 x 68.6 x 43.2 cm
Edition unknown, Georges Rudier Foundry, Paris
Issued by Musée Rodin, Paris
CC 1617

24 *Monumental Torso of the Walking Man*
*c.*1905, cast 1985
Bronze, 110.1 x 67.9 x 38.1 cm
4/8, Godard Foundry, Paris
Issued by Musée Rodin, Paris
CC 1410

25 *The Prayer*
1910, cast 1979
Bronze, 125.7 x 54.9 x 49.8 cm
5/edition unknown, Godard Foundry, Paris
Issued by Musée Rodin, Paris
CC 1553

26 *Dance Movement, pas de deux (type B)*
*c.*1910–11, cast 1965
Bronze, 33.0 x 18.1 x 12.7 cm
10/edition unknown, Georges Rudier Foundry, Paris
Issued by Musée Rodin, Paris
CC 1559

27 *Dance Movement (type D)*
*c.*1910–11, date of cast unknown
Bronze, 32.4 x 10.8 x 9.2 cm
1/edition unknown
Issued by Musée Rodin, Paris
CC 1469

28 *Narcissus*
no date, cast 1985
Bronze, 81.3 x 33.0 x 31.1 cm
8/8, Godard Foundry, Paris
Issued by Musée Rodin, Paris
CC 1402

The Gates of Hell (1880–*c.*1900) and derivatives

29 *Adam with Pillar*
1878–80, cast 1978
Bronze, 41.9 x 12.1 x 12.7 cm
11/12, Georges Rudier Foundry, Paris
Issued by Musée Rodin, Paris
CC 1485

30 *Eve with Pillar*
1878–80, cast *c.*1977
Bronze, 41.9 x 14.0 x 15.2 cm
8/12, Georges Rudier Foundry, Paris
Issued by Musée Rodin, Paris
CC 1486

31 *Third Maquette for The Gates of Hell*
1880, cast 1992
Bronze, 110.1 x 73.8 x 29.8 cm
IV/IV, Godard Foundry, Paris
Issued by Musée Rodin, Paris
CC 1626

32 *The Thinker*
1880, enlarged in 1902–03, cast *c.*1960
Bronze, 200.7 x 130.2 x 140.3 cm
10/12, Georges Rudier Foundry, Paris
Collection: Iris and B. Gerald Cantor
Promised Gift to the Iris and B. Gerald Cantor Center for Visual Arts at Stanford University
CC 6440

33 *The Thinker (reduction)*
1880, reduced 1903, date of cast unknown
Bronze, 37.5 x 19.8 x 28.9 cm
Edition unknown, Alexis Rudier Foundry, Paris
CC 1499

34 *Fallen Caryatid with Stone*
1880–81, enlarged 1911–17, cast 1988
Bronze, 133.4 x 83.3 x 99.1 cm
II/IV, Coubertin Foundry, Paris
Issued by Musée Rodin, Paris
CC 1563

35 ***The Three Shades***
1880–1904, single figure conceived *c.*1880, enlarged individually in 1901, group composition by 1904, cast 1991
Bronze, 191.8 x 191.8 x 106.7 cm
II/IV, Coubertin Foundry, Paris
Issued by Musée Rodin, Paris
CC 1628

36 ***The Three Shades***
1880–1904, single figure conceived *c.*1880, group composition
1904, cast 1981
Bronze, 97.2 x 95.3 x 52.1 cm
10/edition unknown, Coubertin Foundry, Paris
Issued by Musée Rodin, Paris
Collection: Iris and B. Gerald Cantor
Promised Gift to the Iris and B. Gerald Cantor Foundation
CC 1492

37 ***The Kiss***
*c.*1881–82, date of cast unknown
Bronze, 86.4 x 43.2 x 55.9 cm
Edition unknown, Alexis Rudier Foundry, Paris
CC 1689

38 ***The Falling Man***
1882, cast 1979
Bronze, 59.0 x 43.2 x 25.4 cm
8/edition unknown, Godard Foundry, Paris
Issued by Musée Rodin, Paris
CC 1606

39 ***Small Torso of the Falling Man***
*c.*1882, cast 1984
Bronze, 26.7 x 19.7 x 16.5 cm
II/IV, Godard Foundry, Paris
Issued by Musée Rodin, Paris
CC 1571

40 ***Head of Sorrow***
*c.*1882, cast 1956
Bronze, 24.1 x 20.0 x 25.4 cm
Edition unknown, Georges Rudier Foundry, Paris
Issued by Musée Rodin, Paris
CC 1467

41 ***Eve (reduction)***
1883, date of cast unknown
Bronze, 71.1 x 25.4 x 26.7 cm
7/12, Georges Rudier Foundry, Paris
CC 1500

42 ***Ovid's Metamorphoses***
*c.*1885–89, date of cast unknown
Bronze, 33.3 x 40.0 x 26.0 cm
Edition unknown, Perzinka Foundry, Versailles
CC 1192

43 ***Fugitive Love***
before 1887, date of cast unknown
Bronze, 52.7 x 83.8 x 38.1 cm
2/edition unknown, Alexis Rudier Foundry, Paris
CC 1305

44 ***Paolo and Francesca***
1889, cast 1973
Bronze, 30.4 x 56.5 x 37.5 cm
2/8, Georges Rudier Foundry, Paris
Issued by Musée Rodin, Paris
Collection: Iris and B. Gerald Cantor Center for Visual Arts at Stanford University
Gift of Iris and B. Gerald Cantor Collection
CC 658

45 ***Sorrow***
1889, cast 1983
Bronze, 29.2 x 16.5 x 17.1 cm
1/8, Coubertin Foundry, Paris
Issued by Musée Rodin, Paris
Collection: Iris and B. Gerald Cantor
Promised Gift to the Iris and B. Gerald Cantor Foundation
CC 1324

46 *The Creator (bas relief)*
*c.*1900, cast 1984
Bronze, 40.6 x 36.2 x 6.4 cm
II/IV, Coubertin Foundry, Paris
Issued by Musée Rodin, Paris
CC 1568

47 *Toilette of Venus and Andromeda*
no date, cast 1987
Bronze, 50.8 x 36.8 x 59.7 cm
II/IV, Godard Foundry, Paris
Issued by Musée Rodin, Paris
CC 1510

Studies for the Burghers of Calais (1884–1895)

48 *First Maquette (with pedestal) for the Burghers of Calais*
1884, cast 1987
Bronze, 60.3 x 37.7 x 33.0 cm
7/8, Godard Foundry, Paris
Issued by Musée Rodin, Paris
CC 1450

49 *Monumental Head of Jean d'Aire*
*c.*1884–86, enlarged 1909–10, date of cast unknown
Bronze, 67.9 x 50.3 x 57.2 cm
1/12, Georges Rudier Foundry, Paris
CC 15800

50 *Monumental Head of Pierre de Wiessant*
*c.*1884–85, enlarged *c.*1909, date of cast unknown
Bronze, 81.3 x 48.3 x 52.1 cm
8/12, Godard Foundry, Paris
CC 775

51 *Left Hand of Pierre de Wiessant*
*c.*1884–89, date of cast unknown
Bronze, 27.9 x 19.0 x 15.2 cm
Edition unknown, Alexis Rudier Foundry, Paris
CC1610

52 *Second Maquette for Jean d'Aire*
1885–86, cast 1970
Bronze, 69.8 x 24.1 x 24.8 cm
1/12, Susse Foundry, Paris
Issued by Musée Rodin, Paris
CC 16100

53 *Nude Study for Jean d'Aire (reduction)*
1885–86, cast 1976
Bronze, 106.1 x 34.9 x 30.2 cm
4/edition unknown, Georges Rudier Foundry, Paris
Issued by Musée Rodin, Paris
CC 1554

54 *Jean de Fiennes*
1885–86, cast 1983
Bronze, 208.3 x 121.9 x 96.5 cm
5/8, Coubertin Foundry, Paris
Issued by Musée Rodin, Paris
CC 1330

55 *Final Head of Eustache de Saint-Pierre*
*c.*1886, cast 1995
Bronze, 41.2 x 24.4 x 29.2 cm
II/IV, Godard Foundry, Paris
Issued by Musée Rodin, Paris
CC 1685

56 *Pierre de Wiessant (reduction)*
*c.*1886–87, reduction made 1895 or 1899, date of cast unknown
Bronze, 47.6 x 16.5 x 16.2 cm
Edition unknown, Alexis Rudier Foundry, Paris
Collection: Iris and B. Gerald Cantor
Promised Gift to the Iris and B. Gerald Cantor Foundation
CC 1715

Studies for the Monument to Balzac (1891–1897)

57 ***Nude Study for Balzac (reduction, type C)***
probably 1892, cast 1972
Bronze, 76.2 x 42.5 x 34.3 cm
11/12, Georges Rudier Foundry, Paris
Issued by Musée Rodin, Paris
CC 16800

58 ***Bust of Young Balzac***
1893, cast 1988
Bronze, 71.4 x 34.0 x 37.1 cm
II/IV, Godard Foundry, Paris
Issued by Musée Rodin, Paris
CC 1579

59 ***Balzac in a Dominican Robe***
1893, cast 1981
Bronze, 106.0 x 51.2 x 50.8 cm
9/edition unknown, Georges Rudier Foundry, Paris
Issued by Musée Rodin, Paris
Collection: Iris and B. Gerald Cantor
Promised Gift to the Iris and B. Gerald Cantor Foundation
CC 1491

60 ***Study for Balzac (type B)***
1896, cast 1963
Bronze, 28.2 x 8.9 x 10.2 cm
8/edition unknown, Georges Rudier Foundry, Paris
Issued by Musée Rodin, Paris
CC 1476

61 ***Nude Study of Balzac as an Athlete (type F)***
1896, cast 1974
Bronze, 94.0 x 40.6 x 39.4 cm
5/edition unknown, Georges Rudier Foundry, Paris
Issued by Musée Rodin, Paris
CC 1555

62 ***Monumental Head of Balzac (enlargement)***
1897, cast 1980
Bronze, 50.8 x 44.5 x 40.6 cm
9/12, Georges Rudier Foundry, Paris
Issued by Musée Rodin, Paris
CC 1301

Hands (1885–1910)

63 ***Large Left Hand of a Pianist***
1885, cast 1969
Bronze, 18.4 x 25.4 x 12.4 cm
9/12, Georges Rudier Foundry, Paris
Issued by Musée Rodin, Paris
CC 1488

64 ***Large Clenched Left Hand***
*c.*1885, cast 1966
Bronze, 46.4 x 26.4 x 19.3 cm
3/12, Georges Rudier Foundry, Paris
Issued by Musée Rodin, Paris
CC 2120

65 ***Large Clenched Right Hand***
*c.*1885, cast 1965
Bronze, 46.9 x 31.7 x 15.9 cm
Edition unknown, Georges Rudier Foundry, Paris
Issued by Musée Rodin, Paris
Collection: Iris and B. Gerald Cantor
Promised Gift to the Iris and B. Gerald Cantor Foundation
CC 2300

66 ***Small Clenched Right Hand***
*c.*1885, date of cast unknown
Bronze, 14.0 x 11.4 x 6.4 cm
Edition unknown, Alexis Rudier Foundry, Paris
Issued by Musée Rodin, Paris
CC 2160

67 ***Large Clenched Left Hand with Figure***
1906 or 1907, cast 1970
Bronze, 44.5 x 29.2 x 26.4 cm
1/12, Godard Foundry, Paris
Issued by Musée Rodin, Paris
Collection: Iris and B. Gerald Cantor
Promised Gift to the Iris and B. Gerald Cantor Foundation
CC 2240

68 ***The Cathedral***
original stone version executed in 1908, cast 1955
Bronze, 64.1 x 32.3 x 34.3 cm
Edition unknown, Georges Rudier Foundry, Paris
Issued by Musée Rodin, Paris
CC 15600

69 ***Head of Shade with Two Hands***
*c.*1910, date of cast unknown
Bronze, 19.4 x 27.3 x 20.6 cm
2/edition unknown, Alexis Rudier Foundry, Paris
CC 1545

70 ***Right Hand, Fingers Close Together, Slightly Bent***
no date, date of cast unknown
Bronze, 12.1 x 5.4 x 3.8 cm
6/12, Georges Rudier Foundry, Paris
CC 1489

71 ***Right Hand, Middle Fingers Together***
no date, date of cast unknown
Bronze, 10.2 x 5.1 x 3.8 cm
Edition unknown
CC 4290

PRINTS

72 ***The Round*** *c.*1883
Engraving, 29.2 x 19.7 cm
CC 690

73 ***Antonin Proust*** 1885
Engraving, 30.5 x 21.6 cm
CC 670

74 ***Victor Hugo (frontal view)*** 1886
Drypoint, 22.2 x 16.5 cm
CC 669

WORKS BY OTHER ARTISTS

Camille Claudel France 1864–1943
75 ***Bust of Rodin***
1888–92, date of cast unknown
Bronze, 40.0 x 23.5 x 28.0 cm
Edition unknown, Alexis Rudier Foundry, Paris
CC 593

Paul Paulin France 1850–1932
76 ***Bust of Auguste Rodin***
1917, date of cast unknown
Bronze, 38.7 x 29.2 x 33.0 cm
Edition unknown, Valsuani Foundry, Paris
CC 1598

Edward Steichen United States of America 1879–1973
77 ***Portrait of Rodin with The Thinker and The Monument to Victor Hugo*** 1902
Gelatin silver photograph, 33.7 x 42.2 cm
CC 1110

78 ***Portrait of Rodin*** 1910
Photogravure, 24.1 x 16.5 cm
CC 685

MUSÉE RODIN, PARIS

SCULPTURE

79 ***Study of A Woman (Mrs Russell)*** 1890
Marble, 56.2 x 43.5 x 30.8 cm
S 1027

DRAWINGS

80 ***Kneeling Female Nude*** *c.*1890
Pencil, ink and gouache on paper, 17.7 x 11.4 cm
D 4289

81 ***Seated Female Nude*** *c.*1890
Pencil, watercolour on paper, 17.3 x 11.0 cm
D 4290

82 ***Draped Female Nude*** *c.*1890
Pencil, ink, gouache and watercolour on paper, 17.4 x 10.8 cm
D 4296

83 ***Reclining Female Nude*** *c.*1900
Pencil and watercolour on paper, 32.4 x 24.6 cm
D 4611

84 ***Kneeling Female Nude*** *c.*1900
Pencil on paper, 31.2 x 20.4 cm
D 482

85 ***Seated Female Nude*** *c.*1900
Pencil on paper, 20.4 x 31.4 cm
D 484

86 ***Seated Female Nude*** *c.*1900
Pencil, estompe on paper, 31.3 x 20.4 cm
D 493

87 ***Female Nude*** *c.*1900
Pencil, estompe on paper, 31.2 x 19.6 cm
D 501

88 ***Reclining Female Nude*** *c.*1900
Pencil on paper, 20.0 x 31.0 cm
D 511

89 ***Draped, Seated Female Nude*** *c.*1900
Pencil, estompe on paper, 31.1 x 20.2 cm
D 569

90 ***Female Nude*** *c.*1900
Pencil, estompe on paper, 36.0 x 22.7 cm
D 613

91 ***Seated Female Nude*** *c.*1900
Pencil on paper, 31.0 x 20.0 cm
D 654

92 ***Draped, Seated Female Nude*** *c.*1900
Pencil, estompe on paper, 31.2 x 19.7 cm
D 740

93 ***Standing Female Nude*** *c.*1900
Pencil on paper, 31.2 x 20.2 cm
D 748

94 ***Draped, Seated Female Nude*** *c.*1900
Pencil, estompe on paper, 31.0 x 20.0 cm
D 811

95 ***Seated Female Nude*** *c.*1900
Pencil, estompe on paper, 31.1 x 19.9 cm
D 822

96 ***Seated Female Nude*** *c.*1900
Pencil on paper, 19.8 x 31.1 cm
D 922

97 ***Seated Female Nude*** *c.*1900
Pencil on paper, 31.1 x 19.2 cm
D 928

98 ***Seated Female Nude*** *c.*1900
Pencil on paper, 36.0 x 23.1 cm
D 1074

99 ***Psyche*** *c.*1900
Pencil and watercolour on paper, 32.6 x 24.6 cm
D 4630

100 ***Pierrette*** *c.*1900
Pencil and watercolour on paper,
31.7 x 24.2 cm
D 4722

101 *The Sea* c.1900
Pencil and watercolour on paper,
32.6 x 25.2 cm
D 4743

102 *Night Flower (Young Mother and Child)* c.1900
Pencil and watercolour on paper,
25.0 x 31.3 cm
D 4805

103 *Crouching Female Nude* c.1900
Pencil and watercolour on paper,
25.2 x 32.4 cm
D 4808

104 *Draped, Seated Female Nude* c.1900
Pencil and watercolour on paper,
32.8 x 25.1 cm
D 4822

105 *Draped Female Nude* c.1900
Pencil and watercolour on paper,
32.5 x 25.0 cm
D 4837

106 *Annunciation* c.1900
Pencil and watercolour on paper,
32.2 x 24.0 cm
D 4930

107 *Standing Female Nude* c.1900
Pencil and watercolour on paper,
32.5 x 24.8 cm
D 4937

108 *Seated Female Nude* c.1900
Pencil and watercolour on paper,
32.4 x 24.9 cm
D 4952

109 *Seated Female Nude* c.1900
Pencil and watercolour on paper,
33.8 x 20.0 cm
D 5262

FONDATION PIERRE GIANADDA, MARTIGNY, SWITZERLAND

DRAWINGS

110 *Two Kneeling Nudes* c.1900
Pencil and watercolour on paper,
44.0 x 31.8 cm

111 *Standing Nude* c.1900
pencil and watercolour on paper,
50.2 x 32.2 cm

112 *Kneeling Female Nude* after 1900
Pencil and watercolour on paper,
23.5 x 31.0 cm

113 *Female Dancer* 1906
Pencil and watercolour on paper,
32.2 x 25.0 cm

114 *Portrait of a Woman (Portrait of the Countess Nouvre Rohozinska)* 1906
Pencil and watercolour on paper,
31.5 x 24.0 cm

115 *Nude* no date
Pencil and watercolour on paper,
32.5 x 25.0 cm

NATIONAL GALLERY OF VICTORIA, MELBOURNE

SCULPTURE

116 *The Crying Lion*
1881, cast *c.*1905
Bronze, 27.6 x 33.9 x 16.8 cm
Felton Bequest 1909

117 *Jean-Paul Laurens*
1881–82, cast 1905
Bronze, 58.1 x 39.1 x 31.1 cm
Felton Bequest 1906

NATIONAL GALLERY OF AUSTRALIA, CANBERRA

SCULPTURE

118 *First Maquette for the Burghers of Calais*
1884, cast 1973
Bronze, 33.0 x 35.0 x 26.5 cm
9/12, Godard Foundry, Paris
Issued by Musée Rodin, Paris
1974.379

119 *Nude Study for Eustache de Saint-Pierre*
1885, cast *c.*1974
Bronze, 98.0 x 33.0 x 42.5 cm
9/12, Georges Rudier Foundry, Paris
Issued by Musée Rodin, Paris
Promised Bequest of Tony Gilbert 1998
16100

120 *Nude Study for Jean d'Aire*
1885–86, cast 1973
Bronze, 205.0 x 67.0 x 53.5 cm
3/12, Georges Rudier Foundry, Paris
Issued by Musée Rodin, Paris
1974.381

121 *Jean d'Aire*
*c.*1885–86, cast 1974
Bronze, 209.0 x 80.0 x 75.5 cm
7/12, Susse Foundry, Paris
Issued by Musée Rodin, Paris
1974.382

122 *Nude Study for Jean de Fiennes*
*c.*1885–86, cast 1967
Bronze, 203.5 x 131.0 x 42.5 cm
1/12, Georges Rudier Foundry, Paris
Issued by Musée Rodin, Paris
1974.380

123 *Pierre de Wiessant*
*c.*1885–86, cast 1974
Bronze, 206.0 x 92.0 x 99.5 cm
1/12, Susse Foundry, Paris
Issued by Musée Rodin, Paris
1976.64

124 ***Eustache de Saint-Pierre***
1885–86, cast 1984
Bronze, 213.5 x 75.0 x 102.5 cm
I/IV, Coubertin Foundry, Paris
Issued by Musée Rodin, Paris
1985.1227

125 ***Andrieu d'Andres***
*c.*1886, cast 1985
Bronze, 297.0 x 89.0 x 135.0 cm
I/IV, Coubertin Foundry, Paris
Issued by Musée Rodin, Paris
1985.2006

DRAWING AND ILLUSTRATED BOOK

126 ***The Cambodian Dancer*** 1906
Watercolour, 23.0 x 24.2 cm
1984.471

Auguste RODIN, artist
France 1840-1917
Auguste CLOT, lithographer
France 1858–1936
127 ***Le Jardin des Supplices [The Torture Garden]***
by Octave Mirbeau
(Paris: Ambroise Vollard, 1902)
Colour lithograph, letterpress, 32.4 x 25.0 cm
9/200
1988.1475

Editor's Note:
Within each catalogue essay, titles of works are first given in French with English translations and thereafter in English. With illustrations, if the works appear in the exhibition checklist on pages 148–158, then a shortened caption refers the reader to the relevant catalogue number for full caption details.

FURTHER READING

Books and Articles

Rodin, Auguste. *Correspondance de Rodin,* annotated by Alain Beausire, Florence Cadouot and Hélène Pinet, 4 vols, Paris: Musée Rodin, 1985–1992.

Butler, Ruth (ed.). *Rodin in Perspective*, Englewood Cliffs, New Jersey: Prentice Hall, 1980.

Butler, Ruth. *The Shape of Genius*, New Haven: Yale University Press, 1993.

Crone, Rainer (ed.). *Rodin: Eros and creativity*, Munich: Prestel, 1995.

Elsen, Albert. *Auguste Rodin: Readings on his life and work*, Englewood Cliffs, New Jersey: Prentice Hall, 1965.

Elsen, Albert. *In Rodin's Studio*, Oxford: Phaidon, 1980.

Elsen, Albert. *'The Gates of Hell' by Auguste Rodin*, rev.ed. Stanford University Press, 1985.

Goldscheider, Cécile. *Rodin: Catalogue raisonné de l'œuvre sculpté*, Paris: Wildenstein Insititute, 1989.

Grappe, Georges. *Catalogue du Musée Rodin*, Paris: The Museum, 1927, 1929, 1931, 1938, 1944.

Grunfeld, Frederic V. *Rodin: A biography*, New York: Holt, 1987.

Judrin, Claudie. *Rodin: Drawings and watercolors*, New York: Thames & Hudson, 1983.

Krauss, Rosalind. 'The Originality of the Avant-Garde', in *The Originality of the Avant-Garde and Other Modernist Myths,* Cambridge, Massachusetts: MIT Press, 1985, pp. 151–170.

Le Normand-Romain, Antoinette. *Rodin*, Paris: Musée Rodin; Flammarion, 1997.

Pinet, Hélène. *Rodin: The hands of genius*, London: Thames & Hudson, 1992.

Rilke, Rainer Maria. *Rodin*, (Trans. Robert Firmage), Salt Lake City: Peregrine Smith, 1982.

Rodin on Art and Artists: Conversations with Paul Gsell, New York: Dover, 1994.

Steinberg, Leo. 'Rodin', in *Other Criteria: Confrontations with twentieth- century art,* London: Oxford University Press, 1972, pp. 322–403, 417–419.

Tancock, John L. *The Sculpture of Auguste Rodin: The collection of the Rodin Museum, Philadelphia*, Philadelphia: Philadelphia Museum, 1976.

Exhibition Catalogues

The Drawings of Rodin, N.Y. Praeger for Washington, DC: National Gallery of Art, 1971.

Auguste Rodin: Le Monument des Bourgeois de Calais, Paris: Musée Rodin, 1977.

Rodin Rediscovered, Washington, DC: National Gallery of Art, 1981.

Rodin: Sculpture and drawings, London: Art Council of Great Britain/Hayward Gallery, 1986.

Claude Monet–Auguste Rodin: Centenaire de l'exposition de 1889, Paris: Musée Rodin 1989.

Rodin: Dessins et aquarelles des collections suisses et du Musée Rodin, Martigny: La Fondation Pierre Gianadda, 1994.

Rodin à Québec, Québec: Musée du Québec, 1998.

Rodin en 1900, Paris: Musée de Luxembourg, 2001.